Skeptical Feminism

Skeptical Feminism

Activist Theory, Activist Practice

Carolyn Dever

University of Minnesota Press

Minneapolis | London

An earlier version of chapter 4 was published as "The Feminist Abject: Death and the Constitution of Theory," *Studies in the Novel* 32, no. 2 (summer 2000): 185–206; copyright 2000 by the University of North Texas; reprinted by permission of the publisher. An earlier version of chapter 5 appeared as "Obstructive Behavior: Dykes in the Mainstream of Feminist Theory," in *Cross-Purposes: Lesbians, Feminists, and the Limits of Alliance*, ed. Dana Heller (Bloomington: Indiana University Press, 1997), 19–41; reprinted by permission of Indiana University Press.

Published by the University of Minnesota Press
111 Third Avenue South, Suite 290
Minneapolis, MN 55401-2520
http://www.upress.umn.edu

Library of Congress Cataloging-in-Publication Data

Dever, Carolyn.
    Skeptical feminism : activist theory, activist practice / Carolyn Dever.
        p.   cm.
    Includes bibliographical references and index.
    ISBN 0-8166-4252-4 (alk. paper) — ISBN 0-8166-4253-2 (pbk. : alk. paper)
        1. Feminist theory.   2. Feminism.   I. Title.
    HQ1190 .D494 2004
    305.42'01—dc22

                                                                    2003015329

Printed in the United States of America on acid-free paper

The University of Minnesota is an equal-opportunity educator and employer.

12 11 10 09 08 07 06 05 04   10 9 8 7 6 5 4 3 2 1

For Kathryn

Even as we, in the academy, hone our skills at exposing the ways in which experience is produced as experience, there is too little self-consciousness about the ways in which theory is produced as theory.
—Biddy Martin, *Femininity Played Straight: The Significance of Being Lesbian*

Just as all social life is theoretical, so all theory is a real social practice.
—Terry Eagleton, *The Significance of Theory*

Scholarship has, in principle, to be eminently teachable.
—Paul de Man, *The Resistance to Theory*

Contents

Preface

> Abstraction and illusion rule in knowledge, domination rules
> in practice.
>
> —Donna Haraway, *Simians, Cyborgs, and Women*

> A woman seldom runs wild after an abstraction.
>
> —John Stuart Mill, *The Subjection of Women*

In a feminist context, to be described as "abstract" or as putting something in abstract terms is usually a bad sign. The topic often arises in the charged context of accusation—if not of an outright character flaw, then of the perpetuation of an elitist, exclusionary mode of description, or of the failure to engage fully with the matter of social justice. Abstraction persists as a signifier of detachment and high-culture privilege, the opposite of such valued concepts as "concrete," "material," or "particular." In this book, I suggest that skepticism toward abstraction and all that it connotes has been a vital, and vitalizing, component of feminist theories. The feminist critique of abstraction reasserts the stakes of social change in all its concrete, material, and particular implications. It serves as a linchpin in the feminist effort to find new ways of understanding relations between theory and practice.

The critique of abstraction has helped feminists to find new vocabularies and methodologies that challenge patriarchal conventions of the "theoretical." This work has taken place across the range of feminist discourses, as powerfully and creatively in popular and activist feminisms as in the academic discourses usually understood as the source of "feminist theory." In the chapters that follow, I address a range of activist, popular, and academic feminist traditions from the second-wave U.S. women's movement forward in order to consider how such divergent discourses, operating under a shared set of political concerns, construct—and deconstruct—sites of theoretical authority. In the 1970s, the period on which this book is focused, the concept of feminist theory was first coming into being. This process occurred in the context of a political idealism so sensitive to the hierarchical implications of "theory" that feminist theories, in order to be effective, had to account for themselves, had to demonstrate their resistance to theoretical abstraction, even as they produced theoretical abstractions as a matter of course.

Texts from the women's liberation movement are not ordinarily granted much consideration in the canons of feminist theory, yet the uncanonical
status of this feminist work is what makes it so valuable to my argument
here. Precisely because this work is so very critical of feminist theoretical
authority, it demonstrates implications of feminist theoretical authority.
Precisely because it shows how feminists have attempted, from the first, to
theorize differently, it demonstrates both the limitations and the possibilities of new theoretical forms. My interest here is not in reifying a particular
canon of theories or theorists, nor is it in identifying a new tradition of
theoretical canonicity in feminism. I am not concerned to construct a utopia
of the women's movement (or a dystopia, for that matter), or to suggest that
feminist theories produced before academic disciplinary distinctions had
much at all to do with feminism have some kind of pure or originary status.
I aim instead to understand the fate of feminist theoretical authority: how it
is claimed, how its claims are challenged, and how this pattern of assertion,
challenge, and reassertion has provided the ethical system at work behind
feminist concepts of material change.

As I will argue in more detail in the introduction, "theory" has been a
complex and oftentimes ambivalent undertaking for feminists from the earliest moments of the women's movement. Theoretical logic in general and
theorists in particular as figures of authority have been perceived as hierarchical and detached in a social movement dedicated to the critique of hierarchy. They have also, however, been perceived as a vital necessity for a social
movement dedicated to material utility. A concern with the implications of
theoretical detachment and with the abstract representational modes that
bring theory into being transects boundaries that have come to distinguish
different feminist discourses: academics and activists; the women's liberation
movement and poststructuralism; cultural materialists and psychoanalysts;
and, to follow a trajectory that developed in the 1990s, gender theorists,
queer theorists, and feminist theorists. By undertaking to produce a material
history of abstraction across a range of feminist contexts, I treat the often
divisive terms "abstraction" and "theory" as shared and indeed unifying
concerns in order to address the strategies that different kinds of feminists
have devised to make theory matter as a force for political change.

In chapters 1 through 5 of the book, I argue that feminists have addressed
permutations of the theory-practice gap by manipulating fine distinctions
between the feminist mind and the feminist body. I am particularly interested in feminist discourses that *counterpose* mind and body, because they
customarily fall back on the equation of the mind with the intellect and thus
with abstraction; and the body with the material and thus with the practical. This symbolic pattern situates abstraction and materiality in opposition

to one another. But more important, the fact of the opposition itself locates abstraction and materiality in relation to one another, as cohabitants within the same subject and thus as mutually dependent, mutually constitutive, inextricable. By mobilizing these symbolic and intensely charged terms, feminist theories of social change seek to ground abstract claims in a material world. They aim to elude the traps of alienation and detachment in order to produce an ideal, praxis-oriented kind of theory, a theory that is as one with practice. In the consciousness-raising movement alone, female bodily experience, apprehended correctly, tutored women intellectually in a feminism already known on the somatic and emotional levels. This is typical of a pattern that locates feminist theory first in the body and second in the intellect. "Body" is, of course, an abstraction in its own right, its inadequacy to the task of grounding a theoretical argument in inalienable fact doomed to immediate exposé. Yet the persistence of this trope signifies an ongoing feminist resistance to abstract generalizations and thus an ongoing commitment toward ways of engaging and changing the material world.

The heart of the book tracks the emergence of bodily abstractions in a number of feminist contexts—the consciousness-raising movement, psychoanalysis, sexology, novels of the women's liberation movement, and emergent academic literary theories—that have been important to second-wave feminist theories in the United States. These are all discourses that attempt to breach the theory-practice gap, to find ways of putting the material world to work in the production of a feminist vision that manages, somehow, to resist abstracting itself on the road to social change. By focusing on feminist theoretical discourses that predate academic feminist theories, that circle around the gradual academicization of feminist thought, and that weave back and forth across boundaries that have come to distinguish academic, popular, and activist feminisms, I mean to delineate a complex epistemological history of feminism. Feminist debates about the relationship between abstraction and materiality illuminate the politics of theory production. The very persistence of these debates suggests new ways of understanding how "theory" has come to stand for a highly particular form of institutional power.

Through a reading of American feminist Kate Millett, I argue in my introduction, "Feminism, in Theory," for a contentious politics of the theoretical in the U.S. feminist tradition. Millett, following the publication of her literary-critical book *Sexual Politics* in 1969, was canonized on the cover of *Time* magazine as the leader—and the theorist—of the women's movement, in terms very much invested in her status as a figure for the "normal" white heterosexual married, and thus unthreatening, feminist. Her fall from grace a few months later, on the grounds of her public acknowledgment of lesbianism, allegorizes theoretical prestige and the resistance it provokes. Thinking through the implications of Millett's case, I describe in this introduction how particular theoretical discourses have come into a high-canonical status. In the context of this debate, I argue that literary-theoretical methodologies, which offer feminists strategies for the analysis of language informed by issues of power and control, provide an especially useful tool for understanding those very anxieties *about* feminist theory that are endemic *to* feminist theory.

My first chapter, "The Future of an Ideal: Consciousness and the Radical Vision of Women's Liberation," follows impassioned debates about the relationship between theory and practice in the women's liberation movement and the resulting development of the consciousness-raising movement as a mode of praxis, or theory in practice. In the 1970s, feminists used consciousness-raising to mobilize a critique of conventional femininity. They argued that women had been excluded from patriarchal spaces of intellectual labor and imprisoned instead in the patriarchal spaces of heterosexual domesticity. The central tactic of this effort involved an analysis of individual experience and emotion, locating "feminist theory" within the body and mind of each practitioner. Yet even as the canonization of the personal forged powerful bonds among women who had never before seen themselves as a political coalition, it reified particular kinds of experience and emotion as normative. This tension restages rather than resolves the gap between theoretical abstraction and material practice.

The book's second and third chapters focus on aspects of the establishment of a psychoanalytic feminism in the United States. In "The Activist Unconscious: Feminism and Psychoanalysis," I address a sea change in American feminism: whereas at the beginning of the 1970s, Freud in particular and psychoanalysis in general were widely perceived as feminist public enemy number one, by the middle of the decade, psychoanalysis was increasingly cited as an urgently necessary feminist methodology. If the consciousness-raising movement signaled the upward mobility of the feminist consciousness, the embrace of psychoanalysis, I argue, signaled the opposite: through claims to the conflicted powers lurking deep in the unconscious mind, feminists exchanged an emphasis on the real, the empirical, and the knowable for a theory of the acutely unreasonable. It is interesting to realize, then, that this new theoretical model found its most powerful site of articulation in a very old gendered narrative: analyses of motherhood and the determining psychic power of women—or men—who mother. By claiming the power of the maternal body and the maternal function, contemporary feminists follow in the footsteps of their predecessors in consciousness-raising, locating the bourgeois domestic sphere as the first line of offense for feminist politics. Following the native intelligence of the body, the mind and the emotions emerge as the primary site for feminist material intervention.

The feminist colonization of that domestic narrative took another twist in the psychoanalytic theory of female sexuality. I argue in "The Feminist Body Politic: Sexuality's Domestic Incarnation" that discourses of the feminist orgasm, organized to repudiate Freud's theory of the "mature" vaginal orgasm, represented the appropriation of pleasure for political ends. Constructing feminist eroticism as a mode of political action, recent theories of the "feminist body" demonstrate ambivalence about the diverse range of practices from which pleasure might be abstracted. By seeking both the causes and the effects of orgasm, these discourses model the impossibility of a feminist body that is at once universal and endlessly particular. The material body emerges here as the ultimate abstraction.

This is a narrative put into practice in novels of the women's liberation movement. In chapter 4, "The Feminist Abject: Death, Fiction, and Theory," I focus on several best-sellers that, I argue, intervene in the debate about the nature and culture of feminist theory. Feminist novelists at the end of the 1970s wrote stories of messy bodies that intrude on would-be orderly minds, and, in their reinscription of the body-mind dichotomy, they narrated a mode of distinction between materiality and abstraction. More specifically still, in locating women's violent deaths and bodily humiliations in academic contexts, they presented the bodily "real," and the claims of sex, blood, and death, as an unmet challenge to academic feminism.

I take up narratives internal to academic feminism in chapter 5, "Obstructive Behavior: Dykes in the Mainstream of Feminist Theory," in an analysis of the use to which the "dyke"—that is, the trope of lesbian sexuality—has been put in feminist literary theory. I argue that feminist and, more recently, queer theoretical discourses vacillate between appropriation and repudiation of a lesbian iconography, with the lesbian alternately figuring the stakes of materiality and abstraction. This shifting pattern reveals less about lesbianism than about the feminist discourses that use lesbianism as a means to an end—as a way of critiquing theoretical abstraction or, to put it another way, of reasserting the priority of material action.

In the book's conclusion, "Left Justified," I turn Carol Gilligan's theory of gendered voice to the analysis of contemporary feminist arguments about what constitutes a proper, powerful, effective feminist political voice. I am particularly concerned here with the equation of "good feminism" with "good mothering"; that is, heteronormative ideals of femininity, maternity, and nurturing that are equated—symptomatically, I argue—with materiality, clarity, and groundedness. This equation stands in contrast to modes of expression characterized by abstraction and difficulty, their "theoretical" qualities. I trace the equation of "theory" with unfeminine, male-identified speech that, in its butchness, signifies as unmaternal, queer, fallen, failed. This is a particularly telling example of the ambivalent equation of feminist theory with feminist subjectivity, as well as of the ideologies of normative virtue that, perversely, retain their constitutive force.

Finally, a word about this book's historical and cultural archive. This is an examination of the politics of theory production in a number of feminist institutional contexts, including academic interventions in the humanities, social sciences, and sciences; activist discourses about the meaning and scope of feminist politics; and pop-cultural discourses both by feminists and about feminism as a cultural phenomenon. I focus, in general, on feminist discourses that have not made their way into canonical academic feminist theories or have made their way into canonical academic contexts in clouded or ambivalent ways. It is in this sense that *Skeptical Feminism* offers an exploration of the boundaries with which academic feminists have constructed their work, presenting a challenge to feminist canon formation that is tendered in the same progressive spirit that has informed feminist challenges to canonicity in literary and historical contexts.

Although this archive both addresses and uses the "high-theoretical" vocabularies of academic feminist, gender, and queer studies, and at times does so extensively, my goal here is to put these theoretical terms in conversation with other ways of understanding the term "feminist theory." There are practical and even political gains to be achieved through this strategy. It represents one way of responding to the charge to feminists to breach pernicious academic-activist, highbrow-lowbrow divides. It offers insight into the equation of theory with authority, and thus participates in the feminist tradition of skepticism toward the very figures of authority feminists put to use. Finally, my focus on second-wave feminist discourses in the United States is informed by the increasing historical engagement with the history and politics of U.S. civil rights movements. Writing in the context of literary analysis, Fredric Jameson urges critics to "always historicize."[1] I offer this book as one attempt to historicize "theory" and to historicize "feminism," and to suggest that the union of those projects illuminates the force of each.

Acknowledgments

This book owes its greatest debt to the feminist thinkers who people its pages and to those whose work in feminist, gender, lesbian and gay, and queer studies has been so important to me. The American Council of Learned Societies, Vanderbilt University, and New York University provided support and sabbatical time that were instrumental to my research and writing. My thanks to Natalie Kapetanios for research assistance at the beginning of the project and to Shalyn Claggett, Lisa Niles, and Jessi Vernon for help at the end.

This book originated in the experience of teaching several seminars in literary theory to smart, political graduate students who inspired me with the exactingness of their responses. All books emerge from conversations, and this one is no exception. My thanks especially to Sarah Blake, Tita Chico, Margaret Cohen, Lisa Duggan, Lynn Enterline, Natalka Freeland, Teresa Goddu, Phil Harper, Karla Jay, Barbara Johnson, Sharon Marcus, John Maynard, Ann Pellegrini, Diane Perpich, John Plotz, Mary Poovey, Claire Potter, Greta Rensenbrink, Mark Schoenfield, and Hilary Schor. Nan D. Hunter and Judith Roof were careful and challenging readers, and Richard Morrison has been a terrific editor. Brooke Ackerly and Esther Newton shared their work at key moments, for which I am grateful. Dana Heller and Diana York Blaine edited articles that turned into chapters. For contributions to individual chapters, I thank the Faculty Working Group in Queer Studies at New York University and Diane Perpich's graduate seminar on gender and identity in the philosophy department of Vanderbilt University. Thanks to Robin Nagle and Valerie Traub, who offered early opportunities to present material from the book's introduction.

I have been the lucky beneficiary of Jay Clayton's thoughtful reading and of many years of work and play with Marvin Taylor and Michael Gillespie. K-Lea Gifford, Jan Campbell, Christy Brock, Ruth Smith, and Kimberly Christopher have provided an indispensable support system, and Kathryn Schwarz has been extraordinary in every way.

Introduction
Feminism, in Theory

The Politics of Theory

August 31, 1970. Under the banner headline "The Politics of Sex" and a price tag of fifty cents, *Time* magazine presented its latest "cover girl": "Kate Millett of Women's Lib." Millett appears in a very painterly portrait, her eyes burning under heavy dark brows, hair flowing loose, jaw and shoulders braced as if for combat. To her chagrin (it was later revealed), Millett was portrayed alone, contrary to her understanding with the editors of *Time,* who had suggested an impressionistic group portrait of the collective personalities—reflecting the collective politics—of the women's movement.[1] Instead, by representing Millett alone on its cover, *Time* singled out an icon for American feminism. The implications of this selection, mediated by its dramatic retraction several months later, reflected and shaped efforts to locate the women's liberation movement within a coherent set of theoretical agendas.

On August 31, 1970, to mark the fiftieth anniversary of woman suffrage, American feminism went mainstream on the cover of *Time* through the figure of Kate Millett. The cover story suggested that Millett's recently published book *Sexual Politics* was newsworthy because it provided a much needed theoretical instrument to the diverse and often inchoate factions of women's liberation:

> Until this year, . . . with the publication of a remarkable book called *Sexual Politics,* the movement had no coherent theory to buttress its intuitive passions, no ideologue to provide chapter and verse for its assault on patriarchy. . . . In a way, the book has made Millett the Mao Tse-tung of Women's Liberation. That is the sort of description she and her sisters despise, for the movement rejects the notion of leaders and heroines as creations of the media—and mimicry of the ways that men use to organize their world. Despite the fact that it is essentially a polemic suspended awkwardly in academic traction, *Sexual Politics* so far has sold more than 15,000 copies and is in its fourth printing.[2]

It was this book's status as "a polemic suspended awkwardly in academic traction" that merited *Time*'s attention in the first place. *Sexual Politics* gave voice to its political analysis in the context of an authorizing scholarly framework; "academic traction" symbolized, for *Time*, a new seriousness in the women's movement, signifying the newsworthiness of a newly intellectualized—and thus newly substantive—feminism.

Yet even as it invested in feminism's intellectual implications, this cover story supported its argument through a personal profile of Kate Millett—and a suspiciously sanitized one at that. It constructed Millett as a mildly countercultural New Yorker who was at heart a good Midwestern girl, a loving daughter, and a wife. Her "remarkable book" might mobilize an assault on patriarchy, but the story presumed a disconnect between that argument and the argument of Millett's life itself: she was safe and unthreatening, merely an academic whose political effectiveness went no further than aesthetic observation.

Until the follow-up story that *Time* published the next December, that is. The new story reported that Millett, when asked point-blank during a panel discussion at Columbia University, had admitted to being a lesbian: "The disclosure," read the anonymous story, "is bound to discredit [Millett] as a spokeswoman for her cause, cast further doubt on her theories, and reinforce the views of those skeptics who routinely dismiss all liberationists as lesbians."[3] Rescinding in December the very icon status it had bestowed in August, *Time* revealed its original investment in Millett as a safe, and safely "normal," figure. When she was revealed as not only an erotic subject but a transgressively erotic subject, Millett's sexuality discredited her status as spokesperson. In her book *Flying*, published in 1974, Millett insisted that she was never closeted about her sexuality; *Time* had produced a feminist star by constructing a closet around her.[4]

I want to focus here on the coincidence of "cover girl" and theorist, on the history-making emergence of Millett from the molten masses of the women's movement as "the Mao Tse-tung of Women's Liberation" and on the notoriety that her emergence produced. As the original story pointed out, Millett-as-Mao was exactly the "sort of description she and her sisters despise[d]." *Time* reported unironically that feminists rejected "the notion of leaders and heroines as creations of the media—and mimicry of the ways that men use to organize their world." Millett herself speculated that the public question she faced about her sexual life came from feminists infuriated over her heterosexualized *Time* profile.[5] Millett wrote of a conversation with a friend about the *Time* cover story and its aftermath: the friend comments, "They set you up for this, *Time* Magazine, that cover job." "[Y]eah, I know now," Millett replies, adding for the reader, "But I didn't know. Never knew until it was out. My face on the cover. They asked me whose picture they should use. . . . I said no one woman but crowds of them. . . .

Then the shock when the cover was printed, idiots sending it to me for autographs. Just what the movement hates."[6]

The narrative of Millett's rise and fall and the circulation within that narrative of issues of female erotic identity reflect an ongoing ambivalence toward the concept of "theory" in feminist circles. In this book I argue that such ambivalence represents one of the crucial features of feminist-theoretical production, not only in the women's liberation movement and the activist discourses at its heart but also in the academic-theoretical discourses that emerged from and paralleled this activist tradition.

In feminist contexts, the concept of "theory" has at certain moments signified elitism, exclusiveness, and detachment from material politics: Millett on the magazine cover stands apart from the Movement, seemingly detached, aloof, authoritative. At the same time, and often in the same breath, feminists argue for the vital need for rigorous theory, in order to bring about feminist social change and feminist education. Theory is at worst feminism's necessary evil, at best an exhilarating, if fraught, context for the articulation of fresh analytical insights, of new possibilities. The *Time* story vests feminist theory with symbolic authority within the women's movement. It also acknowledges that feminists are focused on dismantling structures of authority. Millett embodies a paradox that circulates again and again in feminist discourses: feminist theory is a form of authoritative discourse whose own authoritative implications must be undone as a function of its political critique.

How, then, have feminists managed to achieve theoretical insights and effective working paradigms without reproducing the very dynamics of authority and elitism they seek to eliminate? How have they managed to talk the talk *and* walk the walk?

In setting Millett up for a fall, an exposure, a debunking, *Time* cannily manipulated the antiauthoritarian ideology already circulating within the women's movement, cleverly pitting feminists against one another. This book describes how that story is imbedded within feminist discourses themselves: I analyze a number of efforts to reconcile the powerfully contradictory challenges of feminist antiauthoritarian authority. The process has been far from debilitating; it has in fact empowered, energized, and nuanced feminist discourses from the beginning of the second wave. Its histories lend insight into political and rhetorical tensions among feminists, and thus into conflicts and continuities that have given shape to contemporary feminist social discourses.

Feminist writers have always acknowledged that "theory" can represent a power formation at odds with the egalitarian political goals that motivate its production; this concern has been a constant in feminist discourses from the early 1970s through the end of the century, in contexts ranging from political activism to literary criticism. As Barbara Christian has suggested, theoretical abstraction is political: if knowledge is power, then the feminist analysis of power must entail the analysis of institutions through which knowledge is produced.[7] Deborah McDowell has argued that the resistance to theory is less concerned with theory per se than with "theory" as one privileged signifier of certain elite forms of practice. McDowell calls for "an insistence that we inquire into why [theory] is so reductively defined and why its common definitions exclude so many marginalized groups within the academy."[8] Mapping the persistent devaluing of African American feminists' work as political or critical, as "practice" rather than "theory," McDowell argues that such "hierarchical arrangements of knowledge" duplicate hierarchies of race and gender. The academic canonization of theory produces a politics of exclusion both within the academy and also between "academic" theories and those generated from contexts other than the scholarly.[9] This phenomenon, McDowell argues, reveals a great deal about the institutional politics of the academy, as well as the limited scope of the feminist theoretical canon: "When the writings of black women and other critics of color are excluded from the category of theory, it must be partly because theory has been reduced to a very particular practice."[10]

This book addresses various authorizing strategies that feminists have employed to produce the "very particular practice" that McDowell identifies as "theory." She suggests that this practice is selectively inclusive, that it constructs an ideological profile through the ideas it chooses to value and to disregard. In the context of McDowell's observation, in the chapters that follow I attempt to address terms by which that feminist ideological story has been produced.[11] All feminisms, I argue—whether in the classroom, on the streets, or in the pages of *Time* magazine or academic journals—that attempt to present a systematic justification, definition, explanation, or hypothesis linked more or less concretely to a body of evidence are "theoretical." This argument underscores the fact that the high-theoretical canon of academic tradition is always in conversation with an array of theoretical modes drawing from other epistemological traditions, whether or not those relations are presented explicitly. José Esteban Muñoz, for one, argues that the queer visual and performance artists of color at the center of his study *Disidentifications* produce valuable contributions to "theory":

> After this tour of different high-theory paradigms, I find myself in a position where I need to reassert that part of my aim in this book is to push against [a] reified understanding of theory. The cultural workers whom I focus on can be seen as making theoretical points and contributions to the

issues explored in ways that are just as relevant and useful as the phalanx
of institutionally sanctioned theorists that I promiscuously invoke throughout these pages. To think of cultural workers such as Carmelita Tropicana,
Vaginal Creme Davis, Richard Fung, and the other artists who are considered
here as not only culture makers but also theory producers is not to take an
antitheory position.[12]

Muñoz describes his challenge to "high-theory paradigms" as "an attempt
at opening up a term whose meaning has become narrow and rigid."[13] Like
both Christian and McDowell, Muñoz links the need for epistemological diversity with issues of racial, gender, and erotic difference. In feminist
contexts beginning with the women's liberation movement and in academic
as well as activist discourses, the homogenizing, hegemonic tropes of theoretical logic have been challenged most consistently, and most effectively,
by such analyses. As Muñoz demonstrates, to point out or even to mobilize
such a challenge "is not to take an antitheory position"; rather, it is to insist
on theory's powerful explanatory force. It is also to address that power cau-
tiously by insisting on the meticulous exposition of the material conditions
in which it is produced.

In feminist contexts, the first step toward the examination of a theory's
material origins frequently comes as a challenge to that theory's abstract
logic, to its position as a discourse detached or abstracted from detail. A
theoretical discourse both requires and presupposes a logic of abstraction:
abstraction is the process by which material evidence is distilled into a narrative, a coherent story that isolates causes, effects, and implications. But
that very process of story making, of constructing an overarching theory
that links multiple sites of material evidence, requires feminists to step back
from the local and the material in order to take a broader view. This is the
double bind of feminist theoretical production: abstraction from the local is,
on the one hand, useful and necessary; on the other, it represents the failure
to account for all the material claims and challenges local evidence presents.
The double bind is also powerfully useful, however. It represents the formative dialectic of feminist theoretical production: feminist theory, I argue, is
an ethical system that requires material challenges to any abstraction. This
is an ethics bound up with a larger critique of power and authority, and also
with the feminist effort to be relevant to all women even while understanding that within the large, abstract category "women," no two individuals
are the same. In a sense, the most oddly powerful and persistent observation
of feminist theory is its very inadequacy to the task at hand.

As Karl Marx suggests, abstraction is first and foremost a means of expression, the way the material world makes itself available for use, exchange,

and circulation. Marx's argument is just as concerned with epistemological terms as with economics; indeed, the two are as one in the discourse of dialectical materialism. Sharon Marcus usefully abstracts Marx's argument, explaining that "abstraction is the synthesis of the particular into a more general concept or system based on resemblance rather than difference."[14] In this formulation, Marcus makes it clear that the very fact of abstraction leaves difference behind, consolidating the "more general concept or system" via homogenization; given the feminist investment in difference, abstraction thus poses a political problem from the very first. Marcus continues, describing "alienation" as "the process by which abstraction *from* the material or the particular occurs."[15] Again, abstraction concerns a detachment from the material sphere. In Marcus's terms, abstraction and alienation are spatial metaphors distinguished from the matter to which they refer but always gesturing back toward the material world that is their reference point. Detached from but referring to the material sphere, abstraction is divorced from but also dependent on matter. Matter requires abstraction for its description and expression; abstraction requires matter for a point of reference.

Working from the examples of Marx and Jacques Lacan, Marcus writes,

> [A]lienation is not the absolute loss of the thing alienated but a means of elaborating a relation to that thing. In the Lacanian notion of the mirror stage, subjects attain an illusory but powerful sense of coherence and selfhood only by alienating themselves into such nebulous objects as mirror images. The mirror stage thus anticipates the symbolic stage, in which the subject is alienated into language, into abstract signifying systems and social exchanges, and into such idealizations as the phallus, which represents lack and "can play its role only when veiled."[16]

Subjects become subjects, in other words, through a process of abstraction and a mechanics of alienation; language, always alienated from the material world to which it refers, produces individual subjects in its own mold. Lacan invokes a range of patriarchal signifiers as tokens of this process, including the phallus, the symbolic, and the Law of the Father, suggesting that the subjects constituted through abstraction and alienation are fully products of a patriarchal system; hence the primal quality that characterizes feminist critiques of and resistance to abstraction.[17] For Lacan, as for Marx, abstraction signifies the alienation by which culture makes itself known to each individual: for Lacan, abstraction is the constitutive trope of patriarchy, just as, for Marx, it is the constitutive trope of capitalism. Thus, the question of how best to understand, to resist, and to utilize abstraction has been a keynote of second-wave feminist theory in the United States; the question is integral to understanding feminists' relationships to language and to power.

Resistance to abstraction and its codifying implications is not identical to a wholesale resistance to or rejection of theory, though it is frequently mistaken as such. Indeed, in this book I argue that feminist challenges to abstraction oftentimes represent a deeply felt ethical conviction: an attempt to make theory an ever finer, ever more material, ever more effective analytical tool. Abstraction has a material function within a feminist theoretical context; it affords advantages by acting as a distancing or globalizing maneuver, even as such distance itself marks detachment from the material issues under examination. Because abstraction is the constitutive condition of language, any concept of material politics, change, or intervention requires abstraction as its mode of expression, regardless of whether the "language" in question is mediated through ink, chalk, pixels, paint, film, videotape, or discursive forms still on the horizon of technology. Throughout the vast range of feminist political interventions, an acute concern with the relationship between abstract expression and the material world that abstraction both constitutes and serves remains a constant. Feminists frequently express this concern in terms of a worrisome gap between theory and practice.

If abstraction gestures toward the material world but also marks our alienation from it, the limits of abstraction define feminist theory's function and effectiveness. David Simpson, in a discussion of theory's ideological underpinnings in Enlightenment Europe, suggests a complex historical past for theoretical methods, "with [their] apparently inevitable appetite for assertions about what is normative, schematically elegant, and describable by acts of pure intellection." Accordingly, in the 1960s, theory and method, Simpson suggests, "were coming under attack from the left itself as symptoms of the problem rather than the solution, as instances of elitism, masculinism, Eurocentrism, and a merely instrumental reason."[18] The production of a theoretical paradigm assumes a global ideal of portability—what Paul de Man calls the expression of "a system of some conceptual generality," of "normative principles."[19] In a feminist context, the construction of overarching principles from local evidence requires the consolidation of resistance, diversity, and internal difference. In other words, the very process of theory making repeats terms already thematically central to feminist debates, including tensions between normativity and alterity, the global and the local, the collective and the individual. Particularly in a feminist context, Simpson suggests, any claim to "autonomous critical knowledge . . . has a bad reputation. . . . [I]t is masculinist (as 'theory' itself is often said to be), exploitative, and Eurocentric, and it is received equally critically by the poststructuralist left whether it emanates from classic capitalism or classic Marxism."[20]

Writing of the risks feminists undertake in reproducing the "epistemological imperialism" they critique, Judith Butler warns, "The effort to *include* 'Other' cultures as variegated amplifications of a global phallogocentrism constitutes an appropriative act that risks a repetition of the self-aggrandizing gesture of phallogocentrism, colonizing under the sign of the same those differences that might otherwise call that totalizing concept into question."[21] As Butler suggests, epistemological models themselves, operating as abstractions, enact colonizing gestures, even or perhaps especially within theories designed to accommodate "difference." This has serious consequences extending even to the erasure of difference—or resistance, or "Otherness"—altogether from an epistemological system. Gayatri Chakravorty Spivak argues that the descriptive rhetoric of explanation also implies just such a homogenizing dynamic: "I call 'politics as such' the prohibition of marginality that is implicit in the production of any explanation. From that point of view, the choice of particular binary oppositions . . . is no mere intellectual strategy. It is, in each case, the condition of the possibility for centralization (with appropriate apologies) and, correspondingly, marginalization."[22]

In her focus on the rhetorics in which explanatory paradigms are produced, Spivak argues that theoretical models replicate imperialist relations of margin and center. There is no avoiding this inevitability, she suggests, but the awareness of it entails an ethical obligation for feminists, addressed only through scrupulous self-interrogation. Judith Butler concurs with Spivak's argument, writing, "Feminist critique ought to explore the totalizing claims of a masculinist signifying economy, but also remain self-critical with respect to the totalizing gestures of feminism."[23] And, as Kate Millett's example suggests, the problem of theory—how to do it, how to do it well, how to elude its doctrinaire or hierarchical or exclusionary associations—has circulated in feminist discourses from the beginning of the second wave. This occurred with particular explicitness in the women's liberation movement, which placed a premium on the egalitarian, inclusive qualities of movement politics. Even the task of defining "feminism" itself, of staking claim to its terms and goals, its objects of analysis, and its metalanguages, was fraught with concern over the limits any such statement of purpose imposed, whether willfully or blindly.

This concern frequently expressed itself, and still does, in discussions of theoretical language as exclusive or privileged. For example, the editorial collective of the French feminist journal *Questions féministes* contended in 1977 that the adjective *theoretical* "too often refers to inaccessible texts that are destined for a privileged social elite" and that "theory" is "synonymous with hermetic, as if the obscure nature of a text established its 'scientific value,' its 'seriousness.'" They proposed a definition of "theory" that emphasizes its pragmatic, democratic qualities:

> We want to rehabilitate the true meaning of theory and by so doing make theory everyone's concern, so that each of us can not only use it but also produce it. We consider as theoretical *any discourse, whatever its language may be,* that attempts to *explain the causes and the mechanisms,* the *why* and the *how* of women's oppression in general or of one of its particular aspects. "Theoretical" means any discourse that attempts to draw political conclusions, that offers a strategy or tactics to the feminist movement.[24]

"Theory" in this model is quite simply an explanatory principle, and "feminist theory" is a particular explanatory principle addressing "the why and the how of women's oppression." Theory offers a vocabulary, a metalanguage, by which feminism might describe itself relative to the "strategy or tactics" it posits for material change. Recognizing the power of this function, the writers aim to enfranchise anyone as a producer as well as a consumer of theory—to replace, as it were, a portrait of one powerful theorist alone on a magazine cover with the crowd of faces for which Millett had originally wished.

To trace the shifting terms of this debate is an effort *Skeptical Feminism* only begins to initiate, but by doing so I aim to open access to the different meanings of feminist praxis over time. In order to situate feminist theory within a material history of its production, I focus on sites at which "the why and the how" of feminist discourses come under interrogation, at which the social significance of feminist ideologies, interpretations, or actions are at stake. This is to construct a very simple definition of "theory," after the pattern of the *Questions féministes* collective, as a form of abstract statement or hypothesis serving the purpose of constructing or enacting a critique; it is also to assume a continuous relationship between the abstract principles of feminist theory and the material implications of feminist political practice. In the context of these assumptions, then, this book poses several questions: Through what specific epistemological and political procedures is "feminism" produced as theory? and is "theory" produced as feminist? How does resistance to theoretical abstraction inflect the terms by which such production occurs? What does a feminist history of theory—or a history of feminist theory, or a theory of feminist history—have to teach us about theory itself as a phenomenon vested with great cultural value?[25]

If theory is the metalanguage of feminism, then feminism can usefully serve as a metalanguage of theory, as a means of understanding the relations of theory and practice in any context, critical and/or political. Feminist theories of politics and of interpretation provide a way of understanding how theoretical paradigms more generally begin to account for the hierarchies they challenge, reproduce, or represent. To historicize the terms by which feminist theory has been produced thus offers insight into the terms "feminism" and "theory" simultaneously, as epistemological and political categories, in relation to one another and as mutually resistant terminologies.

In *Sexual Politics*, Kate Millett presents a series of literary-critical analyses in the chapter she describes as the book's most challenging, "Theory of Sexual Politics," which "attempts to formulate a systematic overview of patriarchy as a political institution."[26] The salient point about "Theory of Sexual Politics," as with any theoretical model, is its vast, even universalizing, scope: striving to achieve "systematic overview" requires the homogenization of local detail in favor of abstract generalizations. In itself, the gesture of homogenization replays a central tension within feminist epistemology and politics, that is, the dialectic between the globalizing imperatives of a feminist collective and the resistant claims of individual differences, often framed within terms of race, class, and sexuality. Again, like the failure of one face on the magazine cover to symbolize the scope and diversity of all feminists' perspectives, a single "theory of sexual politics," however convincing it may be, sacrifices detail to achieve a "systematic overview."

Ann Pellegrini associates homogenization with a politics of oppression and connects the feminist embrace of difference with a wholesale resistance to "subjugation": "[T]he denial or erasure of differences *within* marginalized or oppressed classes has much more often been a tactic imposed from 'above' than asserted from below in the name of liberation. Homogenization, the refusal to recognize particularity, is one of the better-known mechanisms of subjugation."[27] Historian Alice Echols notes that, in the early 1970s, an insistence on homogeneity or sameness worked in the end to undermine radical feminists' analysis, offered in the name of "sisterhood." Echols contends that "radical feminists' emphasis upon women's commonality masked a fear of difference, one which had serious consequences for the movement. Differences—either those rooted in class, race, and sexual preference, or those of skill and expertise—were seen as undermining the movement. When lesbians and working-class women finally pierced the myth of women's commonality, the movement was temporarily paralyzed, thus proving to some that differences were inevitably crippling."[28]

However paralyzing its temporary effects, the "piercing" of that myth was quite arguably a sign of health, a signifier of the growing pains of a feminist epistemology called upon to make ever more rigorous its constitutive terms. Barbara Johnson suggests that the analysis of conflict among feminists makes available a newly heterogeneous feminist logic. This approach slips the trap, Johnson argues, of those heterosexist, patriarchal ways of thought that perceive the only differences that matter to be those that exist between women and men:

> [A]s long as a feminist analysis polarizes the world by gender, women are still standing *facing* men. Standing against men, or against patriarchy, might not be structurally so different from existing *for* it. A feminist logic that pits women against men operates along the lines of heterosexual thinking. But conflicts among feminists require women to pay attention to each other, to take each other's reality seriously, to face each other. This requirement that women face each other may not have anything erotic or sexual about it, but it may have everything to do with the eradication of the misogyny that remains within feminists, and with the attempt to escape the logic of heterosexuality. It places differences *among* women rather than exclusively *between* the sexes.[29]

Johnson urges feminists to face off, literally and figuratively; to pay attention to each other and to respect their internal conflicts as sufficiently serious that they merit full analytical attention. She diagnoses the resistance to this sort of work as a lingering misogyny within feminism and as a vestige of the heterosexist thinking that orients feminists toward masculine and patriarchal objects of analysis. The effort to swap oppositional and thus heterosexist thinking for polymorphous difference and diversity represents, for Johnson, the embrace of a productive indeterminacy: "[T]he project of bringing about change on the basis of a category like 'woman' will eventually encounter the lack of fit between 'woman' and the heterogeneous reality of women."[30] Feminist theory has come into being through the challenges imposed by the "lack of fit" Johnson identifies: the drive to produce powerfully effective, widely applicable epistemological paradigms is mediated by the requirement that such theories resist universal claims, that they account for individual difference. Judith Roof summarizes the double bind, writing that feminist critics "attempt to recognize and comprehend the multiple differences that exist among women and . . . work these different perspectives into a feminist methodology that can allow and theorize multiplicity while remaining politically and intellectually effective."[31] Dissent internal to feminism, especially as it has concerned women's individual diversity, has pushed feminists hard to consider and reconsider their foundational terms, their unconscious politics.

Textual Politics: Theory as a Status Symbol

In her 1985 book *Sexual/Textual Politics,* which situates a concern with the "textual" within Millett's paradigm of sexual politics, Toril Moi contends that "[o]ne of the central principles of feminist criticism is that no account can ever be neutral."[32] Moi's book is organized through a contrast between Anglo-American feminist "criticism" and French feminist "theory," and it deliberately focuses this distinction within the disciplinary politics of literary studies.[33] French feminism, for Moi, exceeds the Anglo-American tradition in its intellectual rigor, whereas the Anglo-American critical tradition unconsciously reproduces pernicious, patriarchal humanist conventions: "My reservations about much Anglo-American feminist criticism are thus not primarily that it has remained within the lineage of male-centred humanism but that it has done so without sufficient awareness of the high political cost this entails" (87). Moi argues, in contrast, that French feminism engages its intellectual precedents more knowingly:

> One of the reasons for the relatively limited influence of French theory on Anglo-American feminists is the "heavy" intellectual profile of the former. Steeped as they are in European philosophy (particularly Marx, Nietzsche and Heidegger), Derridean deconstruction and Lacanian psychoanalysis, French feminist theorists apparently take for granted an audience as Parisian as they are. Though rarely willfully obscure, the fact that few pedagogical concessions are made to the reader without the "correct" intellectual coordinates smacks of elitism to the outsider. This holds for Hélène Cixous's intricate puns and Luce Irigaray's infuriating passion for the Greek alphabet, as well as for Julia Kristeva's unsettling habit of referring to everyone from St Bernard to Fichte or Artaud in the same sentence. (96)

Here Moi raises a serious point concerning the potentially exclusive nature of French feminism's "intellectual profile," whose complexities she implicitly celebrates under the sign of the difficult. "Outsiders" to this tradition did in fact criticize its inaccessibility; but, unlike Moi, I would suggest that such critique is far from equivalent to an antitheoretical or anti-intellectual bias.

After all, there is more than one way to do theory. No single theoretical tradition is fully sufficient to address the analytical challenges posed by feminism; indeed, insofar as the very existence of feminist critique signifies a challenge to conventions of theoretical epistemology, the restriction of "feminist theory" to a single genealogy does a disservice both intellectual and political not only to feminism but to theory as well. Moi's account of French feminism has been justly valued for its insights into an influential, innovative, rigorous, and useful body of theoretical work. Yet that same account establishes French feminism's intellectual value by constructing a foil of Anglo-American feminists' work. As Moi points out, writers such as Cixous, Irigaray, and Kristeva produce and deploy an erudite theoretical vocabulary. However, questions of intellectual pedigree have been quite sensitive within feminist discourses perceived as tightly bound up with elitist patriarchal val-ues; hence the premium placed not only on specialized theoretical vocabular-ies but also on those that appeal to many different audiences.

Making a case for the diversification of the theoretical canon in terms that reflect multiple traditions of identity and education, Barbara Christian writes, "People of color have always theorized . . . but in forms quite differ-ent from the Western form of abstract logic."[34] From another perspective, Susan Brownmiller, at the end of a 1999 memoir about the women's libera-tion movement, argues that by the early 1980s "feminist theory had gone as far as it could go in the twentieth century."[35] Brownmiller's "feminist theory" makes no reference to the philosophical and literary tradition that Moi describes as "feminist theory" in toto. Yet in no sense is Brownmiller's conception of feminist theory, or Christian's, any less theoretical or any less feminist than Moi's.

"Anglo-American feminist critics," Moi argues, "have been mostly indif-ferent or even hostile toward literary theory, which they have regarded as a hopelessly abstract 'male' activity" (70). Arguments such as this one, how-ever, perpetuate a high-culture–low-culture split in feminist discourses.[36] In response to this problem, Biddy Martin writes,

> Some feminist literary theorists tend either to ignore non-academic move-ment texts or to treat them as unreadable, unreadable but classifiable like so-ciological evidence. They become part of the critics' received wisdom about the problems with what is called "radical" feminism. This coheres with the temptation to narrate the history of feminist thinking from what is assumed to be a self-evident center, that is, academic theory, a narrative that almost inevitably marginalizes questions of sexuality and race, when they are, after all, absolutely central from the point of view of other possible histories.[37]

Moi's assumption that Anglo-American feminist critics are not only untheo-retical but antitheoretical as well helps to construct the assumption that aca-demic discourses provide feminism with the "self-evident center" that Mar-tin describes—a center that Martin suggests marginalizes as many issues as it addresses. Moi conflates a particular feminist mode, a subgenre that locates itself within a Western European hermeneutic and philosophical tradition, with the sum total of "theory" in a feminist context, regardless of the ideo-logical assumptions this argument imposes. The Anglo-American resistance to theory, Moi suggests, leads critics to reproduce the very humanist catego-ries they would otherwise seek to dismantle, blind to their implicit gender politics. Suggesting, for example, that Kate Millett's focus on misogynist male writers blinds her to the tactics by which women writers have resisted patriarchy, Moi writes, "Millett's view of sexual ideology cannot account for the evident fact that throughout history a few exceptional women have indeed managed to resist the full pressure of patriarchal ideology, becoming conscious of their own oppression and voicing their opposition to male power. Only a concept of ideology as a contradictory construct, marked by gaps, slides, and inconsistencies, would enable feminism to explain how even the severest ideological pressures will generate their own lacunae" (26). In Millett's paradigm, Moi suggests, patriarchy is irresistible, constant, and universally oppressive to the universal population of "women." Because Millett's theoretical model fails to account for women's resistance to the fissures and instabilities within patriarchal power, Moi contends that it is fatally one-sided.

Sexual/Textual Politics addresses "the relationship between feminist critical readings and the often unconscious theoretical and political assumptions that inform them" (1). Yet that argument, too—any argument, for that matter, including mine—is beholden to unspoken and unconscious assumptions. For example, Moi constructs the terms of her analysis through a homogenization of "French theoretical" and "Anglo-American critical" intellectual traditions, in a context in which "theory" and "criticism" are not value-neutral designations: in their literary criticism, Anglo-American feminists are represented as provincial, naive (if well-meaning), plot-bound, and, at worst, anti-intellectual. Moi elevates "theory"—located within a specifically French cultural and philosophical context—over and against "criticism" in a paradigm that not so subtly reinscribes the hierarchy of intellectualized abstraction over positivist practice.

This argument does not credit theoretical epistemology itself as a vessel of ideological reproduction. Moi's consideration of "alternative" feminist traditions in the Anglo-American context is limited to the following comment: "Some feminists might wonder why I have said nothing about black or lesbian (or black lesbian) feminist criticism in America in this survey. The answer is simple: this book purports to deal with the theoretical aspects of feminist criticism. So far, lesbian and/or black feminist criticism have presented exactly the same *methodological* and *theoretical* problems as the rest of Anglo-American feminist criticism" (86; emphases in original).[38] Such a dismissal of "lesbian and/or black" feminist interventions as identical to "the rest of Anglo-American feminist criticism" underscores bell hooks's contention that feminist theories have generally consolidated the positions of white middle-class feminists at the expense of others: "This has led many women outside the privileged race/class group to see the focus on developing theory, even the very use of the term, as a concern that functions only to reinforce the power of the elite group."[39] From the late 1960s onward, "lesbian and/or black" feminists, hooks included, criticized influential feminists and feminist paradigms, establishing themselves, separately and collectively, as voices of resistance to the feminist claim to speak for all women. Such internal resistance provided a shaping influence for feminist epistemologies in literary-critical as well as political contexts. In not only homogenizing but erasing the significance of "lesbian and/or black" feminist interventions, Moi herself falls into the trap in a maneuver for which she criticizes Millett and other Anglo-American feminists: she draws conclusions about the entire theoretical spectrum of Anglo-American feminism from the evidence of a few normative viewpoints. Critiquing Anglo-American feminism for its simplistic relationship to humanist categories of identity and knowledge, Moi represents that tradition symptomatically, within straightened, whitened categories.

Theory as a Practice of Language; or, Why a Literary-Critical Methodology Is Useful to Feminists

Biddy Martin has suggested that feminist theorists following Millett and Moi within the feminist subgenre of literary studies tend "to equate feminist literary theory with feminist theory *per se.*"[40] In order to suggest strategies for understanding symbolic resistance within feminist theory—as well as to feminist theory—I argue that the slippage Martin points out is both important and revealing; the rather obnoxious assumption that feminist literary theory speaks for all feminist theory in fact reveals something important about how feminists have approached the matter of theory. This concerns the built-in ideological conflict constitutive of feminist theory in the first place, the conflict between the *need* for authoritative paradigms in a political tradition mobilized *against* authoritative paradigms. Literary theory makes available to feminism an analysis of linguistic instability that coheres powerfully with feminism's fundamentally nihilistic theoretical core.

Kate Millett suggests that literature offers its analysts an especially direct entrance into the structuring principles of patriarchal culture: precisely because it is not empirical, literature is a site at which otherwise elusive subtleties of patriarchal power and its abuses, intimate complexities, and internal contradictions reveal themselves to the feminist critic. Precisely because literature is not schematic, she argues, it offers up subtle evidence for feminists' schematic critique of patriarchy. The literary critic is uniquely positioned at the taproot of ideological reproduction: "It has been my conviction that the adventure of literary criticism . . . is capable of seizing upon the larger insights which literature affords into the life it describes, or interprets, or even distorts."[41] Millett sees no discontinuity between "the adventure of literary criticism" and its feminist political implications, and, accordingly, she inaugurates a tradition in which the representational analysis of literature and aesthetics more generally constitutes a material intervention in feminist politics.[42] "[T]he task for politically engaged critics," wrote Biddy Martin more than twenty-five years after Millett, "has to include sustained respect for and access to the love of literature that emerges from the power it has to organize and express fantasies—fantasies that are irreducible to the effects of social and political power, however nuanced our understandings of those effects might be; fantasies hold open a gap, a space, or a gulch that cannot be covered by making subjectivity only an effect of discipline and control."[43]

"Theory" is an ambivalent proposition for feminists, whether it signifies a form of intellectual elitism (consider, for example, bell hooks's critique of academic feminist jargon for its implicit exclusion of readers from diverse educational backgrounds)[44] or an abstract proposition about gender identity (consider the instability of the category "woman" in the context of scientific conflict about the location and meaning of sexual difference).[45] Some have argued that public dissent within feminism plays into the hands of antifeminist factions pursuing a divide-and-conquer strategy.[46] This is a risk, to be sure. But it's also the case that contention, dissent, and internal resistance within feminist discourses might signify the renewal of political commitment through the insistence on ever more rigorous, ever more precise analytical terms. Resistance, wrote Freud, acts as an *"agent provocateur."*[47] In this case, a resistance to theory—in the name of the local or of difference or diversity—provokes the redefinition of feminism's express political agendas. In thus reclaiming political intervention, abstract theory is reoriented in relation to material practice.

Wlad Godzich points out that the logical opposition of "theory" and "practice" is of relatively recent invention; he traces "theory" etymologically to the Greek *theorein,* meaning "to look at, to contemplate, to survey."[48] John Ruskin, who in a different guise plays a major role in Millett's *Sexual Politics,* notes tellingly that the opposite of *theorein* is *aesthesis:* "The mere animal consciousness of . . . pleasantness I call Aesthesis, but the exulting, reverent, and grateful perception of it I call Theoria."[49] For both Godzich and Ruskin, the distinction between *theoria* and *aesthesis,* or theory and the aesthetic, is analogous to the split between public and private, the empirical and the affective, the mind and the "mere animal consciousness" of bodily response. Implicit within this logic is a distinction between the detached methodical, empirical systems of *theoria* and the intuitive engagements of *aesthesis.* This echoes Millett's suggestion that literature and other forms of aesthetic production offer unique insights into patriarchal power. Millett suggests that because literature, an aesthetic object, is unstable and unempirical, it reveals subtleties and internal contradictions concealed within more empirical data.[50] Literature exceeds codified theoretical logic, and its

affective, excessive qualities offer strategies for subverting prescriptive ideologies. Millett presents a useful paradox: a schematic theory generated from
unschematic evidence. Indeed, in this aspect of her work, Millett predicted
one of the major tactics that later feminists used to disrupt the patriarchal
conventions of theory production. Like Millett, they worked assiduously to
ground their theoretical conclusions not in data conventionally viewed as
consistent, empirical, or reasonable but in data drawn from the intuitive,
the emotional, the experiential, and the aesthetic. This work supports a
larger feminist investment in generating normative principles about the pernicious implications of normative principles.

Godzich, noting that the word *theoria* is "always a plural collective,"
presents a narrative of origins for the political authority vested within theory
production. Tellingly, for feminism, the theorist in this fable is a functionary
of the state, and "theory" itself serves ideological ends. I quote this story at
length:

> [T]he act of looking at, of surveying, designated by *theorein* does not desig-
> nate a private act carried out by a cogitating philosopher but a very public
> one with important social consequences. The Greeks designated certain in-
> dividuals, chosen on the basis of their probity and their general standing in
> the polity, to act as legates on certain formal occasions in other city states or
> in matters of considerable political importance. These individuals bore the
> title of *theoros,* and collectively constituted a *theoria.* . . . They were sum-
> moned on special occasions to attest the occurrence of some event, to wit-
> ness its happenstance, and to then verbally certify its having taken place. . . .
> In other words, their function was one of see-and-tell. To be sure, other
> individuals in the city could see and tell, but their telling was no more than
> a *claim* that they had seen something, and it needed some authority to adju-
> dicate the validity of such a claim. The city needed a more official and more
> ascertainable form of knowledge if it was not to lose itself in endless claims
> and counterclaims. The *theoria* provided such a bedrock of certainty: what
> is certified as having been seen could become the object of public discourse.
> The individual citizen, indeed even women, slaves, and children, were ca-
> pable of aesthesis, that is perception, but these perceptions had no social
> standing. They were not sanctioned and thus could not form the basis of
> deliberation, judgment, and action in the polity. Only the theoretically at-
> tested event could be treated as a fact. The institutional nature of this certi-
> fication ought not to escape us, as well as its social inscription.[51]

In Godzich's fable, theory represents the voice of the institution, of the state.
Theory represents privileged vision, a state-sanctioned "bedrock of certainty"
or authorized facticity; and the theorist himself, a patriarch standing apart

from women, slaves, and children, serves the judicial and indeed ideological function of the state, defining reality and authorizing "deliberation, judgment, and action." In a subtle reinscription of characteristics conventionally associated with the male and the female, the theoretical state apparatus privileges the public over the private, the empirical over the affective, the abstract over the material. Following an etymological fable such as this one, the resistance to theory would seem to be a logical prerequisite of feminist political identity.

If *theoria* is a hegemonic concept constructed in contrast to *aesthesis*, then the feminist embrace of aesthetic critique as a mode of political action might be seen as a means of accommodating this distinction: the women, children, and slaves cut out of *theoria* but in touch with *aesthesis* might use that alternative means to erode the official version of the "real," to undermine the concept of *theoria* itself. Thus, "the adventure of literary criticism" takes on a whole new set of implications. In the context of such an adventure, Paul de Man, discussing resistance provoked by literary theory and its practitioners, contends that "the main theoretical interest of literary theory consists in the impossibility of its definition."[52] Within the terms of de Man's argument, the very literary concerns of literary theory have the capacity to disrupt the hegemonic implications of *theoria* itself. "Theory," for de Man, represents the effort to organize knowledge systematically, to generalize outward about abstract or universal implications—the "normative principles" (6)—of particular events, concepts, or methods. The leap to abstraction is not equal to diminished accessibility; indeed, de Man aligns theory with pedagogical usefulness: "As a controlled reflection on the formation of method, theory rightly proves to be entirely compatible with teaching, and one can think of numerous important theoreticians who are or were also prominent scholars" (4). Literary theory in this context represents "the rooting of literary exegesis and of critical evaluation in a system of some conceptual generality" (5), even as literature itself, as the aesthetic object of such systematizing efforts, is necessarily resistant to the procedures of general codification.

For de Man, this concerns the linguistic implications of literary exegesis; literary critics in the post-Saussurian tradition conceive of language as a system of signs that refers always (and only) to its own limitations, to the gap between the abstract signifier and the material referent: "[N]o one in his right mind will try to grow grapes by the luminosity of the word 'day'" (11). Thus, as the enterprise responsible for "controlled reflection" on the implications of language, literary theory is constituted entirely within the terms of its epistemological failure, riding the circuit of self-referentiality as a form of negative-knowledge production. This is in sharp contrast with epistemologies in the scientific tradition, which preserve an investment in their positive implications—an investment, in other words, in their success, not their failure, as working generalizations.

Such essential negativity is the founding condition of all literary-theoretical enterprises and a reason, I suggest, for literary theory's historic usefulness to feminists inside and outside literary disciplines, inside and outside concepts of "discipline" altogether. De Man writes,

> It may well be . . . that the development of literary theory is itself over-determined by complications inherent in its very project and unsettling with regard to its status as a scientific discipline. Resistance may be a built-in constituent of its discourse, in a manner that would be inconceivable in the natural sciences and unmentionable in the social sciences. It may well be, in other words, that the polemical opposition, the systematic non-understanding and misrepresentation, the unsubstantial but eternally recurrent objections, are the displaced symptoms of a resistance inherent in the theoretical enterprise itself. (12)

For de Man, "literature" is "the place where this negative knowledge about the reliability of linguistic utterance is made available"; literature speaks of language itself and thus, however unreliably, of epistemology in its most general sense (10). Literary theory, replete with tautological implications, emerges as the theory of all theoretical enterprises, composed as they are of linguistic utterances and representational practices.[53] Within the terms of this logic, literary theory, for de Man, is metatheory, in science and politics as much as literature: in its concern with language, literary theory addresses the representational signs through which generalizations are produced—and, crucially, by which those generalizations confront their failings and limitations.

Resistance, as de Man suggests, is a "built-in" component of this sublimely unstable analytical mode. Extending the implications of de Man's argument, I suggest that linguistic instability is, perversely, the reason for the historical importance of literary theory to feminism. Feminism, too, encounters a built-in resistance that has to do with language as a system of abstraction: just as "no one in his right mind will try to grow grapes by the luminosity of the word 'day,'" no one in her right mind would assume that a feminist theory of gendered power would suffice in itself as a means of redistributing power. Theory serves as a means to that end, and a powerful one at that. As a form of abstraction, however, and as an artifact of language, it is not an end in itself.[54]

Nevertheless, literary theory's linguistic self-consciousness also offers insight into the motives of feminist theoretical resistance. Any number of important feminist theoretical interventions have addressed the matter of language directly. In 1987, Mary Daly produced *Webster's First New Intergalactic Wickedary of the English Language,* following in a long tradition of radical feminist resistance to the misogyny implicit within colloquial language; in a related vein, Alice Walker's proposal for a "womanist" movement implicated feminism in racist and classist politics, proposing, through the act of symbolic renaming, a new tradition of inclusiveness reshaped through the contributions of African American women.[55] Daly and Walker view language, as well as literature, suspiciously, as a symptom of the gendered hierarchies that their various feminist praxes are designed to combat. Their work has effected material changes in the popular understanding of language: my computer's grammar-checking program, for instance, will prompt the revision of the universal male pronoun in favor of gender-specific or gender-neutral usage. In contrast to de Man, for whom language is a self-referential circuit constituting its own negation, feminist theorists of language view it first in relation to its ideological effects, as the vehicle of immediate material implications. It is from this point that feminists engage in their own form of deconstructive practice, often through appropriative political strategies such as renaming, punning, or inventive spelling. This tactic dismantles the hegemony implicit within language by attacking at the level of the word itself. "Contests for the meanings of writing are a major form of contemporary political struggle," Donna Haraway writes in an argument focused specifically on the narrative and linguistic innovations of feminist women of color.[56] This perspective invests still more fully in the material implications of language than de Man's deconstructive argument would suggest.

There is, however, a sense in which de Man's concern with the internal resistance of language engages a tenet of the feminist theoretical enterprise. De Man argues that literary theory is constituted through its own resistance, and that both its metatheoretical importance and the backlash against its claims are conditioned by the terms of that resistance. Feminist theory models a similar ambivalence; indeed, I suggest that this very ambivalence is foundational to its effectiveness. Organized through internal paradoxes, feminist theories operate through built-in sites of resistance that produce a logical circuit of self-referentiality, an agon motivated by a core ideological discontinuity between the epistemological goals of theory making and the political goals such theory production serves. *Time* magazine's canonization of scholar Kate Millett as "theorist" emblematizes much of this ambivalence: in the name of "theory," *Time* singled out a leader to stand for the women's movement as a whole, putting one face on the cover as opposed to the crowd of faces Millett had envisioned; in Millett, *Time* identified the public, authorizing, and representative *theoros* who certified the existence of the new women's movement. Not only does this move represent the women's movement within the terms of an epistemological hierarchy in which "theory" sits firmly on top, it also enfranchises *theoros* with authority to speak for the general population of those concerned with feminist ideas.

In a political movement concerned with women's attempt to find a voice, both literally and figuratively, the media construction of Millett as representative voice is anathema: within the larger contest for a voice, how can a single theoretical model "speak" for the feminist aggregate? For that matter, what are the terms by which the aggregate is composed? Does feminism work on behalf all women? North American white middle-class women only? all gendered persons? radical separatists only? Where and how and of what constitutive terms is "gender" located, anyhow?[57] Millett explicitly disavowed the suggestion that she spoke for all feminists; but in its canonization of Millett, *Time* simply literalized canonizing implications built into the theoretical project itself. Feminism practically, politically, necessarily resists generalization. But its success as a material critique of culture demands the generalizing principles inherent within the theoretical project, for pedagogical purposes, for strategies of political organization, and for the provision of interpretive models, material aid, the raising of funds, and the securing of grants—for the very reproduction of the ideological antistate apparatus. If "theory" stands in a definitional or hypothetical relationship to the body of knowledge to which it refers, the parameters and the very goals of "feminism" retreat endlessly from generalizability, recoiling from the very epistemological premises of "normative principles." "Theory" is the necessary error of feminism, the move to generalization that it so foundationally resists.[58] This is the grounding paradox of feminist theory, the resistance that turns it back on itself.

Paul de Man argues that literary theory's self-interrogating, self-annihilating qualities offer both its most powerful site of intervention and the most powerful grounds of resistance to its implications. For de Man, linguistic instability exposes the limitations inherent within any given theoretical proposal. Feminist theory, whether consciously literary or not, is similarly tautological and continually metalinguistic, contesting the grounds of its own existence and taking into account the necessary cost at which its principles are articulated. In the context of this argument, the most important component of feminist theory, regardless of the disciplinary or political context from which it emerges, is that metatheoretical quality, precisely because the moment of self-interrogation exposes built-in limitations. The site of resistance or epistemological failure represents the potential for progress, the need to reinvent, that lends both frustration and rigor to feminism, both as an intellectual enterprise and as a political movement. "Theory," writes Bruce

Robbins, "makes politics strenuous and rare. Rare, because it is not always already there to be unearthed but must be ventured out for. And strenuous, because effort must be expended both in seeking the right face of the antagonist and in composing a resistant subject to confront it."[59] It is the very contrariness of the feminist theoretical enterprise that signals its increasing rigor: the exactingness with which local concerns rise up to challenge and to resist normative theoretical claims tests and strengthens the liberal project of feminist thought.

Coda

June 29, 1998, the cover of *Time* once again. Disembodied on a black background float four faces, all in a row, instead of just one. The first three are in black and white: Susan B. Anthony, Betty Friedan, and Gloria Steinem. In color, on the extreme right, the face of a television actress named Calista Flockhart; above her head, the name of the character she played at the time, Ally McBeal; below her head, in the region of her chest, a single question, printed in red: "Is Feminism Dead?"

Among ads for liquor, cars, and airlines appeared the story, titled "Feminism: It's All about Me!" followed by the teaser "Want to know what today's chic young feminist thinkers care about? Their bodies! Themselves!" Like all obituaries, this one was of course belated, the story situating the demise of feminism in the extinction of the very scholarly apparatus emblematized in Millett's *Sexual Politics;* author Ginia Bellafante writes, "[I]f feminism of the '60s and '70s was steeped in research and obsessed with social change, feminism today is wed to the culture of celebrity and self-obsession."[60] This story suggests that the latest trends in feminism—such as raunchy, sexually explicit celebrations of "grrrl power"—are a consequence of recent shifts in the academy that distance feminism "from matters of public purpose":

> "Women's studies, a big chunk of it at least, has focused increasingly on the symbols of the body and less on social action and social change," explains Leslie Calman, a political-science professor and director of the Center for Research on Women at Barnard College. Moreover, gender studies, the theoretical analysis of how gender identities are constructed, have become increasingly incorporated into women's studies or turned into rival departments of their own. In April, Yale University renamed its Women's Studies Department the Women and Gender Studies Department. (60)

The suggestion in this, the penultimate paragraph of a six-page cover story, is that the increasingly theoretical nature of academic feminism has created an educational vacuum; that in its emphasis on representation, on gender construction and "symbols of the body," it has failed to educate younger generations about feminist issues as issues of social justice.

Bellafante calls this the "Camille Paglia syndrome," suggesting that although the argument about women's sexual accountability proposed in Paglia's 1990 book *Sexual Personae* "was powerful and full of merit," when it was "deployed by lesser minds it quickly devolved into an excuse for media-hungry would-be feminists to share their adventures in the mall or in bed" (58–59). Underscoring the shaping force of theory on feminist history but suggesting that recent, less academically inclined feminists have somehow betrayed a heritage of intellectual seriousness, Bellafante writes, "We would never have had Ginger Spice if we hadn't had Germaine Greer" (57). The implication is that as feminism gets more and more embedded within popular culture, it will continue to get dumber and dumber. Bellafante does not take up the possibility that pop-cultural feminism, with its broader scope of influence than academic feminism, might have a serious point to make about the class-accessibility of feminist theory; nor does Bellafante credit the possibility that "duh feminism" might have any serious point—most obviously about concerns she herself emphasizes, including sexuality, economics, and power—at all.[61]

This, needless to say, is an obituary for feminism as incomplete as the announcement of its birth on August 31, 1970. But what would a biography of the twenty-eight-year life span that intervened suggest? "It's not surprising," writes Bellafante, "that Old Guard feminists, surveying their legacy, are dismayed at what they see. 'All the sex stuff is stupid,' said Betty Friedan. 'The real problems have to do with women's lives and how you put together work and family.' Says Susan Brownmiller, author of *Against Our Will*, which pioneered the idea that rape is a crime of power: 'These are not movement people. I don't know whom they're speaking for. They seem to be making individual bids for stardom'" (60).[62]

The denouement constructs the biography within fearfully symmetrical terms. The plot elements are identical. Instead of being part of a bildungs-roman, a story of "women's lives and how you put together work and family," Betty Friedan, like the editors of *Time* who canonized Kate Millett as feminism's Mao only to revoke the honor when her sexual identity was publicly revealed, finds herself in a narrative nightmare of transgressive sexuality, of erotic politics whose concerns are somehow detached from or even threatening to the icon of a happy home life. Meanwhile, Susan Brownmiller mourns the loss of collective movement politics; again recalling Millett, pictured alone instead of within a collective on that earlier cover, contemporary feminists "seem to be making individual bids for stardom."

In the article "What Ails Feminist Criticism?" which was also published during the summer of 1998, Susan Gubar describes the genealogy of her argument in answer to the title question, an argument that originated in a lecture titled "Who Killed Feminist Criticism?" "I used a murder-mystery title," Gubar writes of her original title, "to fuel suspicion that feminist criticism's evolution would circumvent the happily-ever-after of the love plot to arrive at the demise demanded by its major narrative competitor."[63] But this argument met with resistance, Gubar reports: audiences disliked the notion of an obituary for feminism, which they found premature. Instead Gubar plotted feminist history along the lines of a love story, its protagonist weak but virtuous. In response to her new title's question, "What ails feminist criticism?" Gubar seeks "one diagnostic phrase summing up the net effect of rhetorics of dissention." The diagnosis: "a bad case of critical anorexia" brought on by dissent and resistance from factions within feminism that have diffused feminism's focus as well as its effectiveness: "For racialized identity politics made the word *women* slim down to stand only for a very particularized kind of woman, whereas poststructuralists obliged the term to disappear altogether. How paradoxical that during the time of feminist criticism's successful institutionalization in many academic fields it seems to be suffering from a sickness that can end in suicide" (901).

Reflecting the premium feminists have placed on an image of consensus, Gubar writes of the intellectual endeavors of the 1970s in utopian terms of unity: "Many Western narratives begin with Edenic scenes, so let me start the story of feminist criticism in the paradise of a roused, indeed, 'raised,' consciousness" (882).[64] In response to Marianne Hirsch and Evelyn Fox Keller's point that "from its earliest days, feminist theory was in fact characterized by a marked multiplicity in its goals, and in its stated functions," Gubar counters, "I am arguing that there was more solidarity and coherence in the seventies than [in feminism's] later evolution" (888 n. 1).[65] A primary challenge to this ideal of solidarity, Gubar suggests, was the work of African American, lesbian, and postcolonial feminists, who mobilized analyses of feminism's racial—and implicitly racist—politics by pointing out "the propensity of feminists to use the word *women* to mean 'white women'" (888).[66] Gubar responds with a strong call for feminists to return to original ideals of cooperation, coalition, and collaboration (900), with the goal of "heal[ing] feminist discourse of the infirmities that made us cranky with one another" (902).

For *Time* magazine, the failure of feminist intellectuals to translate theory into practice betokens the death of feminism. In Gubar's narrative, the death drive is no less fatal: feminism's institutional success within the academy has pushed our heroine to the brink of suicide, her love plot turned tragedy by virtue of "racialized" and dissenting opinions. *Time* and Gubar speak of and to the academy as profoundly different entities, but each stakes claim to the single indictment of "theory": guilty in perpetrating the demise of feminism.

My argument differs. Both of these narratives describe a life completed between 1970 and 1998. My story is not about a life at all, and still less about a life lived in twenty-eight short years. "Feminism" is an ethical, ideological, theoretical abstraction constituted in relation to material culture—to lifestyle, arguably, in its most debased forms, and to social justice in its ego ideal. In both 1970 and 1998, the terms by which this dialectical relationship is constituted remain the same: sexuality and transgression; the tension between collective politics and the claims of the individual, between "woman" as a collective plural designation and "woman" singular; and the ambivalent status of the "intellectual," the academic, in the context of the mass marketplace. The dialectical nature of feminism requires constant translation, the engineering of a balance between theory and practice, abstraction and materiality. The fact of this slippage is registered within theoretical models themselves, in the internal critique of hierarchy, and in resistance to and dissent against the totalizing implications of theoretical claims. *Time* and Gubar present narratives of repetition with a difference, narratives of two dates, August 31, 1970, and June 29, 1998—of two academic-theoretical epochs, the 1970s and the 1990s—that make the same case. Replete with dissent, with disagreements about style and substance and the social agendas of the political inquiry called "feminism," these narratives are symptomatic yet vital examples of the epistemological procedures of feminism, in theory.

1

The Future of an Ideal
Consciousness and the Radical Vision of Women's Liberation

Beginning in the 1990s, feminist historians including Flora Davis, Alice Echols, Karla Jay, Susan Brownmiller, and Ruth Rosen began to address the brief, dynamic, influential period of women's liberation in the United States.[1] In this chapter, I build on their work by examining the fate of the "theory" paradox in the women's liberation movement. As I have suggested, in the egalitarian political context of feminist critique, the need to produce an explanatory master narrative of feminist history, ideas, and goals is in tension with the feminist critique of master narratives per se as a patriarchal and thus oppressive mode of representation.

In the women's movement, this was a conflict explicitly played out in discussions about the relationship between theory and practice. Feminist activists identified the need for a rigorous body of feminist theories to address key political issues and to open up new ways of thinking about women, gender, and power—but they also wanted to avoid the trap of limiting feminist vision to these theoretical approaches alone. In order to construct theoretical models in a genuinely feminist vein, and in order to avoid patriarchal conventions of theoretical mastery, feminists mobilized alternative approaches to political analysis. The consciousness-raising movement, as I will argue, was a product of this effort to produce a "rigorously unrigorous" approach to feminist theory. By concerning itself with women's personal experience and personal emotions as the authoritative evidence needed to ground a political movement, consciousness-raising deliberately flew in the face of theoretical convention by putting "feminine" forms of knowledge to work for women's liberation. This was a complex strategy that was, in many ways, powerfully effective. But insofar as it quite deliberately

27

recycled conventions of femininity as the basis for women's experience, it risked reasserting patriarchal norms of femininity—especially those of normative heterosexual middle-class identity—in the process. In this chapter, I suggest that consciousness-raising served as a source of genuine ideological awareness and thus resistance for women in the early 1970s. I also suggest that the process worked against itself by inadvertently reconstituting those very codes of feminine constraint from which it originated and which it sought to eliminate.

Femininity and the Consciousness-Raising Movement

In the period of women's liberation, and to some extent still, "consciousness-raising" was a metaphor for the crucial process of awareness building that had to precede any political action. Within the women's movement, that work frequently took place in the many consciousness-raising groups that flourished in the United States in the late 1960s and early 1970s. In contexts ranging from activist movement cells to private homes in suburbia, women came together for group discussions about the personal effects of their political circumstances. Many groups organized particular meetings around a general topic, then invited participants to discuss individual experiences relating to, and feelings about, that topic. The payoff of the discussion was catharsis and connection, the achievement of an "aha moment" that enabled each participant to link her private experiences to those of others in the room and from there to the larger political situation of women in patriarchal culture. Fueled by nascent identification, the feminism of each woman gained depth and nuance as she was mobilized to work toward change for all women. By this process, a movement of intensely linked but individually empowered feminists was born.

Consciousness-raising was a mode of activism that aimed to blur any distinction between the abstract and the material, the personal and the political, the individual and the collective. The process prized consensus among all its participants, equality of voice, and the full validity of each woman's perspective. These priorities were supported by the format, which usually called for participants to sit in a circle facing one another, a configuration that emphasized the equal status of each person and that, just as important, enfranchised no single person as the leader of the group. This physical arrangement supported one of the primary political points of the consciousness-raising movement: women were there to learn from one another and to develop their political vision from the analysis not of external authorities (political theorists, for example) but of their personal experiences. This represented the embrace of women's indigenous knowledge and the presumption that, although each woman was different, the shared experience of femininity created a powerful core continuity in the group as a whole.

It also created several difficulties. First, ideals of consensus and commonality potentially created a new taboo in disagreement and potentially silenced dissenting perspectives.[2] Second, the extent to which the women present could understand and identify with all women was at least potentially limited by the range—or, more perniciously, the homogeneity—of the women present in the room. Generalizations extracted from the testimony of particular women's experiences threatened to replicate wholesale uninterrogated assumptions, and because many consciousness-raising groups were composed of self-identified white middle-class heterosexual women, the method risked insinuating white middle-class heterosexual identity as a template for all women. Finally, the focus on individual experience raised questions about how to implement consciousness-raising as a political tactic in the public arena. There was no doubt that the raised consciousness worked as a form of private activism, empowering individual women psychologically for feminist action, but the translation of an individual's psychological empowerment to widespread social change proved more difficult. It is ironic that consciousness-raising, which originated as an activist mode of theory production, was ultimately stymied by the process of translating theory into practice.

In 1978, Kathie Sarachild, a member of the women's liberation group New York Radical Women, wrote, "To be able to understand what feminist consciousness-raising is all about, it is important that it began as a program among women who all considered themselves radicals."[3] In Sarachild's account, feminist consciousness-raising originated in meetings of the New York Radical Women as members tried to develop a methodology to encourage "radical thinking and radical action," "to get to the root" of women's circumstances. The idea emerged from skepticism concerning, and distrust of, conventional models of political theory, in which feminists generally identified an implicit misogyny. The method offered not only a forum for the development of feminist theories but also, as Sarachild wrote, "a method of radical organizing tested by other revolutions."[4]

Contemporary discussions of the techniques, implications, and failings of consciousness-raising almost invariably engaged questions of what feminism was meant to do and how such goals might be achieved; thus, implicitly and often explicitly they entered into the heart of tensions within the term "feminist theory." "'Consciousness-raising,'" wrote Juliet Mitchell in a 1971 account of the U.S. women's movement, "is speaking the unspoken," an act derived from the Chinese revolutionary practice of "speaking in bitterness," of the "bringing to consciousness of the virtually unconscious oppression; one person's realization of an injustice brings to mind other injustices for the whole group."[5] Gerda Lerner describes "feminist consciousness" in terms of women's resistance to tokens of their subordination as a group; the key here, again, involves women's identification of one another as allies rather than competitors. Lerner writes, "I define feminist consciousness as the awareness of women that they belong to a subordinate group; that they have suffered wrongs as a group; that their condition of subordination is not natural, but is societally determined; that they must join with other women to remedy these wrongs; and finally, that they must and can provide an alternate vision of societal organization in which women as well as men will enjoy autonomy and self-determination."[6]

The power of consciousness-raising involved the catalytic potential built into women's *self*-consciousness as feeling beings. Esther Newton and Shirley Walton, writing in 1971, described the consciousness-raising experience in the terms of religious conversion: the women they interviewed "stated that c-r had given them a heightened understanding of the world and their own experience; a sense of new clarity, a sense that through 'consciousness' about themselves as women, the whole world looked different and less mysterious."[7] Newton and Walton suggested that the euphoria accompanying such heightened clarity of vision was crucial to the widespread success of feminist organizing. The women's lib movement generally privileged "cells," small groups that were local, potentially isolated, and deliberately nonhierarchical. Consciousness-raising enabled a cathartic process that helped to create a sense of unity within the disparate, fragmented pockets of activity that constituted the women's movement.[8] The "sisterhood" that emerged involved a powerful new sense of self. "Women should be sensitive to the fact that the movement itself is a deeply spiritual event which has the potential to awaken a new and post-patriarchal spiritual consciousness," wrote Mary Daly in 1971. ". . . Sisterhood is an event that is new under the sun. It is healing, revolutionary, and revelatory."[9] The metaphorical importance of "sisterhood" in this period suggests a material benefit to the c-r movement: raising the consciousness of individual women and of husbands, parents, the government, the media, bosses, and teachers required first the forceful expression of women's common condition.

Feminists, in other words, faced the initial challenge of convincing women that they needed feminism; that such a need occupied the very center of their personal, everyday lives; that it was political; and that it was sufficiently important to merit energy and activist attention. Claims to the urgency of feminist issues were frequently dismissed as frivolous or not sufficiently time-sensitive to warrant distraction from other radical causes. Why focus on the problems of women, rhetorically asked Kathie Amatniek (later known as Kathie Sarachild), when thousands were being slaughtered in the Vietnam War? "Sisters who ask a question like this are failing to see that they really do have a problem as women in America . . . that their problem is social, not merely personal . . . and that their problem is so closely related and interlocked with the other problems in our country, the very problem of war itself . . . that we cannot hope to move toward a better world or even a truly democratic society at home until we begin to solve our own problems."[10]

To mobilize women widely, movement activists built on analyses of the domestic sphere first undertaken by Betty Friedan and Alice S. Rossi, using a rhetoric of affect and empathy in order to authorize women to think of their area of expertise—if nothing else, the day-to-day events and circumstances of their lives—as worth taking seriously.[11] Consciousness-raising groups thus addressed a need for women's "sisterhood"—a need that was both psychological and politically pragmatic, as it offered women who were isolated through bourgeois domestic conventions a framework for understanding potential loyalties to one another. Like the ideology of *fraternité* in the French Revolution, "sisterhood" provided a metaphor for women's solidarity even while constructing radical terminologies within the explicitly bourgeois codes of family.[12] In this sense, the sisterhood metaphor itself begs as many questions as it addresses: even as feminists critiqued the family as a legitimate, and legitimating, metaphor and as a formidable psychological force, they acknowledged the family's determining powers by honoring it in citation.[13]

Consciousness-raising groups functioned as a countermeasure to, and a critique of, women's containment within heterosexual convention; by building homosocial affiliations among otherwise isolated middle-class women, feminist theorists proposed a resulting shift in all women's ability to analyze their material circumstances as women and to work toward change. The feminist analysis that produced this strategy perceives knowledge itself as patriarchal and heterosexist. "Sisterhood," by contrast, provides a kind of psychological support toward the end of an intellectual need. In 1971, Jo Freeman wrote that, for women,

> the agents of social control are much nearer to hand than those of any other group. No other minority lives in the same household with its master, separated totally from its peers and urged to compete with them for the privilege of serving the minority group. No other minority so thoroughly accepts the standards of the dominant group as its own and interprets any deviance from those values as a sign of degeneracy. No other minority so readily

argues for the maintenance of its own position as one that is merely "different" without questioning whether one must be the "same" to be equal.[14]

As Freeman's analysis suggests, the women's movement, through the mechanism of consciousness-raising, attacked the larger context of women's identification. By engineering a shift in the conventionally heterosexual woman's
identification with her husband toward her identification with other women,
c-r groups sought to awaken women to the false consciousness that had previously guided their lives. Marriage, within this analysis, is claustrophobic;
women, the oppressed minority, are kept close to the master's hand, and such
control of their bodies extends inexorably toward control of their minds as
well, as women internalize their oppressed status as somehow "natural."

In Freeman's analysis, consciousness-raising groups acted against *but
also presumed* normative codes of identity and identification: women, in this
account, were always already married, middle-class, and restless, and the
movement recognized a desire to disrupt this condition. This assumed a great
deal about the life circumstances women brought to the c-r circle and about
the feminist vision with which they would leave. In this context, replacement
of marriage with "sisterhood" as feminism's prevailing domestic metaphor
is especially complex. How literally is the "woman-identified woman," to
use Adrienne Rich's phrase, meant to take the effort of identifying with her
sisters?[15] What is the relationship between identification and desire? Does
the fact of women's mutual love and recognition, fostered so centrally in
the ethical system that is consciousness-raising, lead inevitably to lesbian
separatism? If not, why not? How might women mobilize dissent from, or
resistance to, a program of radical individualism that presumes upon inalienable core similarities?

Freeman's argument further suggests that marriage pits women against
one another in a competition damaging to feminist solidarity. The shift in
primary allegiance from husband to sisterhood affords women a means
of understanding more fully the limitations of marriage; the middle-class
woman, newly bonded in sisterhood with women of other classes, races,
and personal circumstances, is then thrust forth into activism by virtue of
her conscience. This strategy overwrote the differences presumed by—and
indeed, prescribed by—heterosexual isolation, but the emphasis on women's
common ground risked capitulating to homogeneity; where did women's
empathy and identification end? The difficulty of answering this question
was compounded by the status of empathy as a prime factor informing
action in this arena of the women's movement. Ideally, motivated by her
empathic identification with her sisters, the consciousness-raised woman
would work to dismantle the power structure that kept them all down.

Dana Densmore wrote of this shift, "To have sympathy with women is by implication to condemn the circumstances that oppress them, and those circumstances are the male power structure."[16] Yet the translation from sympathy and condemnation to material change proved difficult. Densmore suggested that consciousness-raising should ideally provoke women to the repudiation not simply of marriage but also of the material securities that heterosexual marriage presumably affords. Newton and Walton pointed out, however, that although consciousness-raising provoked such conclusions, c-r groups themselves were not equipped with material resources that would support middle-class women compelled to remove themselves from the marriage relationship.[17] Densmore constructed a logical path that, if followed, would have radical implications: the formerly complacent woman, her consciousness newly raised, would be compelled to extrapolate exponentially from sisterly identification to radical action on behalf of that sisterhood. This extrapolation would presumably include the wholesale critique—and rejection—of the social context that had produced the woman and that continued to oppress her. Such a passage from affect and identification to activism for revolutionary change represented an uncompromising, idealistic, all-or-nothing vision: resistance meant selling out to a false, and fallen, consciousness.

The C-R Movement: A New Way of Doing Theory

Women's access to different forms of knowledge is shaped by the conventions of heterosexual femininity, argued the theorists of consciousness-raising. Pamela Allen suggested that conventional theoretical knowledge is implicitly heterosexist and relegates women, solely by virtue of their gender identities, to an ancillary, passive role: "We have come to see that women are relegated to a private sphere, dependent both psychologically and financially on their husbands. The [consciousness-raising] group is a first step in transcending the isolation. Here, sometimes for the first time in her life, a woman is allowed an identity independent of a man's. She is allowed to function intellectually as a thinker rather than as a sex object, servant, wife, or mother. In short, the group establishes the social worth of the women present, a necessity if women are to take themselves seriously."[18] The emerging feminist intellectual described by Allen and others comes into being in an oddly doubled relation to patriarchy. Even as women are excluded from conventionally male intellectual spaces, they are at the same time confined within conventionally male-dominated domestic spaces. The feminist claim to a primary female homosociality is thus the move that challenges patriarchal heterosexism *and* the move that begins to construct an arena for feminist theory. Accordingly, this early articulation of feminist theory collates the intellectual and domestic spaces of patriarchy and challenges them as one. The argument that the personal is political extends to the methods by which nascent feminist theory constructed itself.

The consciousness-raising movement intervened at a level of individual empowerment, progressed from there to coalition building, and from there to the initiative for material change. This was a form of theory production that emerged from a feminist context in which "theory" was a sensitive and often volatile issue. The grounding of feminist theory in the familiar circumstances of women's experiences, their everyday lives, was a strategy that emerged from resistance to theory as a detached, esoteric, hierarchical practice—that is, as anything but familiar, experiential, or everyday. Kathie Sarachild, in the preface to a collection of essays produced by the radical feminist group Redstockings and abridged in 1978, described the problem:

> The radical feminist interest in developing and disseminating theory—in raising and spreading consciousness—was scorned, even attacked, by the liberal feminists and non-feminist left alike, who were always calling for "action" and for whom no amount of action we engaged in was ever even acknowledged. They were always posing it as analysis vs. action, and priding themselves in being the activists, or the "politicos," or the steady, on-going workers who accomplished tangible, concrete gains "in the community," "in the nation," for themselves, or what not. They always implied that the radical, "theory" people . . . didn't take any action, didn't produce any actual changes in the everyday lives of women.[19]

Reflecting the activist hierarchy Sarachild describes here, and recalling her frustration at the Redstockings' investment in developing theory, Rita Mae Brown wrote in 1997, "I believe an ounce of work is worth a pound of theory. . . . [And] back then it was mostly theory since no one wanted to risk anything until the ideology was absolutely in place."[20] "'Don't agonize, organize' was a favorite one-liner," Sarachild reported, suggesting that "when stated as 'Don't analyze, organize' a lot of the punch goes out."[21] For Ti-Grace Atkinson, in 1970, the formulation of an argument—any argument—was a radical feminist act: "[A]t this time, the most radical *action* that any woman or group of women could take was a feminist analysis. The implications of such an analysis [were] a greater threat to the opposition to human rights for women than all the actions and threatened actions put together up until this time by women."[22] Atkinson resisted the suggestion that feminists who place analysis before action are overly cautious or conservative; in Atkinson's view, analysis is a radical act far more powerful than activist interventions that proceed without a well-formulated program.

For feminists such as Atkinson and Sarachild, the urgency of developing analysis, whether in tandem with or as a precursor to feminist action, not only was fundamental to identifying and achieving the long-term goals of cultural revolution, but also involved a claim to a form of intellectual labor conventionally perceived as masculine, and accordingly it involved the appropriation of "theory"—because it was a privileged form of knowledge and because it was imperative to the achievement of feminist goals—in the name of the feminine. Allen argued that abstract logic is part of a heterosexist system that assigns women only abstraction's opposite, intuition, consigning them to subjective rather than objective thought processes: "We have had to face realistically the inability of many of us to think conceptually. This inability comes from being encouraged to stay in the private sphere and to relate to people on personal levels even when working. . . . The complexity of women's situations necessitates our bringing information outside our individual experiences to bear on our analysis of women's oppression."[23] "Thinking conceptually" is a form of gendered thought and, more specifically still, a form of thought associated with patriarchal conventions of masculinity. Women's "inability" to engage in conceptual thought, Allen suggests, is fostered by middle-class heterosexism, its isolation of women, and its encouragement of women to "relate to people on personal levels" rather than in the abstract. Allen underscores the political urgency of thinking in abstract terms, of defining goals for the women's movement and planning actions strategically in order to achieve those goals. This involves, for her, a hybrid strategy: the combination of conventional study with the analysis generated from women's own experiences, with their concern for the emotive and the personal. Each perspective has limitations, Allen suggests, that will be overcome in such a combination; rigorous theory, for feminists, must start by reappraising the value of the kinds of knowledge credited as "natural" to women. In this account, the production of feminist theory is in itself a mode of resistance to patriarchal devaluations of femininity. It also presumes, however, a highly particular understanding of femininity that constructs women within specific parameters of class and sexuality. The idea of using patriarchal conventions of femininity to debunk patriarchal conventions of femininity had great power. However, it also worked subtly to foreclose on the perspectives of women whose "femininities" differed from the middle-class, heterosexual convention, and for this reason it threatened to reinsinuate a very conservative vision of femininity as the status quo.

Feminists such as Sarachild argued, however, that engaging in this deliberative process alone was a form of radical praxis toward revolutionary ends. Theorizing was presented as a material feminist intervention, political not only in itself but also as an icon of resistance to patriarchal assumptions about the feminine mind. "The opposite of 'feminine' is 'intellectual,'" wrote an American student quoted in a British women's liberation newsletter.[24] Dana Densmore wrote to parody the qualities that distinguish man—not to be confused with woman—from beast: "Man also has a capacity for abstract reasoning. He constructs theoretical systems for the pleasure of the intellectual adventure and the beauty of the system. Moreover he has a unique consciousness of the world and his place in it. He has philosophy. He seeks to know and to understand and to experience for the sake of knowledge and the understanding and the experience, solely to expand his consciousness."[25] To Valerie Solanas, it was impossible to detach women's conversation, and even their appropriation of the intellectual, from the competitive economy of heterosexual exchange:

> Trained from early childhood in niceness, politeness and "dignity," in pandering to the male need to disguise his animalism, [a woman] obligingly reduces her "conversation" to small talk, a bland, insipid avoidance of any topic beyond the utterly trivial—or, if "educated," to "intellectual" discussion, that is, impersonal discoursing on irrelevant abstractions—the Gross National Product, the Common Market, the influence of Rimbaud on symbolist painting. So adept is she at pandering that it eventually becomes second nature and she continues to pander to men even when in the company of other females only.[26]

The "nice," pandering femininity that Solanas describes here is not, however, one that described her own subject position as a public feminist and the narrator of the *S.C.U.M. Manifesto*, which was quite deliberately and performatively rude and crude. This suggests that an ideal of feminine (anti-)intellectual virtue circulated quite explicitly in discourses of women's liberation. Put to use powerfully in some circles, the icons of femininity were repudiated in others.

Activists of the women's liberation movement were guided by an ethical belief that theory in the abstract, in the absence of practice, was worthless. For this reason, theoretical paradigms were evaluated scrupulously relative to their practical implications. This, Nancy Hartsock argued, was a departure from the liberal traditions out of which feminism emerged. The "Male left" had never comprehended the hierarchical, patriarchal status of theoretical abstraction, and accordingly had failed to understand the political urgency behind its subversion: "'Theory' meant reading and studying a few sacred texts which are frequently recited but seldom connected with reality. 'Practice,' in contrast, meant organizing other people (never one's self) by applying textbook teachings to their situations."[27] Hartsock emphasized an organic, even symbiotic relationship between feminist theory and feminist practice: "Feminists argue that the role of theory is to take seriously the idea that all of us are theorists since we 'engage in practical activity and in [our] guiding lines of conduct there is implicitly contained a conception of the world, a philosophy.' The role of theory, then, is to articulate for us what we know from our practical activity, to bring out and make conscious the philosophy embedded in our lives" (75–76).[28] "Theory," in this context, is achieved through the fusion of the intellectual and the activist; ultimately, Hartsock wrote, feminist theory is quite simply "the articulation of what our practical activity has already appropriated in reality" (75). In feminist action is feminist theory, Hartsock contended, endorsing the Marxist mode of praxis by locating a coherent philosophy within the action itself and granting that the process of "conceptualization" must occur in order to create a feminist program for future action.

For Hartsock, the problem of theory, of abstraction or conceptualization, was one of expression: feminist activity itself constitutes a coherent philosophy, she suggested, and "theory" is the expression of that philosophy in terms that help "to make the next steps clear" (76). In its ideal, feminist theory will retain its authenticity even in the process of abstraction; authenticity grounded in experience is the felt quality against which abstraction is judged. "Experience," therefore, presumes a common ground shared by feminists and potential feminists. By identifying what is shared, a theoretical paradigm serves both an explanatory and a planning function, accounting for what is already in place and offering a means of understanding future change. Hartsock argued that conventional texts of political theory served little purpose in the women's liberation movement, because they spoke neither of nor to women. This helps to explain the importance of individual experience to the consciousness-raising movement: the embrace of women's indigenous knowledge as both the basis for feminist theory and feminist theory in its own right stands as a challenge to the intellectual elitism implied in patriarchal traditions of theory. The popularization of theory served as a tactic for constituting a coherent women's liberation movement, and then for motivating this new, huge, diverse constituency toward grassroots social action.

The consciousness-raising movement emerged from the feminist ideal of theory production as a mode of activist practice, as the strategic continuity of method and message. Consciousness-raising represented a politics of empathy, the creation of emotional union and thus political coalition among women and potentially between women and other oppressed groups. "Consciousness-raising," writes Carla Kaplan, "could be an exercise in participatory democracy, a 'training' reinforced in leadership-building practices such as rotating chairwomen and avoidance of designated spokeswomen."[29]

Acting as what Kaplan calls feminism's "basic training" program, the c-r movement had a great deal to do with the enormous growth of a feminist constituency in the late 1960s and the early 1970s, a time in which democratic access to the core terms of women's liberation was vitally connected to the development of a critical mass of activists.[30] "Women's Liberation," wrote Juliet Mitchell in 1971, "is crucially concerned with that area of politics which is experienced as personal. Women come into the movement from the unspecified frustration of their own private lives, find that what they thought was an individual dilemma is a social predicament and hence a political problem. The process of transforming the hidden, individual fears of women into a shared awareness of the meaning of them as social problems, the release of anger, anxiety, the struggle of proclaiming the painful and transforming it into the political—this process is *consciousness-raising*." Through the consciousness-raising process, Mitchell concluded, "a personal incident that was condemned to the oblivion of privacy is examined as a manifestation of the oppressed conditions women experience: the personal is seen to be a crucial aspect of the political."[31] The fusion of the personal and the political is famous as a feminist slogan and tactic, but Mitchell's comment underscores the ethical imperative involved in the gesture: the claim that the personal is the political gives value to evidence previously "condemned to the oblivion of privacy," evidence previously discredited as significant or political or interesting at all. Again, this is a politics grounded in the psychology of individual empowerment. It rests on the presumption that within each individual woman lurks a latent political activist. That potential activist awaits her powerful animation, needing only the awareness of the misogynist regime under which she lives to come into powerful being.

"The way in which women become involved in feminist politics follows a natural progression," wrote the collective that produced the journal *Ain't I a Woman?* in 1972. "As we move beyond examining our personal lives and hassles, we look for ways to correct the injustices; as we find the injustices to be inherent in the political system of this country, and after spending varying amounts of energy and effort in effecting change, we recognize total change to be necessary. The work we engage in at this point of consciousness we must see within the framework of some larger strategy leading to and eventually accomplishing a revolution."[32] The sequence of development described here is key and represents the expected progression—as well as the fragility—of the feminist theory-practice continuum. This sequence starts with the personal, with the analysis of "lives and hassles," a process that prompts a corrective impulse. This in turn prompts, first, the realization that the injustices in question are endemic within the entire political system and, then, the inevitable conclusion: feminists must seek "total change" promised in revolution, for there is no use treating the part when the entire system is hobbled by disease. Turning on the claim that the personal is political, this sequence develops from small picture to large, from the concrete to the abstract. As a logic for the production of feminist theories, it is precisely coextensive with the process designed to produce feminist theorists: resting on the claim that the personal is political, feminist paradigms are insistently grounded in the identities, the psychologies, and the experiences of their practitioners.

This is a logic as powerful as it is fragile. Its effectiveness inheres in its empowerment of each individual as singular and significant to feminist political action. Its fragility inheres in the same terrain, however, as both everyone and no one in this leaderless movement was responsible for the risks entailed in revolution. Political change, as described in this model, required individuals to make a quantum leap from an understanding of the significance of "lives and hassles" to a personal commitment to changing the entire system that had produced those lives and those hassles in the first place. If feminism was to be about more than lifestyle, if feminist analysis was to be about massive social change rather than the empowerment of a few isolated individuals, the leap from understanding to action was imperative.

The Problematic Power of Experience

There was a risk in grounding the political so fully in personal experience. Critics have argued that feminists' strategic appropriation of "experience" attacked the symptom rather than the source of the problem, the ripple effects of patriarchal oppression rather than the patriarchal system that caused those ripples. Historian Joan W. Scott contends that the privileging of experiential narrative inadvertently plays into—and ultimately reinforces—systems of power by presenting historically specific categories of identity within an ahistorical and universalizing narrative frame. Because of its narrowness, its necessarily limited perspective, personal experience, uncontextualized, can fail to account for the conditions under which it was produced: "[T]he evidence of experience, whether conceived through a metaphor of visibility or in any other way that takes meaning as transparent, reproduces rather than contests given ideological systems—those that assume that the facts of history speak for themselves and those that rest on notions of a natural or established opposition between, say, sexual practices and social conventions, or between homosexuality and heterosexuality."[33] Scott suggests the urgent necessity of analyzing the filters that produce individuals' "experiences" as such. Indeed, in a Foucauldian context, and in the poststructuralist models developed in the wake of Foucault, "personal experience" is only mistakenly vested with social authority, its "authenticity" only a vestige of ideological formations inaccessible to the individual. Foucault de-authorizes experience by insisting, always, on its situation within the tangled operations of social order: he contends that experience is a symptom, not a source, of the workings of power.[34] For radical feminists in particular, experience is a site of analysis and thus intervention. Although in both contexts the personal is clearly political, the ends to which such a critique of power is directed differ dramatically.

Chandra Talpade Mohanty cautions feminists to avoid conceiving of "experience" as if the term were self-explanatory. "How does location," she writes, ". . . determine and produce experience and difference as analytical and political categories in feminist 'cross-cultural' work?"[35] To radical feminists of the women's movement, "experience" was a term that worked doubly, not as evidence for the stability or knowability of the female subject but as a means of defining that subject's historical contingency, and specifically the means by which she had been produced as "oppressed" and the tactics she had used to resist that condition. Because experience was conventionally an unauthoritative, even delegitimized, abjectified, and unprestigious form of knowledge, it could be claimed as an acceptable mode of authority within contexts concerned to undermine conventions of social authority. And because it revealed the individual's implication within a larger social order, it provided her with a way of understanding how that social order invisibly constructs and exploits categories of personal identity. "Experience" was rhetorically powerful because, in the abstract, it was a form of evidence readily available to all women, and as such it empowered individuals to generate their own theories of gender and the social relations of power.

This is an idealized model, to be sure, for in practice "experience" is far from neutral. What emerged as a problem from the start was the status of erotic, racial, and class difference within the range of women's common experience. Recall Pamela Allen's suggestion that consciousness-raising starts by enabling women to transcend the isolation imposed on them by middle-class American domesticity. When a woman gets to her consciousness-raising group, she is newly "allowed to function intellectually as a thinker rather than as a sex object, servant, wife, or mother. In short, the group establishes the social worth of the women present, a necessity if women are to take themselves seriously."[36]

Allen's account presumes that the women in her group are wives and mothers, that they are "servants" to others within their homes, and that they experience patriarchal sexuality as "objects." But if a consciousness-raising group predicates its theory on a woman who is "a sex object, servant, wife, or mother," what, then, is the status—the social worth—of a woman who isn't? If she is less fully, or differently, positioned in the heterosexual and labor economies than this example of consciousness-raising presumes, is her consciousness already raised? irredeemable? different altogether? capable of participating in the theoretical advances that follow? The process of discussion leads, Allen suggests, to women's social and intellectual empowerment. The first two stages of this process, in which women describe their feelings and then their experiences, lead seamlessly to the last two: to the analysis of their thinking and then to the abstraction of theoretical hypotheses. This is, in some real sense, teleological, with analytical and then theoretical knowledge represented as "higher" products, generated from a universal, and universally degraded, point of departure. Allen resists the hierarchical implication that she sets up here, insisting that "analyzing and abstracting are only valid processes if they continue to be rooted in the present feelings and experiences of participants"; "one does not graduate through the various processes until one is abstracting to the exclusion of all else" (98).

Abstract reasoning is a mode that imposes, and presumes, psychological distance. Allen argues that the achievement of such distance is, in the end, vital to feminist efforts: "[A] certain distance must exist between us and our concerns. When we remove ourselves from immediate necessity, we are able to take the concepts and analysis we have developed and discuss abstract theory. . . . We see this abstracting experience as the purest form of Free Space" (98). Analysis of the big picture—"the totality of the nature of our condition," as Allen puts it (98)—begets access to the rarified sphere of "Free Space." To Allen, "distance" enables acts of the imagination that constitute feminist vision, and such imaginative capacities are a prerequisite to women's eventual achievement of social change. Until now women have been excluded from such thought processes through social conditioning that rewards an emphasis on the immediate rather than the abstract. That conditioning, with its resulting impairment to the imagination, is part of what has kept women down.

In response, the women's liberation movement sought strategies to insure women's political *upward* mobility. Consciousness-raising discourses partook of metaphorical implications of the vertical: women's resistance to being kept "down"—economically, psychologically, and legally—found expression in the imagery of a consciousness on its way "up." And where the consciousness went, feminists banked that lasting material changes would follow.

There is, however, an economics to this system of metaphors that only underscores tensions in the c-r movement between the radical and the bourgeois: What sort of social change does this political, theoretical movement seek? How forcefully do feminists want to rock the boat of heterosexual domestic privilege? Feminism's symbolic upward mobility comes in response to the disaffection implied in "false consciousness"—in women's oppression as a class collective within an economic system that profits from keeping them disenfranchised. Yet, as the twin ethics of upward mobility and individualism should suggest, this is a political model very much invested in bourgeois conventions of ambition. In this context, the very methodology of consciousness-raising prized the leaderless, collective, egalitarian group dynamic as its symbolic ideal, as an explicit attempt to reconfigure masculine models of achievement and ambition.[37] "When we remove ourselves from immediate necessity, we are able to take the concepts and analysis we have developed and discuss abstract theory." Invoking the politics of class through an image of "immediate necessity," Allen affiliates "abstract theory" with a context of great privilege, even luxury. Using the grinding minutiae of the everyday to get to this point, feminist thinkers have the opportunity to liberate themselves from the dirty, demanding immediacies of the ordinary. Thus, the distance implied by abstraction is a vestige not only of patriarchal power but also of class status; within this metaphorical structure, the production of theory is what one does when one is fat and happy, gifted already with five hundred pounds a year and a room of one's own, to invoke Virginia Woolf's argument for the material necessities vital to the work of the woman writer.[38] Indeed, Allen's representation of the "abstracting experience as the purest form of Free Space" lends an air of physical and intellectual freedom to the process. Within the feminist context, however, the "purity" of such transcendence is purchased at the cost of "immediate necessity"—if not actually negating the significance of the immanent, then certainly relegating it to a subordinate role. Allen accounts for this by appropriating abstraction in the name of experience, enabling women "to build (and to some extent, experience) a vision of our human potential": the trick is to make the abstract servant to the "real" (98).

Radical in their implications and accessible in their tactics, consciousness-raising groups, and consciousness-raising as a privileged metaphor of the women's liberation movement, invited women to extrapolate analogically from personal experiences to the condition of women more generally, from a private context of home, hearth, and bedroom to a public sphere in which personal insights bore the fruit of widespread and material social change. The "feminism" of each woman was something produced personally from within the lone, private self but through a gesture of empathetic identification linking that self to a collective and universal population of women. Thus empowered, each individual would act with and as the collective, impelled to action because, as a woman newly attuned to the meaning of that fact, she had a personal stake in creating social change on behalf of all women. "We identify with all women," wrote the Redstockings in 1970. "We define our best interest as that of the poorest, most brutally exploited woman. . . . We repudiate all economic, racial, educational or status privileges that divide us from other women. We are determined to recognize and eliminate any prejudices we may hold against other women."[39]

Experience is the linchpin of the process of identification that the Redstockings describe: "We regard personal experience, and our feelings about that experience, as the basis for an analysis of our common situation. We cannot rely on existing ideologies as they are all products of male supremacist culture. We question every generalization and accept none that are not confirmed by our experience."[40] This critique clearly distinguishes women's personal experiences from "existing ideologies" and therefore suggests that women, as feeling, thinking beings, have somehow escaped the shaping influence of ideology. Here and elsewhere, each woman's personal experiences, and especially her feelings, represent a uniquely authentic site from which to launch cultural revolution; in this accounting, however, "experience" presumably means the same thing for each person. Because it is uniquely unscarred by false consciousness, "experience" constitutes a uniquely feminist epistemological authority for the Redstockings. Consciousness-raising is the method of focusing and extracting the implicit theoretical value of this authority: in the consciousness-raising laboratory, political theories are tested against participants' personal knowledge before the authentic is put to use and the false is rejected.

The Redstockings' construction of a site of authenticity within each individual woman—and thus within the collective population of women—performs a tremendously important piece of theoretical work and suggests how and why consciousness-raising was so effective as a metaphor for feminist goals and as a tool of cultural and, eventually, political reform. At the same time, however, the Redstockings' exemption of experience from ideology foregrounds logical contradictions especially obvious in the context of their argument that the personal is political: personal experience would seem to be constituted exactly within the ideological spheres of a "male supremacist culture."

Through the claim to experience, the Redstockings claimed women's uniqueness as a category; and, through the vehicle of that uniqueness, they presented a means by which ordinary women might resist their conscription within a larger, and largely invisible, system of social control. In an argument that both anticipated and shaped central terms of c-r theories and practices, Simone de Beauvoir suggested that women's lives are conscribed to "repetition and immanence," to the demands of the body and to the present moment; the scope of the male subject, in contrast, is far broader—

futuristic, abstract, its transcendence constructed through, and in contrast to, women's immanence.[41] In this sense, the Redstockings' program made a virtue of necessity, appropriating the concrete materiality of women's daily experiences as theoretical matter, consolidating women's loyalties to one another, and fusing inextricably the personal and the political. The claim to the primacy of individual experience was tactical and, in the sense that it was designed to persuade, it was rhetorical, aimed at the construction of a universal feminist franchise.

This is the expression of a radical ideal within the women's liberation movement: the construction of feminist theory *as* feminist practice. "Our feelings will lead us to our theory, our theory to our action, our feelings about that action to new theory and then to new action," wrote Kathie Sarachild. For Sarachild, feminist theory is the midpoint of a cycle that starts with feelings and ends with action, a process that is necessarily followed by a reinvestment in the intuitive and its analysis. Sarachild's formulation exploits the very codes of knowledge with which women have been credited in patriarchal convention—codes of knowledge that have been devalued as a result: "We're saying that women have all along been generally in touch with their feelings (rather than underneath them) and that their being in touch with their feelings has been their greatest strength, historically and for the future."[42] Sarachild suggests that women's emotions, and in particular their anger, have always offered them a primal, if uncredited, form of knowledge; women's very sensitivity, she contends, offers an analysis of oppression and its resulting injustices. Thus, consciousness-raising undertakes the task of pointing out to women what they already know, of constructing feelings as the site of authentic and authoritative knowledge, and therefore of constructing the potentially abstruse work of feminist theory firmly within the quotidian details of ordinary women's ordinary lives.

"Consciousness-raising—studying the whole gamut of women's lives, starting with the full reality of one's own—would . . . be a way of keeping the movement radical by preventing it from getting sidetracked into single issue reforms and single issue organizing," writes Sarachild. "It would be a way of carrying theory about women further than it had ever been carried before, as the groundwork for achieving a radical solution for women as yet attained nowhere." Though consciousness-raising emerged from a desire to reject conventional theoretical models as implicitly antifeminist, Sarachild strategically authorizes the consciousness-raising methodology through a claim to its scientific virtues: "The decision to emphasize our own feelings and experiences as women and to test all generalizations and reading we did by our own experience was actually the scientific method of research. We were in effect repeating the 17th century challenge of science to scholasticism: 'study nature, not books,' and put all theories to the test of living practice and action."[43] In this account, theory and practice are inextricable. Consciousness-raising represented a form of reality testing that borrowed from scientific methods by which abstract hypotheses are tested through practical experimentation: "study nature, not books." Although Sarachild emphasizes the testing process to which theoretical abstractions are subjected, it is noteworthy that "living practice and action"—considerable abstractions in their own right—constitute the equivalent of "nature," being implicitly more authentic, and thus more authoritative, than "books." By affiliating feminist consciousness-raising with the empirical procedures of science, Sarachild begins to address an underlying but persistent concern that feminist theory is not sufficiently cerebral, thus not rigorous, thus not respectable.

Sarachild claims empiricism as a credential, a prestigious form of knowledge that also, in its presumed engagement with the material, represents a form of skepticism appealing within a radical feminist context. Implicit in Sarachild's argument, however, as in the framework of the consciousness-raising movement, is the idea that "feelings and experiences as women" provide the means for feminists to appropriate empiricist, scientific methods. The theory of consciousness-raising deploys an ethic of emotional authenticity as the means of entering social and political conflicts. The c-r movement enfolds the personal within the political while maintaining a primary stake in the personal as the interpretive lens through which an individual may gain access to the large ideological structures that constitute the social whole. Privileging the personal, and especially the emotive, as an interpretive lens that is powerful precisely because it is popularly accessible to women, this feminist theory mobilizes radical skepticism. It substitutes emotion for intellection as the site of authoritative response, and debunks hierarchies of knowledge by appropriating not only authority but also authenticity on behalf of women who are attuned to the political significance of their experience. Because the emotional, with its emphasis on empathic, subjective knowledge, has been so culturally affiliated with the feminine, it provides Sarachild with a uniquely grassroots feminist credential for undermining patriarchal discourses of science.

Through these terms, activists of the women's liberation movement began to construct emotion as the fulcrum of the theory-practice relationship: feeling, action, and experience signify a form of knowledge available to everyone, and especially to women, all of whom were born and raised in this alternative epistemological tradition regardless of their familiarity with the canonical texts of philosophy, politics, or economics. As Nancy Hartsock suggests, the value of theory inheres in its portability: theory provides an analysis whose terms transcend the local circumstances of any given situation; valid across a range of situations, it is the connective tissue of a far-flung, disparate, local, atomized, grassroots political movement.[44] By advocating the implicitness of theory within feminist practice as within femininity, Hartsock and other feminists begin to identify the experience of feelings—passion, anger, rage—as that connective tissue. Women's experience provides an entryway to further analysis and thus links disparate subjects under a shared philosophical rubric. Experience is a unifying methodology in the women's liberation movement: it is the abstract grid against which unique hypotheses are tested and through which their shared characteristics are given meaning.

Taking It to the Streets: How to Put C-R to Work for Feminism

Motivated by the anger and the empathy that characterize the newly raised consciousness, the feminist subject recognizes herself within the abstractions of political theory. "Controlled, directed, but nonetheless passionate," wrote Susi Kaplow in 1971 of the channeling effects of consciousness-raising groups, "anger moves from the personal to the political and becomes a force for shaping our new destiny."[45] Women's liberation privileged a form of theory that originates in the gut, in opposition to the cool detachment associated with abstraction. The tactical embrace of feelings and experience as the staging ground for feminist analysis represents an example of subversion from within: feminists strategically deployed conventions of the feminine in order to undermine such representations by reclaiming the terms as their own.

Sarachild described consciousness-raising as "an ongoing and continuous source of theory and of ideas for action,"[46] a method of organizing and empowering women through radical introspection. This contrasted with what she called "mindless activism": "the call for 'action' can sometimes be a way of preventing understanding—and preventing radical action. Action comes when our experience is finally verified and clarified."[47] The "Ain't I a Woman?" Collective of Iowa, another analytically inclined feminist group, concurred with Sarachild's emphasis on theory building as a crucial component of activism. A contributor to the collective's newsletter who called herself Radical Feminist 28 wrote,

> [Feminist] organizations must develop theory out of which to act. Our analysis must separate the bases of our oppression from its consequences. Only in this way can we avoid the dangers of reformism and opportunism within the Movement. Action which is separated from a developing analysis of the whole runs the risk of either betraying real feminist interests now or in the future, or of consuming valuable time on projects which haven't

the potential for effecting the necessary revolutionary change. Without a commitment to feminist theory, we will be doomed to continuing sporadic, unconnected action.[48]

The resistance to "mindless activism" foregrounds a major tension, for even in the earliest consciousness-raising groups, challenging questions emerged about how feminists might make the translation from theory to practice: How might the extrapolation from the personal experience of an individual woman to the circumstances of different women, or women in general, occur? And how might one individual feminist bridge the gap between a relatively private context—her own raised consciousness—and the massive social change that her raised consciousness newly demands?

A typed and mimeographed 1972 newsletter from a Long Island women's center described the centrality of concepts of womanhood and femininity to its political mission. Each meeting of the center's c-r group focused on a question that would help the group work toward the long-term goal of defining the idea of "woman," for example, "What is femininity?" "How have I been taught to be a woman?" "What is woman's place?" and "What are my attitudes toward other women?" The newsletter described the methodology involved in its activist implementation of these questions:

> After talking and listening, we begin to learn that we are not isolated in our reactions and that our experiences and feelings can be seen as being a universal phenomenon, often based on the social conditioning peculiar to a female. . . . A C.R. group affords a woman the opportunity to express her feelings about the past and prevailing attitudes society imposes on her sex. She becomes more acutely aware of the urgent need to *act* to improve the quality of her life. It helps her overcome her sense of isolation from other women and she feels less of a personal failure as her self-esteem is raised in direct proportion to her consciousness. She feels the support from other women, for perhaps the first time in her life.[49]

This description is quite explicit in its construction of consciousness-raising as a technique for listening. Listening builds in each individual woman empathy for the other women in the group; empathy in turn builds a network of support among women; that network in turn fosters in each individual "the urgent need to *act* to improve the quality of her life." The newsletter describes a process of political mobilization that occurs on the psychological plane; it locates individual empowerment, occurring in a context of group support, as the necessary groundwork for the production of feminist analysis. That feminist analysis, however, is focused on a recursively individual context: the activist produced in this vision of consciousness-raising concerns herself with the urgent need to act to improve the quality of *her* life—not the quality of the lives of others, nor the system that produces concepts of "quality of life" in the first place. Empathy forged in the crucible of the c-r circle recurs, at least in this description, to the sole benefit of the individual participant.

Built into the initial formula for consciousness-raising was an idea for social action that continued the techniques of awareness building on a more public stage. Sarachild wrote, "The kind of actions the group should engage in, at this point, we decided—acting on an idea of Carol Hanisch, another woman in the group—would be consciousness-raising actions . . . actions brought to the public for the specific purpose of challenging old ideas and raising new ones, the very same issues of feminism we were studying ourselves."[50] Such actions took place in a number of now notorious contexts, including the 1968 Miss America Pageant protest and the 1970 sit-in at the editorial offices of the *Ladies' Home Journal*. "Zap actions," explained Hanisch, "are using our presence as a group and/or the media to make women's oppression into social issues."[51] "Zap actions" used symbolic representation as a means of education; like consciousness-raising groups, they worked evocatively, dramatizing the circumstances of women's oppression in order to increase public awareness of and concern for those issues.

The feminist group WITCH (an acronym that originally stood for Women's International Terrorist Conspiracy from Hell) undertook a number of prominent actions, including a 1968 Halloween hex on the New York Stock Exchange and a 1969 hex on the New York Bridal Fair in Madison Square Garden. In 1977, Robin Morgan, a founding member of WITCH, described the group's restlessness: "[W]e were . . . newly aroused and angry about our own oppression as women—and we wanted to *move*. It seemed intolerable that we should sit around 'just talking' when there was so much to be done. So we went out and did it."[52] Each of these actions worked through a logic related to that of the consciousness-raising group, aiming to raise the public, collective consciousness by putting symbols of femininity to work for feminism.[53] The hex on the stock market on Halloween, for example, was intended to underscore women's economic inequalities, and feminists utilized notions of mystical, witchy, supernatural femininity as their symbolic vehicle. Morgan wrote of this hex, "[T]o liberate the daytime ghetto community of the Financial District, the Coven, costumed, masked, and made up as Shamans, Faerie Queens, Matriarchal Old Sorceresses, and Guerrilla Witches, danced first to the Federal Reserve Treasury Bank, led by a High Priestess bearing the papier-mâché head of a pig on a golden platter, garnished with greenery plucked from the poison money trees indigenous to the area" (75). The coven wended its way through other Manhattan venues from there, ending by taking over a meeting about the media and "creating a genuine discussion on theater, media, ideas, women, the revolution, and other topics relevant to Halloween" (77). As Morgan noted, the stock market responded to its hex by dropping 1.5 points on Halloween and a full 5 points the next day (76).

The hex on the bridal fair at Madison Square Garden, on February 15, 1969, used theatricality to similarly disruptive ends. Morgan reported that "women demonstrators assembled, about a hundred strong, to leaflet, picket, perform guerilla theater, and cast a hex on the manipulator-exhibitors. Some of the demonstrators carried signs reading: *Always a Bride, Never a Person, Coffee Causes Chromosome Damage, Ask Not for Whom the Wedding Bell Tolls,* and *Here Comes the Bribe.*" Demonstrators also performed a "pledge of disallegiance" at a "WITCH Un-Wedding Ceremony" on the morning of the bridal fair: "We promise to love, cherish, and groove on each other and on all living things. We promise to smash the alienated family unit. We promise not to obey. We promise this through highs and bummers, in recognition that riches and objects are totally available through socialism or theft (but also that possessing is irrelevant to love)" (81). This demonstration attempted to reveal the capitalistic, bourgeois aspects of the marriage industry, to expose "the Dracula face of capitalism behind all the orange blossoms." The heart of the attack, Morgan wrote, "was aimed at the institution of marriage itself, and at the structure of the bourgeois family, which oppresses everyone, and particularly women" (81).[54]

Morgan wrote retrospectively of the limitations of these acts as theoretical interventions, suggesting that they were governed more by the passions of the moment than by a fully articulated agenda: "[W]e in WITCH always meant to do the real research, to read the anthropological, religious, and mythographic studies . . . but we never got around to it. We were too busy doing actions. We also meant to have more consciousness-raising meetings—but we were too busy doing actions. We meant to write some papers of theory and analysis—but we were too busy doing actions" (72). The WITCH collective was prompted in its emphasis on action by two factors, Morgan suggested: its members identified politically with the "confrontational tactics of the male Left" and stylistically with the "clownish proto-anarchism of such groups as the Yippies" (72). Spurred by anger about their oppression as women, the group fused its identifications into a form of activism that used theatricality as a confrontational tactic. As Morgan suggests, this was activism as political theater. By using symbolism in this highly representational mode of protest, WITCH members suggested that activism itself works as an abstract enterprise. Self-conscious in their theatricality, these feminist interventions attempted to revise the canons of representation, to use dissident representational strategies in order to challenge accepted narratives of social order.

The history of the WITCH protests and of other modes of activism in this period reveals an important investment in the appropriation of cultural icons—brides, money, the *Ladies' Home Journal*—on feminism's behalf. Intellectual work, and in particular that icon of intellection known as theory, was a powerful symbol that feminists sought just as urgently to appropriate, as an end in itself and as a means to the larger end of furthering feminist interests. Sarachild and the Redstockings laid claim to women's right to study, to contemplate, to analyze: "In the beginning we had set out to do our studying in order to take better action. We hadn't realized that just studying this subject and naming the problem or problems would be a radical action in itself, action so radical as to engender tremendous and persistent opposition."[55] The dismissal of consciousness-raising included ridicule of its frequent focus on "minor" domestic concerns and accusations that it served as therapy or self-help and failed to produce "rigorous" analytical thought.[56] But the standards of rigorous analysis posed a political problem for the women's movement, not from the resistance to thoroughness or an inclination toward the analytical; quite the contrary. The problem inhered in the terms by which theoretical rigor was conventionally assessed—terms, for instance, that would exempt the personal, the emotive, the experiential, and the equation of personal and political from the "serious" category altogether. Hence, consciousness-raising as a form of radical education, as much an "action" on the local level of the individual consciousness as the WITCH hexes or the Miss America Pageant protest, was in the public eye. In the end, "studying," like consciousness-raising and zap actions, had a performative function: Sarachild contends that, in the women's movement, any gesture toward "naming the problem" was a form of radical praxis.

In the period when second-wave feminism was first defining itself, the problem of how patriarchal culture has organized categories of knowledge presented a challenge: feminist attempts to define a social movement worked rigorously to avoid reproducing patriarchal ways of doing business. Consciousness-raising served as a method for feminist organizing and feminist analysis, and as a filter for the consolidation of feminist awareness about the key political issues at stake. It also, however, served as a metaphor for the work that needed to be done before social change could occur, work to build awareness both in the lives of individual women and in the arena of public consciousness. For a brief time, consciousness-raising symbolized a utopian ideal, an attempt to claim an emotional and intellectual franchise for all women; to provide a context in which the rapid spread of grassroots feminism could take place with a measure of coherence; and to offer a model for the synthesis of theory and practice that was urgently necessary for the continued growth and the idealistic integrity of the women's movement. By locating feminist theory in the affective and experiential domain of the individual woman, feminists boldly sought to create a new form of knowledge: an epistemology uniquely reflective of women's perspectives. The prime category of its analysis, "woman," quickly proved to be far more complex and contrary than unifying. Insofar as it provides a theory of how feminist theory might conceivably work, however, consciousness-raising, as movement and as metaphor, persists, its traces discernible in the vexed idealism of the feminist theories that have followed.

2

The Activist Unconscious
Feminism and Psychoanalysis

The consciousness-raising movement in feminism was, at its core, a theory of the politics of emotion and experience. By initiating a powerful link between women's emotional lives and their political circumstances, consciousness-raising links the production of feminist theory with women's psychological perceptions; emotions are both of the mind and of the body, and thus they serve as a symbolic discourse in which feminists can mediate the relationship between materiality and theoretical abstraction.

Feminists negotiated the connection between the psychological and the political with still more complexity in their volatile engagement with psychoanalysis during the women's liberation movement. The claim that the personal is political required intense exploration of the matter of personal life, particularly the entanglements of domesticity, desire, and eroticism that also concerned Freud and other psychoanalysts. In the context of this convergence of interests, feminists initially raged against psychoanalysis, arguing that its presumptions were blatantly misogynist. Soon thereafter, however, psychoanalysis became an important feminist methodology. This chapter explores the terms by which feminists undertook that transition. What are the ideological implications of this dramatic shift, and what does it tell us about the diverse agendas of the women's movement as it ranged from the streets to the academy, from the marketplace to the bedroom to the mind? What does it tell us about the shifting meanings of "feminist theory" and the shifting meanings, too, of women's intellectual, emotional, and embodied lives in relation to feminism's larger political aims?

Since the early days of women's liberation, psychoanalysis has been central to feminism, but initially, embodied in the figure of Sigmund Freud, it was a central negative, a symbol of Western culture's inbuilt misogyny and the psychological and material oppression that kept women down; feminists invoked psychoanalysis most frequently in order to describe what they were revolted by and revolting against. But by the mid-1980s, in part because of the influence of French feminist and Lacanian theories, feminists had found in psychoanalysis a theoretical tool of great value: it enabled a range of textual and cultural analyses in feminist academic work on literature, history, and film; and in both academic and political contexts it provided a common vocabulary that helped to forge alliances between feminists and those working in related areas, particularly in the emergent fields of lesbian, gay, and queer studies.

In this chapter, I argue that the gradual development of a specifically feminist psychoanalytic methodology through the 1970s signaled a shift in feminist theory production more generally. This shift manifested itself in a new emphasis on one particular abstraction: the unconscious mind. The unconscious enabled a new kind of feminist analysis of power, of the body, of sexuality and desire, and of social organizations such as the family that so centrally defined women but that feminists were working so centrally to denaturalize. Because the unconscious was invisible, unempirical, and in some very real sense unknowable, it represented a new kind of evidence for feminist theorists, an abstract concept with potent material consequences. It also allowed a new flexibility in feminist interpretations of power and desire—a new flexibility that implicated desire in the constitution of power. True to the history of feminist debates about abstraction in general, however, the process of putting the abstraction "unconscious" to use was not unambivalent, as I will argue in more detail later in the chapter.

The unconscious was a political activist in the psychoanalytic feminism of the mid-1970s. Feminists argued that intervention for genuine, lasting social change had to occur first at the level of each individual's unconscious mind; then and only then would radical change in the world at large be possible. In the context of this argument, psychoanalytic theory offered a framework for understanding how women and even feminists have been programmed for complicity with patriarchy. More important still, it suggested how a new understanding of that unconscious complicity can initiate a form of resistance to patriarchy. I trace the development of this argument from the early feminist rejections of Freud's essentialism and misogyny to the argument for an insurgent unconscious presented by Jane Gallop in the early 1980s. In between, I focus on the work of feminists Kate Millett, Gayle Rubin, Juliet Mitchell, Dorothy Dinnerstein, and Nancy Chodorow to demonstrate how their connections and disagreements helped to consolidate a feminist psychoanalytic methodology. Millett, Rubin, and Mitchell engaged in a serious reconsideration of the meaning of the female body as a material phenomenon and a symbolic abstraction. These negotiations about the symbolic power of the female body led to the work of Dinnerstein and Chodorow, whose focus on the cultural power of the mother put that female body to work in the context of the domestic sphere; mothers, they argued, have formidable psychic power that in the past has been a tool of patriarchy. By claiming maternal power as a tool of feminism instead, Dinnerstein and Chodorow began to suggest how the activist unconscious might effect material social change.

Like discourses of consciousness-raising in the women's liberation movement, feminist psychoanalysis engages questions of affect and emotion, concerning itself with the mind in order to develop a psychology of both politics and power. As I suggested in the previous chapter, feminist discourses of consciousness-raising utilize an imagery of vertical ascent, of upward mobility, as the means of claiming a politics of personal intimacy: a raised consciousness signals a heightened awareness of the feminist issues in each woman's private life, and thus opens a pathway for her work as a theorist of those issues and as an activist relative to their implications. Feminist psychoanalysis appropriates a related but contrasting logic, utilizing intimate questions of the private—of sexuality, motherhood, and the politics of the domestic sphere—to initiate political critique. Similarly concerned with the private home as patriarchy's origin in individual lives, psychoanalytic approaches to feminism deploy a discourse of individual interiority, exploring an imagery of depth in order to excavate patriarchy's roots. Feminists now identify these roots as buried just as deeply within their own psyches as they are within those of the most egregious misogynists. Psychoanalytic feminism, therefore, provides a means of analyzing how unconscious minds and unconscious desires—even those of feminists—invisibly collude with patriarchy. In this it represents a new frontier for feminism.

This shift also signifies a new approach to the question of how power works, particularly how it works within individual subjects who are necessarily products of the culture they seek to transform. When feminists turned to psychoanalytic theories of power and desire in the mid-1970s, they did so in part to interrogate their culture's stubborn resistance to the logical premises of their arguments—arguments which seemed on the surface fair, equitable, and reasonable, but which met with resistance nonetheless. The embrace of psychoanalysis represented a move away from "reasonableness," from the logical, as a grounding premise of feminist theory.[1] In the context of consciousness-raising, for example, it had proved very difficult to move from talk to action, from theory to practice, and therefore to wholesale social change. Psychoanalytic feminism, however, offered an answer to this puzzle: it suggested that feminists, too, might have something at stake in the maintenance of patriarchal convention; that, even unbeknownst to themselves, they might stand to gain from the continued protections of patriarchy. Psychoanalysis offered feminists a discourse of sexuality, subjectivity, and the distribution of power in the context of individual development. Still more subtly, though, it offered new tactics of analysis for issues of entrenchment, resistance, and the unconscious—for all the invisible but nonetheless palpable workings of gendered power.

Big Bad Daddy

In many ways, the feminist resistance to Freud in particular and to psychoanalysis in general is a matter of common sense. In describing the castration complex as the origin of female sexuality and subjectivity, Freud suggests that the female body is, by definition, inadequate, the scarred, warped inferior to the male body with its boastful phallic equipment and the attending privileges that result. To add insult to injury, Freud can be seen to suggest that the sum total of feminine accomplishment is written on women's bodies—that anatomy is destiny and that women's status as second-class citizens is a token of the natural order of things.

Freud's essays "Femininity" and "Female Sexuality" work as highly efficient teaching tools in women's studies classrooms, provoking students to produce in their own words trenchant critiques of bodily essentialism. Such critiques involve an understanding of the body as a cultural artifact and of gender roles as the socially constructed product of ideological struggles, far from "natural" and, insofar as they are constructed, available for emancipating, deconstructive analyses and acts.[2] "Resistance," wrote Freud in 1915, ". . . [acts] as an *agent provocateur*."[3] As the feminist resistance to Freud in the late 1960s aided the expression of nascent feminist theory, so too did such resistance serve as provocateur to feminists working within the women's liberation movement.

Freud was an important figure for the women's movement, because his work was so centrally concerned with women, with sexual desires both conventional and transgressive, and with the social production of femininity. Because much of what he had to say on these topics reads, at best, as obnoxious and, at worst, as ferociously misogynist, Freud offered a pushing-off point for the consolidation of a new feminist antiessentialism. Feminists writing in resistance to Freud targeted his representations of the female body and, taking such representations personally, got personal themselves about what Freud had at stake in maintaining the patriarchal status quo. Linda Nussbaum (Kingsman), for example, in a 1972 issue of *Echo of Sappho*, wrote, "Many of Freud's fundamental ideas in psychoanalysis depend upon a belief in male supremacy probably caused by his relations with women in his personal life. For instance, such theories as penis envy and clitoral vs. vaginal orgasms in women served to put women in a subservient role. Freud's writings mention women as castrating, secretive, masochistic, deprived, insincere and inferior to men. Freud's entire sexuality theory is built entirely from a male model and the male point of view."[4] In a 1973 article titled "Mr. Freud's Castration Fantasy," Dana Densmore was similarly preoccupied with the psychological complexes that contributed to Freud's theory of penis envy—an idea Densmore found not only ludicrous but also unaesthetic:

> Women have often wondered about the interpretation Sigmund Freud put on their physical and psychic experiences. However, part of the problem seems to lie in a mistake he apparently made not in interpretation but in *fact*. Apparently, in his intense phallocentric fantasies, he came not only to project his own fear of castration onto women, attributing to them the idea that their own streamlined structure was *like* a mutilation in its freedom from the dangling protuberances that the little girls looked askance at in their brothers; he actually came to believe that a physical mutilation, a castration, had occurred in *fact*. Who performed this cruel act, which was to mortify her for the rest of her life, he does not conjecture. Apparently it is done in utero, since at the moment of birth it is observed—alas!—the dastardly deed has already been done.[5]

Nussbaum (Kingsman) did not elaborate on the "relations with women in [Freud's] personal life" that would have caused him to produce the theory of penis envy, nor did Densmore unpack her analysis of Freud's "intense phallocentric fantasies." But it is noteworthy that, in both cases, Freud's fiercest critics used Freudian interpretations, perversely enough, to assail Freud himself: focusing on his motives, Nussbaum (Kingsman) and Densmore alike suggested that Freud was the (perhaps) unwitting tool of private, unresolved psychic conflicts. Densmore's article concluded with these questions: "What do we have to say about someone whose sick fantasies have so taken over his mind that he comes to believe that they *are reality*? Is there a psychiatrist in the house?"[6]

These writings should only underscore the sense in which feminism was, from the first, a psychoanalytic theoretical practice, even when that engagement was expressed through—and as—resistance. Germaine Greer, for instance, titled her pathbreaking 1970 book *The Female Eunuch*, appropriating the castration complex to describe the damage patriarchy inflicts on the female body: "[T]he sex of the uncastrated female is unknown."[7] Similarly, Valerie Solanas, in the *S.C.U.M. Manifesto* (1971), wrote, "Women . . .

don't have penis envy; men have pussy envy," subverting the psychoanalytic argument through the trope of reversal by deploying its core formulations against itself.[8] In the previous chapter, I described second-wave feminism as a political movement organized around the interrogation of the personal. Psychoanalysis quite similarly seeks out the private origins of public conflict—as well as the psychic damage inflicted on the private reaches of the unconscious mind as a result of an unstable social order. Expressing a characteristic claim on the private, Laurel Limpus wrote in the early 1970s that women's oppression is "both psychological and ideological; it concerns people's definitions of themselves and of each other and of the roles that are possible between them."[9] And in an introduction that accompanied Solanas's *S.C.U.M. Manifesto,* Vivian Gornick explained that "the battle for women's liberation is not necessarily a battle for economic and legal reforms; it is a battle for minds and feelings and psychologies. It is a battle in a war that is unmistakably political, and in which territory won is going to be psychological and cultural change."[10] Even the Marxist feminism forged in the women's liberation movement was both psychological and psychoanalytic: time and again, analyses of women's economic status, including studies of marriage, motherhood, labor, and prostitution, shifted into discussions of women's psychological development.[11] Many feminisms circulated in the 1970s, but they consistently engaged arguments against the psychological programming that compels women to conform to a patriarchal norm. "When we . . . consider the liberation of women," wrote Naomi Weisstein, "we naturally look to psychology to tell us what 'true' liberation would mean: what would give women the freedom to fulfill their own intrinsic natures."[12] Feminist political change thus requires the reappropriation of women's developmental trajectory from girlhood up; hence the attraction to, and aggravations of, the Freudian model.

The claim that the personal is political suggests the importance of psychology as a conceptual tool for modern feminism. Psychoanalysis offered a methodology by which that tool could be implemented, as well as a cultural icon, Freud, who focalized a range of feminist resentments and enthusiasms. The theoretical significance of psychology met with resistance in the women's movement, especially from Marxist feminists who perceived such a preoccupation with the personal as a mark of bourgeois privilege, and the equation of selfhood and political change as a pernicious form of complacency. In 1964, for example, Alice S. Rossi argued that feminists had been co-opted by the "pervasive permeation of psychoanalytic thinking in American society": "Our society has been so inundated with psychoanalytic thinking that any dissatisfaction or conflict in personal and family life is considered to require solution on an individual basis. . . . In the process the idea has been lost that many problems, even in the personal family sphere, cannot be solved on an individual basis, but require solution on a societal level by changing the institutional contexts in which we live."[13] Consciousness-raising groups, as collective enterprises, represented one tactic through which feminists attempted to combat the isolation imposed by bourgeois domesticity and the American individualist ethic. But c-r groups, too, were concerned with radicalizing individual women, operating on the assumption that the mass cultural phenomenon that was consciousness-raising would, in the end, produce psychological change in the collective populace of women. This, too, is psychology as radical praxis. To this end, feminist resistance to Freud ultimately worked to consolidate a feminist theory through the trope of opposition.

From the outset, this development involved the use of Freud to reclaim the female body, in practical terms, in legal terms, and, in a more abstract context, epistemologically. Greer wrote, "We know what we are, but know not what we may be, or what we might have been. The dogmatism of science expresses the status quo as the ineluctable result of law: women must learn how to question the most basic assumptions about feminine normality in order to reopen the possibilities for development which have been successfully locked off by conditioning."[14] Greer's argument suggests that the "body" inherited by women in the early 1970s *was* in fact castrated—castrated by a ruthlessly patriarchal culture that had shaped it in service to a heterosexual ideal. Science, Greer contended, had succeeded in passing off the vested interests of heterosexual patriarchy as "the ineluctable result of law"—as natural, inevitable, and unavoidable.

A major component of the feminist critique of psychoanalysis is the scathing rejection of its claims to scientific objectivity and method, a rejection that participates in the ongoing feminist analysis of the ideological bases of scientific fields including medicine, biology, and psychology. In the terms of this critique, Freud appears as a hack, as in Densmore's representation of him as a hysteric in the grip of "sick fantasies" that made him incapable of distinguishing between interpretation and fact. Naomi Weisstein was similarly critical of psychologists who mistook cultural constructs for scientific fact: "Freudians and neo-Freudians, Adlerians and neo-Adlerians, classicists and swingers, clinicians and psychiatrists in general have simply refused to look at the evidence against their theory and their practice, and have used as evidence for their theory and their practice stuff so flimsy and transparently biased as to have absolutely no standing as empirical evidence." Psychology, Weisstein concluded, "has looked for inner traits when it should have been looking at social context."[15] Kate Millett identified psychoanalysis as a wolf in sheep's clothing, an ideological agent disguised in the ostensibly neutral—and prestigious, and "masculine"—clothing of scientific objectivity.[16]

In *Sexual Politics,* Millett led the charge in the feminist demonization of Freud. Millett approached Freudian psychoanalysis as an ideological system, seeking, like other feminists, the relationship between patriarchal oppression and the deep psychic structures of femininity. Freud, too, pursued this link, but in Millett's analysis his work helps to consolidate an ideology of feminine "normalcy" that helps to keep women in their place. In this paradigm, the political flows directly from the personal, and nostalgia for the family ideal is the prime factor in maintaining rigid gender hierarchies: patriarchy, Millett writes, remains "in force as a thoroughly efficient political system, a method of social governance, without any visible superstructure beyond the family, simply because it [lives] on in the mind and heart where it . . . first rooted itself in the conditioning of its subjects, and from which a few reforms [are] hardly likely to evict it" (177).

Feminism and psychoanalysis share a foundational concern with the domestic, but initially critics such as Millett perceived their agenda as directly opposed to that of Freud. Freud was, in Millett's notorious formulation, "beyond question the strongest individual counterrevolutionary force in the ideology of sexual politics" in early-twentieth-century Western Europe, a time and place of sexual revolution (178). For Millett, as for other feminists, the critique of Freud centered on the topic of interpretation. Millett praises the "validity" of Freud's clinical work (179) but describes the "real tragedy of Freudian psychology" as a problem of interpretation (178); unwittingly influenced by ideological conventions of feminine normalcy, Freud "did not accept his patient's symptoms as evidence of a justified dissatisfaction with the limiting circumstances imposed on [her] by society, but as symptomatic of an independent and universal feminine tendency" (179). Psychoanalytic interpretation, therefore, works in defense of that "universal" femininity, blind to the powerful ideological forces that retain a vested interest in the domestic doctrine of separate spheres.

For Millett, as for other feminist respondents to Freud, the most damaging of these interpretations concerned the female body and its status within psychoanalytic terminology as damaged goods lacking the all-powerful penis: "Freud assumed that the female's discovery of her sex is, in and of itself, a catastrophe of such vast proportions that it haunts a woman all through life and accounts for most aspects of her temperament. His entire psychology of women, from which all modern psychology and psychoanalysis derives heavily, is built upon an original tragic experience—born female" (180). In Freudian psychoanalysis, psychic well-being originates in the possession of a phallus. Women are therefore doomed eternally to seek out whatever pathetically inadequate phallic stand-ins the world is prepared to yield forth—first the clitoris, for example, and still later an infant son. Simply by virtue of the fact that they possess female bodies, women are entirely incapable of achieving "wholeness," psychic well-being, or even adequacy.[17]

In Millett's reading, Freud argues that women have no hope of achieving parity with men because of the bodies they're born with. Dispossessed of the phallus, "woman is thus granted very little validity even within her limited existence and second-rate biological equipment: were she to deliver an entire orphanage of progeny, they would only be so many dildoes" (185). A woman has only one legitimate form of ambition, conformity with the cultural ideal of motherhood, which enables her to live out her masculinity vicariously through her son. In search of other phallic substitutes, however, the Freudian woman seeks an ersatz masculinity that is, in the end, ridiculous; Millett writes that ambitious women "do not seek the penis openly and honestly in maternity, but instead desire to enter universities, pursue an autonomous or independent course in life, take up with feminism or grow restless and require treatment as 'neurotics.' Freud's method was to castigate such 'immature' women as 'regressive' or incomplete persons, clinical cases of 'arrested development'" (186).

For Millett, the Freudian phallus is at once actual and metaphorical—a male body part *and* a signifier of male privilege. This is, for Millett, both the value and the failure of psychoanalysis as a mode of cultural interpretation. The theory of penis envy, she contends, has potential—largely unrealized—as a means of describing the effects of a male-supremacist culture on women's developmental well-being:

> [G]irls are fully cognizant of male supremacy long before they see their brother's penis. It is so much a part of their culture, so entirely present in the favoritism of school and family, in the image of each sex presented to them by all media, religion, and in every model of the adult world they perceive, that to associate it with a boy's distinguishing genital would, since they have learned a thousand other distinguishing sexual marks by now, be either redundant or irrelevant. Confronted with so much concrete evidence of the male's superior status, sensing on all sides the depreciation in which they are held, *girls envy not the penis, but only what the penis gives one social pretensions to.* (187; emphasis added)

Millett, in a direct anticipation of the post-Lacanian feminist interpretation of the phallus, rejects Freud's anatomical literalism. In exchange, she proposes a theory of conventional femininity as psychological, not bodily, trauma. Such trauma is not innate to femaleness; it is inflicted on the individual girl or woman by a culture that systematically devalues her sex and her gender, and that expresses that degradation in the language of bodily value. The phallus is a symbol of cultural power, Millett suggests, and its potency as a symbol exists solely in its ability to confirm a distinction between the haves and the have-nots. Freud, Millett suggests, was not "sufficiently objective to acknowledge that woman is born female in a masculine-dominated culture which is bent upon extending its values even to anatomy and is therefore capable of investing biological phenomena with symbolic force. In much the same manner we perceive that the traumatizing circumstance of being born black in a white racist society invests skin color with symbolic value while telling us nothing about racial traits as such" (180).

In Millett's view, Freud failed to comprehend the symbolic value of his own argument, lapsing instead into a simplistic misinterpretation of the female body as "castrated" rather than degraded within "a masculine-dominated culture." Time and again, Millett uses the word *tragic* to describe the opportunities missed by Freud and by later psychoanalysts who, in their efforts to explain the workings of femininity in culture, fatally mistook effect for cause. Through a misperception that blames women for their oppression within a patriarchal system and reinforces patriarchy as a given, and thus natural, social order, "the effect of Freud's work . . . was to rationalize the invidious relationship between the sexes, to ratify traditional roles, and to validate temperamental differences" (178). Freud's misogyny, Millett suggests, is an issue to be taken into account, but so is the status of his theories as "a prototype of the liberal urge toward sexual freedom": "By an irony nearly tragic, the discoveries of a great pioneer, whose theories of the unconscious and of infant sexuality were major contributions to human understanding, were in time invoked to sponsor a point of view essentially conservative. And as regards the sexual revolution's goal of liberating female humanity from its traditional subordination, the Freudian position came to be pressed into the service of a strongly counterrevolutionary attitude" (178). Millett is, in the end, ambivalent about Freud. What remains to be salvaged in his work are theories of the unconscious and the related extension of the analysis of human sexuality into infancy, both of which contribute practically to political efforts emerging in the revolution. However, Freud's arguments are easily interpreted as explanations and thus justifications of patriarchy's "natural" order. The sense in which his work is revolutionary with regard to the material status of what Dorothy Dinnerstein calls "human sexual arrangements"[18] requires the feminist reader to refuse to take Freud literally—to understand the body as a symbolic rather than a material entity, as a metaphor and an abstraction rather than a literal fact. In a description of the irritating flexibility of psychoanalytic discourse, Simone de Beauvoir wrote in 1952, "Words are sometimes used in their most literal sense, the term *Phallus,* for example, designating quite exactly that fleshy projection which marks the male; again, they are indefinitely expanded and take on symbolic meaning, the phallus now expressing the virile character and situation *in toto.*"[19] In the end, the distinction between the phallus as a literal, bodily fact and the phallus as a symbol divided feminists in their arguments about why psychoanalysis might or might not be useful. Kate Millett acknowledges the power of the phallus as symbol, but the sticking point for her is the fact that a discourse of the phallic symbol reinforces a culture of phallic prestige. For Millett, "phallus" represents the fusion of maleness and cultural power. It implies by extension that women are a disenfranchised class and that their subordinated status is inscribed on the female body. In Millett's view, then, the phallus—literal fact or abstract symbol—is overvalued and misogynist, and therefore severely limited in its ability to contribute to feminist change.

The Feminist Real

The feminist appropriation of psychoanalytic theory began in the mid-1970s, when Juliet Mitchell and Gayle Rubin both published vigorous arguments in defense of Freud's feminism. "Psychoanalysis is a feminist theory manqué," Rubin wrote, even as she also credited the fact that "[b]oth psychoanalysis and structural anthropology are, in one sense, the most sophisticated ideologies of sexism around."[20] The mid-1970s work of theorists such as Mitchell and Rubin represents a development in feminist analytical methodologies, a major change not only in how feminists perceived—and used—Freud but also in the use to which they put analyses of the female body and female sexuality. Not coincidentally, Mitchell and Rubin were both readers of Jacques Lacan. In the United States, where psychoanalysis was a highly medicalized field, the Lacanian context for an emergent psychoanalytic feminism represented a major departure. As Rubin wrote, "In France . . . the trend in psychoanalytic theory has been to de-biologize Freud, and to conceive of psychoanalysis as a theory of information rather than organs. Jacques Lacan, the instigator of this line of thinking, insists that Freud never meant to say anything about anatomy, and that Freud's theory was instead about language and the cultural meanings imposed upon anatomy."[21] From the mid-1970s onward, feminists developed their psychoanalytic methods through an intermittent engagement with Lacan, but always in an intellectual context informed by Lacan's complex reading of Freud, language, signification, and ideology, and the understanding of "psychoanalysis as a theory of information rather than organs." Unleashed from constraints imposed by the equation of anatomy and destiny, feminist analyses of eroticism, desire, and domesticity flourished alongside theories of language and signification.

Juliet Mitchell, writing in 1974, first presented an argument diametrically opposed to Millett's. "The greater part of the feminist movement has identified Freud as the enemy," Mitchell began.[22] In the densely argued analysis that followed, Mitchell undertook two major correctives: vigorously justifying the ways of Freud to feminists; and proposing, counter to the feminist theoretical mainstream, worth to the psychoanalytic framework. "[A] rejection of psychoanalysis and of Freud's works is fatal for feminism," she wrote, creating a distinction between the psychoanalytic theories of Freud and the populist theories of Freud's followers in psychoanalysis and the mainstream media. "However it may have been used," she continued, "psychoanalysis is not a recommendation *for* a patriarchal society, but an analysis *of* one. If we are interested in understanding and challenging the oppression of women, we cannot afford to neglect it" (xiii; emphasis in original).

Mitchell makes a new case for Freudian psychoanalysis as a descriptive, rather than a prescriptive, interpretation of gender roles and the domestic ideologies through which they are constructed. Such an analysis must be pivotal to feminist theories of social change, Mitchell contends. In support of Freud, Mitchell reads his representations of male and female bodies through terms strategically different from those of her feminist predecessors. Like Beauvoir, for example, Mitchell argues for the metaphorical status of the Freudian body and particularly of the ever offensive phallus around which Freud's theories of gender determination are organized:

> [I]n "penis-envy" we are talking not about an anatomical organ, but about the ideas of it that people hold and live by within the general culture, the order of human society. It is this last factor that also prescribes the reference point of psychoanalysis. The way we live as "ideas" the necessary laws of human society is not so much conscious as *unconscious*—the particular task of psychoanalysis is to decipher how we acquire our heritage of the ideas and laws of human society within the unconscious mind, or, to put it another way, the unconscious mind *is* the way in which we acquire these laws. (xiv; emphases in original)

This thinking represents a watershed moment in the evolution of feminist theory, a transition in feminism from an emphasis on *consciousness*—and on the social benefits that accompany the raising of consciousnesses, both individual and collective—to a new emphasis on the workings of the *unconscious*. Mitchell argues that "the ideas and laws of human society" are inscribed deep within "the unconscious mind"; and from the unconscious mind those human ideologies, the ideas and laws that constitute culture, might be challenged or might be reinforced. Such an emphasis on unconscious functioning shifts the interpretive lens of feminist theory from the empirical context implied in the emphasis on consciousness to a newly interpretive mode. Mitchell's emphasis on the unconscious initiates a new level of abstraction to the feminist methodology, embodied—or perhaps disembodied—in the concept of the phallus: not "an anatomical organ," the phallus represents for Mitchell an ideology, patriarchy, that is organized around a symbol, the anatomical organ. Those very Freudian concepts—the castration complex and penis envy—that are so universally loathed by feminists for their apparent denigration of women are tools, Mitchell argues, for storming the phallic fortress itself, for revealing the very fragility of the phallic regime, and for capitalizing on the anxiety with which its boundaries are patrolled.

By initiating a feminist psychoanalytic method, Mitchell resists the interpretation of psychoanalysis within the terms of a predetermined story line, the tired plot in which "anatomy is destiny." Instead she reads it as theory, in highly abstract terms in which realistic figures such as "the body" are metaphors for—symptoms of—the otherwise unknowable roilings of the unconscious mind. Through the trope of abstraction and in the figure of the unconscious, Mitchell recuperates psychoanalysis as a highly flexible, highly abstract, and thus useful means of entry for the feminist analysis of gender, culture, and power. In *The Female Eunuch*, Germaine Greer writes, "Probably the best way to treat [psychoanalysis] is as a sort of metaphysic but usually it is revered as a science."[23] Mitchell follows this logic, making psychoanalysis useful by reading it metaphysically and by reading it against the grain of the empirical emphases implied by the term "science." Mitchell's critique of American feminists' reading of Freud turns on their failure to comprehend the meaning of the unconscious: "Most hostile critics of Freud implicitly deny the very notion of an aspect of mental life (expressed in its own 'language') that is different from conscious thought-processes. Other psychologies are about consciousness, psychoanalysis is dealing with the unconscious" (8). Freud's emphasis on the power of the unconscious mind makes psychoanalysis a valuable tool to critics attempting to undermine the apparently fixed and rigid social categories of gender identity. Instead of reading Freud for this revolutionary potential, feminists have become accustomed to "reading Freud's descriptions as prescriptions" (108) and therefore to dismissing Freud as a proponent of oppressively "Victorian" gender arrangements.

The construction of Freud as a rank misogynist is, Mitchell suggests, a phenomenon of the postwar United States. Psychoanalytic theory was influenced by a number of psychoanalysts who immigrated here to escape Nazi persecution. Mitchell argues that this group, which included Karen Horney and Helene Deutsch, imported to the United States a preoccupation with "the impasse of biological determinism" (298), in which psychoanalytic theory in the States remained stuck for decades to come. This development was reinforced by a related phenomenon that Mitchell perceives as central to the empirical emphasis of U.S. psychoanalysis: in the United States, unlike in Europe, practicing psychoanalysts were required to hold medical credentials, a requirement for which the American psychoanalytic establishment initially fought in order to distinguish psychoanalysis from the "charlatans and quacks" operating in popular psychology. Mitchell concludes, "This stipulated medical qualification may have assisted the anatomical-biological bias so strong in Anglo-Saxon psychoanalysis and thus, I believe, contributed to the reduction of its theory" (299).[24]

Feminist theory, too, was "reduced" by a similar bias toward the empirical, Mitchell argues, suggesting that the American psychoanalytic tradition has been impoverished by a chronic underemphasis on unconscious processes: "Desire, phantasy, the laws of the unconscious or even unconsciousness are absent from the social realism of the feminist critiques. With Millett, as with other feminist studies, empiricism run riot denies more than the unconscious; it denies any attribute of the mind other than rationality. As a result it must also end up denying the importance of childhood experiences. The feminist's children are born directly into the reality principle; not so Freud's" (354). Mitchell's argument against an autonomous reality principle went to the heart of a concern central to American feminism in the 1970s: specifically, the complex relationship between theory as a mode of intellectual abstraction and the "social realism" on whose behalf feminist theory is meant to intervene. In her critique of "empiricism run riot" in the era of women's liberation, Mitchell valorized more than the feminist embrace of desire and fantasy; by emphasizing the determining function of the unconscious, she attempted a strategic reformulation of the feminist body as newly abstract and metaphysical.

"The feminist's children are born directly into the reality principle; not so Freud's." Into what universe, then, are Freud's children born, if not one constituted by the familiar waymarks of "reality" or "empiricism"? Into one governed by the unconscious, Mitchell would suggest, and in this shift of emphasis she posits a new feminist epistemology. A theoretical model oriented around the unconscious presumes that nothing is as it appears to be. It undermines the very grounds on which the "reality principle" is presumed to operate, understanding the phenomenal universe—the body, for example, or the phallus more specifically—as nothing more than the signifier of unconscious conflicts projected outward. In this paradigm, anatomy is not destiny; rather, what Freud describes in anatomical terms—the hegemony of the phallus, the castration complex, penis envy, hysteria, the transition in young women from aberrant clitoral to "normal" vaginal orgasms—are psychological, not anatomical, processes. "[T]he bodily symptoms of hysteria," Mitchell explains, "were physical expressions of mental ideas" (8). In this context the body is a metaphor, *the* metaphor, for otherwise inaccessible psychological developments.[25] The body is simply the external, material expression of internal conflicts and processes.

By urging feminists to abandon the "empirical" basis of evidence and of their theories in favor of the abstract unconscious, Mitchell proposes that feminists recapitulate a transition from "social realism" to abstraction that Freud himself undertook. As Jeffrey Moussaieff Masson contends in his controversial book about Freud, Freud's abandonment of the seduction theory represented "a trend away from the real world"—a transition that Masson views very much in the negative but which is of crucial importance to Mitchell's view of psychoanalytic feminism.[26] Freud's abandonment of the seduction theory, as well as his corresponding "discovery" of the unconscious, is conventionally credited as the founding moment of modern psychoanalysis, its inception as a flexible, functional theoretical methodology. Mitchell suggests that, to achieve theoretical maturity, feminism too must undertake such an epistemological shift; again, this involves a discourse of abstraction rather than material specificity. Mitchell describes the terms of Freud's transition:

> Studying hysteria in the late eighties and nineties, Freud was stunned to hear women patients over and over again recount how, in their childhood, their fathers had seduced them. At first he gave an explanation in which the repressed memory of *actual* childhood incest was reawakened at puberty to produce the neurosis. He then realized that the whole thing was a phantasy. And in essence this is the step that . . . his feminist critics will [not] take with him, nor allow him to take. . . . Desire, phantasy, the unconscious or even unconsciousness are absent from the social realism of . . . feminist critiques. These criticisms are, therefore, in this respect not so much anti-Freudian as pre-Freudian. (9; emphasis in original)

Here Mitchell deliberately infantilizes feminist critiques of Freud, I suggest, as not so much anti-Freudian or pre-Freudian as naive Freudian, reminiscent of Freud's own investment in the "real" at a very early moment in his career. Following that stick with a carrot, in relating this account Mitchell urges feminists to identify with, and thus make, the transition that Freud himself made in favor of desire, fantasy, and the unconscious, abandoning the physical for the mental, the empirical for the abstract, the narrative of seduction for a new language altogether—the playful, oblique, often anti-social and disturbing lexicon of the unconscious mind.

Psychoanalyzing feminists, Mitchell argues that their resistance to Freud leaves them fixated at an early developmental moment, demonstrating a fear of progress. This is, to be sure, a tactical mischaracterization of the feminist readers of Freud whose work preceded Mitchell's 1974 account: clearly theorists including Kate Millett, Germaine Greer, and Shulamith Firestone comprehended the distinction between conscious and unconscious processes in Freud. It was not a lack of understanding that fueled liberationists' resistance to Freud; as my earlier account of Millett's reading of "tragic" Freud should suggest, Millett and others could not—would not—read past misogynist implications of a theory that construes all female bodies as damaged. Although Mitchell's case for the importance of psychoanalysis to feminist theory is justifiably influential, her representation of women's liberationists as theoretically naive, their "innocence" even pathological, reflects a common rhetorical pattern of generational demonization. Millett et al. were less developmentally delayed in their use of psychoanalysis than they were strategically different: just as they demonize Freud in order to make a rhetorical point about the body and the political structures that extend from it, so Mitchell demonizes them for the identical purpose.

For Freud, the discovery of the unconscious signified an entirely new understanding of the body and the interpretations of nature and culture predicated on the body. Mitchell's psychoanalytic feminism proposes such an epistemological shift as well, and this implicates, at its very core, the question of what counts as the "evidence" on which feminist arguments rely. In his early studies of hysteria, Freud was surprised to hear women describe over and over again incidents of childhood sexual abuse, and, in Mitchell's words, "[a]t first he gave an explanation in which the repressed memory of *actual* childhood incest was reawakened at puberty to produce the neurosis." On its face, Freud's interpretation seems quite reasonable, particularly in the context of a feminist movement deeply concerned to hear women's voices and to grant women the authority of their experience. Indeed, Freud himself grew skeptical of paternal "seduction" only, and perhaps counterintuitively, when it began to appear to be a very common experience. At that point, "Freud found that the incest and seduction that was being claimed never in fact took place"—that is, that the neurotic adult women who claimed childhood sexual abuse were expressing, instead, a long-repressed childhood erotic desire for the powerful father figure (9).

Here Freud abandoned his earlier mode of prima facie interpretation for a far more skeptical interpretive practice: he read the evidence that he saw and heard not as the transparent reflection of a known, shared reality but as symptoms of unknown, and otherwise unknowable, desires, fantasies, and fixations. "In a sense," says Mitchell, "Freud discovered the unconscious by default. It had to be there—nothing else could account for what he found" (254). Perversely, then, the very flexibility of the unconscious makes it a fundamentally accountable tool for Freud: it works as an explanatory mode because it provides a way of explaining otherwise contradictory evidence. Mitchell writes, "Psychoanalysis makes conscious the unconscious, not only as a therapeutic technique, but also as the task of its theory. It reconstructs the unperceived, fragmented and incoherent myths and ideas held within the unconscious mind, it makes them coherent and presents them as what they are: myths, representations of ideas, ideology—the word is difficult to find as each has a debased meaning" (368–69). The psychoanalytic method, Mitchell suggests, is not merely something Freud implemented in the psychotherapeutic context; as "theory," it provides a mode of reading that is extravagant in its flexibility and thus in its usefulness. It enables the psychoanalytic interpreter to connect apparently unconnectable dots in order to find in the pattern revealed ideologies or ideas or myths—to find, in other words, the cultural biases that quietly and behind the scenes construct apparently objective reality.

Mitchell's claim to the importance of psychoanalytic theory for the feminist movement originated in—indeed, depended on—such abstraction. But the establishment of a positive function for psychoanalysis within U.S. feminism required first a feminist social context sufficiently well established that the claim to objective reality could be forsaken. It is not surprising that Mitchell was able to make a case in 1974 that seemed counterintuitive even to a would-be sympathetic critic such as Kate Millett, who had written *Sexual Politics* in 1969. By 1974, American feminists were primed for a new approach to psychoanalysis in a way that they had not been earlier. By this point the social, political, and interpretive meaning of "the body" had expanded dramatically, because of the mainstream popular appeal of the women's liberation movement; because of women's unprecedented access to medical and scientific information about their bodies in contexts including the book *Our Bodies, Ourselves*, by the Boston Women's Health Collective; and because of such legal developments as the January 1973 Supreme Court decision in *Roe v. Wade*, which decriminalized first-trimester abortions. The slogan of abortion-rights activists in the United States was borrowed from Margaret Sanger: "A woman has the right to control her own body."[27] In the women's liberation movement to this point, feminist theories of the body, and of women's voices and stories, had focused on their moral, ethical, and legal right to self-determination. In the period following *Roe,* however, feminists began to approach issues of women's legal relationship to the body somewhat differently: they now began to consider issues of "bodily control" as abstractions and as matters of life and death. This was a shift that helped to make feminists newly amenable to a psychoanalytic feminism that read the body differently, as a symbol, a symptom of otherwise unknowable unconscious conflict. Psychoanalytic feminism in the United States in the mid-1970s began to produce, and to make use of, the body itself as an abstraction.

The Feminist Phallus

Gayle Rubin, writing in 1975, approached the question of a psychoanalytic feminism through Marxism and structuralism, and in this she paved the way for later feminist analyses—including those of Dorothy Dinnerstein and Nancy Chodorow—of family systems as symptoms of patriarchal power and potential sites of resistance for women. For Rubin, psychoanalytic feminism picks up where Marxist feminism leaves off, because psychoanalysis offers a means of understanding the psychosocial pressures that produce individuals as women and men within the system of economic circulation that Marxist feminists describe. The Marxian critique of capitalist oppression convincingly demonstrates that women's work, in the home and in the industrial sphere, is vital to the production and reproduction of a patriarchal social economy. But Rubin suggests that this doesn't explain much about women themselves, about the processes that determine individual women's conscription within the social network. In her reading of Claude Lévi-Strauss's *The Elementary Structures of Kinship,* Rubin argues that social organization is based on an incest taboo, specifically on the requirement of exogamy; the incest taboo is enforced through the control and exchange of women's bodies. The "traffic in women," Rubin writes, "is a shorthand for expressing that the social relations of a kinship system specify that men have certain rights in their female kin, and that women do not have the same rights either to themselves or to their male kin."[28] This kinship system requires not only heterosexuality of its subjects but heterosexuality aimed monogamously and exogamously, outside the immediate family context; it requires a social differential based on male and female gender roles; and, in order to ensure the paternal lineage, it requires female married chastity.

For Rubin, Lévi-Strauss provides an analysis that, although not feminist in itself, has important implications for feminist theory. "The 'exchange of women' is a seductive and powerful concept," she writes. "It is attractive in that it places the oppression of women within social systems, rather than in biology. Moreover, it suggests that we look for the ultimate locus of women's oppression within the traffic in women, rather than within the traffic in merchandise" (175). Kinship systems, and the economic structures they produce and intersect, rely on the traffic in women in order to reproduce themselves. Rubin underscores kinship as a theory of economics *and* sexuality: the two terms are inextricable, mutually constituting and renewing one another, and no discussion of anatomy alone, or of biology, or of money markets, is capable of accounting for the complex interdependency that results.

Psychoanalysis supplements structural anthropology by offering a means of analyzing the many frailties and contingencies on display as kinship systems labor to reproduce themselves: "Anthropology, and descriptions of kinship systems, do not explain the mechanisms by which children are engraved with the conventions of sex and gender. Psychoanalysis, on the other hand, is a theory about the reproduction of kinship. Psychoanalysis describes the residue left within individuals by their confrontation with the rules and regulations of sexuality of the societies to which they are born" (183). Psychoanalysis, in other words, is about the flaws in the system—about how men become men and women become women, and about the resistance of individuals during the process by which they are educated in the rules of social engagement. The work of Freud and Lévi-Strauss "enables us to isolate sex and gender from 'mode of production,' and to counter a certain tendency to explain sex oppression as a reflex of economic forces," writes Rubin. "Their work provides a framework in which the full weight of sexuality and marriage can be incorporated into an analysis of sex oppression. It suggests a conception of the women's movement as analogous to, rather than isomorphic with, the working-class movement, each addressing a different source of human discontent" (203).

This is obviously a departure from previous feminist approaches to psychoanalytic theory, and for Rubin its efficacy is bound up in the combined power of psychoanalysis and structural anthropology. This is an argument of great influence. On the surface, feminist theories in the United States, especially those emerging from the analysis of language and representation and from the disciplinary context of the humanities, take up Rubin's challenge primarily through the psychoanalytic mode. But the shaping influence of structuralism is palpable across the range of such feminist theories; this is especially conspicuous in North American feminists' concern with institutional formations—especially the family and its larger reproductive significance—in analyses generated later in the 1970s, before the widespread feminist engagement with French feminism and poststructuralism. As this suggests, the feminist tradition in the United States originates in an engagement with structuralism that offers the political theories of structuralism a far more social-scientific orientation than does the European tradition.

From the first, however, the nurturing of an American psychoanalytic feminism involved a departure from the scientific tradition of American psychoanalysis in favor of a more European psychoanalytic emphasis on the symbolic; in this, American feminist psychoanalysis is always already Lacanian. Commenting on the medical-establishment context of American psychoanalysis, Rubin stresses that "the clinical establishment has fetishized anatomy": "Transforming moral law into scientific law, clinical practice has acted to enforce sexual convention upon unruly participants. In this sense, psychoanalysis has often become more than a theory of the mechanisms of the reproduction of sexual arrangements; it has been one of those mechanisms. Since the aim of the feminist and gay revolts is to dismantle the apparatus of sexual enforcement, a critique of psychoanalysis has been in order" (184). Suggesting that psychoanalysts themselves, beginning with Freud, have been almost willfully blind to the radical implications of their own theoretical discoveries, Rubin argues that psychoanalysis in fact "contains a unique set of concepts for understanding men, women, and sexuality. It is a theory of sexuality in human society. Most importantly, psychoanalysis provides a description of the mechanisms by which the sexes are divided and deformed, of how bisexual, androgynous infants are transformed into boys and girls" (184–85). In its capacity to explain the origins and development of gendered and erotic difference, psychoanalysis supplements Marxist theories of labor, entering the analysis of "reproduction" at the level of its implications for the individual child, who mysteriously grows up to act as a willing and complicit cog in the capitalist machine.

One of the radical insights offered by psychoanalysis, which emerges especially vividly when it is read as a description of social processes and not as a prescription of desired behavior, is the radical contingency of the heterosexual "norm." Freud's developmental theories trace the powerful mechanisms by which the wildly diverse, polymorphous infant gets wedged into conformity with a socially acceptable category—girl, boy—and rigidly directed toward the choice of erotic object appropriate for that gender identity. In this, psychoanalytic theories demonstrate their value for feminist inquiry: they map the perversity and the frailty of the "normal."[29]

In the women's liberation movement, the feminist payoff of this observation was the immediate repoliticization of the personal. Psychoanalysis offered new ways of interpreting the function and meaning of the family, of individual gendered bodies and sexualities, and of abstract concepts of desire. In its analysis of femininity as an identity grounded in "pain and humiliation," to use Rubin's words (197), psychoanalysis offered feminists new terms for arguments against the rigid social conventions that produce this effect; importantly, though, at the same time it offered the means of analyzing women's conscious or unconscious complicity with those conventions—and of comprehending the paradox of women's staggering psychological power within the same social network credited with their oppression. For Rubin, psychoanalytic theory further presented a means of linking the women's and gay rights movements through the argument that the social control of women's sexuality originates alongside kinship networks' investment in maintaining a taboo of homosexuality in men and women alike.[30] "As a description of how phallic culture domesticates women," Rubin writes, "and the effects in women of their domestication, psychoanalytic theory has no parallel. And since psychoanalysis is a theory of gender, dismissing it would be suicidal for a political movement dedicated to eradicating gender hierarchy (or gender itself). We cannot dismantle something that we underestimate or do not understand. The oppression of women is deep; equal pay, equal work, and all of the female politicians in the world will not extirpate the roots of sexism" (197–98). In the mid-1970s, after nearly a decade of feminist theory and practice in the United States, Gayle Rubin and other psychoanalytically inclined feminists argued that gender hierarchy was not yet understood, and suggested that prominent battles of the women's liberation movement—for equal pay, for equal work—only scraped the surface of the problem. To this point, the prevailing imagery of feminist theory in the United States had involved the upward mobility of consciousness-raising. But feminism was about to go down deep: theories based on the raised consciousness now made way for theories attendant to the depth of the dark, unconscious mind.

An Argument for Male Mothering

In *The Mermaid and the Minotaur: Sexual Arrangements and Human Malaise*, published in 1976, Dorothy Dinnerstein uses a psychoanalytic framework to gain what she describes as a deeper understanding of human "sexual arrangements," or "the division of responsibility, opportunity, and privilege that prevails between male and female humans, and the patterns of psychological interdependence that are implicit in this division."[31] Her goal is to understand the apparent intractability of those gender arrangements: after a decade of radical critique by New Left and feminist activists, why has the conventional nuclear family remained intact as the cornerstone of patriarchal convention? "The stone walls that activism runs into have buried foundations," she writes (12), and those foundations are entrenched in the unconscious, in the primal dramas of infantile love and helplessness from which every person first learns what it means to be a human being.

Dinnerstein's analysis turns on the concept of consent: why, she asks, do men and women, even avowed feminists aware of what is "intolerable in our gender arrangements . . . go on consenting to such arrangements?" (6).

The gender arrangements of Western culture are represented by the arche-types "mother" and "father," and the neurotic individual—which is to say, every individual—within that culture is always, at some level, "infant." The argument for the "normalcy" of the nuclear family is rooted deep within the human unconscious, Dinnerstein suggests, and the prospect of social change depends fundamentally on an understanding of the unconscious investment in maintaining things the way they are—and in the profundity of individu-als' resistance to change: "What at this point most basically enforces our consent . . . is something more deeply mutable than the defenders of the present arrangements, lay and scholarly, would have us think: It is not, most basically, our anatomy, or our hormones. It is not some mysteriously genetically determined remnant of the mechanisms that guide the ecologi-cally adaptive relations of male and female gorillas, chimps, and baboons. Neither does it bear any magic and sacred relation to the needs of infants and young children: indeed, it violates some of the most vital of those needs" (7). As this quotation suggests, Dinnerstein argues that the gender conven-tions of Western culture are not rooted in the body—not in anatomy, nor in hormones, nor in genes, nor in a presumed biological dependency between newborn human beings and their mothers. Ours is a culture that has a great deal invested in that "magic and sacred relation" of Madonna and child, but its "magical and sacred" qualities clothe ideology in a thin rhetoric of physi-cal dependency. Even feminists leap to the defense of sacred maternity: "It is one thing to want change in the educational, vocational, and legal status of women; it is quite another thing to start tampering with Motherhood" (76).

At the heart of Dinnerstein's argument, however, is the contention that, as long as "Motherhood" remains in place as the inviolable icon of femi-nine power, the sexual double standards that feminists have committed to fight will also remain securely in place: "[N]o societal compromise which changes other features of woman's condition while leaving her role as first parent intact will get at the roots of asymmetric sexual privilege" (76). The patriarchal system is, at its roots, grounded in the domestic conventions that assign women the important function of caring for infants; not only male and female gender identities but also sexuality, misogyny, and individuals' investment in achieving and wielding power originate in the sublimated, but never resolved, dynamics of the mother-infant relationship. "The primitive cornerstone of human solidarity is also the primitive cornerstone of human pathology," Dinnerstein writes (77). The fact that this pathology is wired into the heads and unconscious minds of human infants means that it is il-logical, primal, and symbolic.

Proposing such a challenge to the integrity of this system—"tampering" with the sacred family unit—is precisely what Dinnerstein proposes to do.

The goal of her book is to explore "how the prevailing sexual arrangements can be re-examined, in a spirit of respect for the complexity of our own emotional situation, as part of the process of withdrawing our consent from them" (233). To that end, this is her activist conclusion: men must take on the labor of child care, and especially of infant care, on terms that are equal to women's. The hand that rocks the cradle rules the world, she contends—but there is no earthly reason that the hand must necessarily be attached to a female body: "[T]he meaning of maternity itself (its present meaning, which is by no means eternal, by no means intrinsic to or inseparable from our status as live-bearing mammals) must also change. And for this in turn to happen, man's hand must be as firm on the cradle as woman's" (128).

This is a deceptively simple thesis. It is offered not in the terms of Marxist critique that informed earlier feminist demands for equal male participation in housework and child care. Unlike critics in the women's liberation movement who situated the nuclear family within a capitalist patriarchal system, Dinnerstein does not propose the dismantling of the nuclear family, nor does she take up the consequent adjustment in economic arrangements required by equal male mothering. At the heart of Dinnerstein's proposal is an attempt to restructure power arrangements by intervening at the source of their construction, in infancy, with the belief that patriarchal ideologies are a psychopathology addressed only by alterations to the psychological programming carried on in the domestic arrangements that almost invariably govern infancy. In this context, she suggests that the "sexual arrangements" of modern culture, including the capitalist engine of the patriarchal system, are the vestiges of a psychological—indeed, a psychopathological—regime that can and must be toppled.

However, "our consent is far less simple to withdraw than many feminists would like to believe," Dinnerstein writes. "The law, custom, economic pressure, educational practice, and so on that stand in the way of change—essential as it is to identify and fight each of these on its own level—are the symptoms, not the causes, of the disorder that we must cure" (7). As long as they fail to perceive, and to act against, the unconscious roots of "cultural malaise," feminists are complicit in the maintenance of what is, in the end, a profoundly misogynist system. It is not enough to fight that system in its visible incarnations—in the law, for example, or education; for Dinnerstein, the very survival of the human species depends on the birth and nurturing of an entirely new kind of person, a person whose developmental drama, with its variant cycles of helplessness and empowerment, joy and sorrow, pure love and violent hatred, is negotiated not just relative to women but to women and men. Dinnerstein contends that such reprogramming will forever change the cultural meaning of power, of love and desire, and is the only means to the end of truly radical, permanent social change.

This is a new form of argument for feminist theory, a new approach to perceptions of women and social change, largely because of its attitudes toward—and its use of—psychoanalytic theory. Unlike that of her predecessors Millett and Mitchell, Dinnerstein's feminism is expressed not through an attack on, nor a defense of, Freud's attitudes toward women, their bodies, and their psychosexual development. Influenced by psychoanalytic object-relations theory, and especially Melanie Klein's work on the symbolic status of the mother in the project of infantile development, Dinnerstein uses psychoanalysis structurally, as a means of understanding how the major patterns of everyday life reproduce patterns and attitudes embedded in the human mind during infancy.[32] Hers is neither a psychoanalysis nor a feminism preoccupied with the phallus; instead, Dinnerstein is concerned with psychoanalytic insights into the mother's power, into the love for, and hate of, women that emerges from infantile perceptions of the omnipotent mother.[33] The simultaneous and conflicting infantile love and loathing of women gives form to all later human understanding; all ideologies—all understandings of the body, of social power, and of sexual desire—find shape within this primal ambivalence. The ideological investments originated in infancy and imported into adulthood through the vehicle of the unconscious will change only when the caretaking structures of infancy are reconfigured. Only when women are off the hook, when not just women but also men are the figures against which infants act out their primal rage and adoration, will unconscious structures change, too. Dinnerstein describes "the mother-raised human's fear and resentment of female authority": "Every . . . proof of our weakness and fragility silently activates a rage that goes far back to our first encounters with the angry pain of defeat. *If these first encounters had not taken place under all-female auspices, if women were not available to bear the whole brunt of the unexamined infantile rage at defeat that permeates adult life, the rage could not so easily remain unexamined; the infantilism could more easily be outgrown*" (190–91; emphasis in original). Dinnerstein is concerned less with getting men to share the practical labor of infant care (though this is a hidden benefit, to be sure) than with redistributing the long-term burdens of the overdetermined emotional relationship an infant constructs with a primary caretaker, a figure who just so happens, in most cases, to be a woman.

Dinnerstein shares Juliet Mitchell's frustration with the feminist tradition of Freud-demonization: "I am disturbed, like other radical critics of our gender arrangements, by the sexual bigotry that is built into the Freudian perspective. But I am disinclined to let the presence of that bigotry deflect my attention from the key to a way out of our gender predicament that Freud, in a sense absent-mindedly, provides. Feminist preoccupation with Freud's patriarchal bias, with his failure to jump with alacrity right out of his male Victorian skin, seems to me wildly ungrateful" (xxix). Indeed, Dinnerstein suggests that the feminist resistance to Freud masks a deeper resistance to the really revolutionary implications of his theoretical insights, however absentminded. At the center of Freud's theory is an understanding of family structure on which Dinnerstein predicates her own theoretical position: "Freud's contribution has radically deepened our awareness of certain central structural defects in human life, one of which is the immense strain imposed both on male and on female personality by the fact (a fact whose effects stem from certain cognitive and emotional peculiarities of humans: they do not occur in other animals) that the main adult presence in infancy and early childhood is female" (xxx).

The legacy of psychoanalytic object-relations theory enables Dinnerstein to read Freudian psychoanalytic theory not as a ritual of phallus worship but as an analysis of the immense determining importance of infantile development and, in the context of infancy, of the formidable power vested in the mother—a power symbolically transposed to women more generally. She creates a distinction between "the conservative psychoanalytic spirit of understanding why things must be the way they are" and "the revolutionary psychoanalytic spirit of thinking out how they can be changed" (44). Dinnerstein sees Freud's own work, notwithstanding its radical implications, as descriptive of, rather than disruptive of, the status quo. Although this point is debatable, given Freud's persistent concern with the precariousness of the status quo—his description of the formidable challenges facing a girl's development into heterosexual womanhood, for example—Dinnerstein is unwilling to throw the baby out with the bathwater, to sacrifice psychoanalytic insights because the terms of the social critique did not predict later feminist analyses.

Dinnerstein's argument registers a number of developments within the canon of feminist theory. Benefiting from analyses such as Mitchell's, Dinnerstein can make use of Freudian psychoanalysis as radical theory without first defending its legitimacy. And from the insights of psychoanalytic object-relations theory, Dinnerstein moves seamlessly into the practice of psychoanalysis as a mother-centered, not a phallocentric, theoretical tool. By analyzing women's "consent" to prevailing misogynist gender arrangements, and by suggesting that even radical feminists extend such consent insofar as they resist challenges to conventions of parenting and ideals of motherhood, Dinnerstein introduces a new analysis of ideology. Counter to previous feminist analyses of patriarchal oppression, which generally represent men as the agents of power and women as its passive victims, Dinnerstein focuses her inquiry on the power—both actual and symbolic—that women possess within patriarchy. In other words, she suggests that women are not the passive oppressed, that they have a stake in patriarchal gender arrangements, and, insofar as they are agents of cultural power, that they have the power to change the system. However radical their politics, Dinnerstein suggests, men and women alike consent in many ways to the maintenance of the status quo.

Dinnerstein's theory is admittedly ethnocentric; feminists from the first had resisted Freud's assumption that the domestic arrangements he observed in a bourgeois capital of Western Europe were universal, global, and for all time. Of her own argument, Dinnerstein writes that "it is mainly couched, in its literal details, in terms of the nuclear family of contemporary white-middle-class America. *Its central points are meant, however, to be usefully translatable to any human situation in which women preside over life's first stages and men are at the same time present as emotionally significant figures for young children*" (40; emphasis in original).

Dinnerstein's argument also assumes a fiercely normative ideology of the heterosexual and the middle-class. In her insistence on the urgent necessity for gender diversity in the earliest stages of child care, Dinnerstein ironically renormalizes—indeed, makes newly utopian—the conventional middle-class ideal of the heterosexual nuclear family, marked off from the cultural ideal only by a strategic redistribution of its labor practices. In purely pragmatic terms, not all children have two parents of opposing genders; some have more than two, and some have fewer, with gender configurations that are similarly mobile. On the one hand, Dinnerstein's vision of the ideal radical family—its psychological implications notwithstanding—looks a lot like the familiar ideal of twentieth-century suburban middle-class white American culture. On the other hand, in her identification of melodramatic passions, of the "human malaise" behind that ideal family portrait, and of the determining cultural power of the mother in the center, Dinnerstein models a structurally focused strategy of psychoanalytic reading. She suggests that individual women and men make a political choice when they situate themselves within a conventional nuclear family. This is not necessarily a conscious choice, but it is a choice nonetheless. Dinnerstein puts psychoanalysis to use for feminism by arguing that where there's choice there's resistance; in her emphasis on the unconscious consent with which men and women conspire to maintain their human malaise, she locates the first battle for a feminist future in the unconscious mind.

A Grammar of Mothering

The radical premise of Nancy Chodorow's influential 1978 book *The Reproduction of Mothering* emerges in the first sentence of the first chapter: "Women mother."[34] This book undertakes to examine the odd persistence of this fact (so often taken for granted and perceived as "natural"), the origin of psychological stability, and the orderly social relations that follow. Even on the level of syntax, Chodorow works to defamiliarize the "natural" homology of woman and mother, for in the statement "Women mother," *mother* is a verb, not a noun. By making *mother* an action word rather than an object word, Chodorow democratizes the labor of mothering itself, demonstrating that, at least in the flexible medium of language, the act of mothering is available to any agent who should happen to be so inclined. This ruptures the assumption that *mother* is a synonym for the noun *woman* and the related assumption that there is an innately womanly quality—chemical, or perhaps biological—at the heart of the mothering act. Instead, by recasting *mother* as a verb, Chodorow shifts emphasis to the performative rather than the identity-bound qualities of mothering; the fact that women are the agents most associated with this act is random, a historical accident taken for granted by a culture lulled into complacency.

"Women mother." The statement also represents a strong claim on behalf of women. In Chodorow's formulation, women are the subject of the sentence, the agents who labor, who act on and through the verb *mother*. Presumably they act in other contexts, too: implicit here is the claim to iteration, the suggestion not only that women mother but also that they act as the subjects of other sentences, the agents of other verbs. "Women mother" is a statement bereft of sentimentalizing adjectives and adverbs. Grammatically, this underscores its status as an observation about a particular kind of work, enacted in general by a particular kind of subject. In the context of psychoanalytic theory, which conventionally narrates the role of mother exclusively from the perspective of her child, the animation of women as grammatical subjects and agents in their own right, as figures with interests, roles, and spheres of action that may include but must exceed mothering, opens a new arena of analytical possibility.

The Reproduction of Mothering is concerned not only with the question of why women mother but also with the question of why they continue to do so, generation after generation, in the context of rapidly changing social institutions, including the family, and wildly expanded understandings of the term "woman." Like Dinnerstein, Chodorow wonders why modern culture continues to define women primarily or even exclusively as mothers—or as not-mothers, for those women who do not have children—when women are having fewer children than in previous generations and thus dedicate less time to the labor of motherhood. Chodorow contends that this tendency, as well as women's persistent self-identification relative to motherhood, goes far deeper than their socialization in conventions of femininity and cannot be changed by the "quick-fix" approach advocated by feminists concerned only with behavioral change:

> Role-training, identification, and enforcement certainly have to do with the acquisition of an appropriate gender role. But the conventional feminist view, drawn from social or cognitive psychology, which understands feminine development as explicit ideological instruction or formal coercion, cannot in the case of mothering be sufficient. In addition, explanations relying on behavioral conformity do not account for the tenacity of self-definition, self-concept, and psychological need to maintain aspects of traditional roles which continue even in the face of ideological shifts, counterinstruction, and the lessening of masculine coercion which the women's movement has produced. (33–34)

The association of mothering and femininity is sufficiently tenacious that Chodorow, like Dinnerstein several years earlier, concerns herself with the unconscious investment retained by women, and also by men, in the maintenance of "traditional roles." In this context psychoanalysis offers an interpretive lens, enabling Chodorow to analyze family structures in order to gain access to the issues at stake in a counterintuitive investment in the traditional: "Psychoanalysis provides an analysis and critique of the reproduction of sex and gender. Freud and his followers demonstrated how sexual repression in the family produces the potentially bisexual, polymorphous perverse infant as a genitally heterosexual, monogamous adult, with boys appropriating their masculine prerogatives and girls acquiescing in their feminine subordination and passivity" (41).

The family, in other words, produces males as masculine and females as feminine, working from the rather unpromising raw material of infantile incoherence. Psychoanalysis describes how this process takes place, and, by arguing that it does so through family sexual repression, it underscores the real—and, for feminists, crucial—instability of gendered sexualities. Such instability produces wide variation within the conventional categories of male masculinity and female femininity, held in check by ideologies that dictate the "normal" range within which that variation may take place. This gets at the heart of Nancy Chodorow's psychoanalytic methodology: hers is a reading of the family as a form of industry, invested in the production of appropriately gendered adults, who will in turn be concerned with the reproduction of the same process in serial form, and so on, generation after generation. The family, Chodorow's analysis suggests, is a self-replicating form, the reproduction of mothering its self-replicating medium. Women are the figures who mobilize the productive-reproductive process.

Writing in 1978, Chodorow benefited from the now-established tradition of feminist psychoanalytic theory; predecessors such as Dinnerstein had paved the way for the political analysis of the domestic sphere, and Mitchell's vigorous arguments for a Freudian feminism enabled Chodorow to adopt a psychoanalytic approach without apology. This is not to suggest that Chodorow lets either Freud or Mitchell off the hook. Arguing for the value of feminist critiques of Freud—"We must face up to the Freudian excesses" (142)—Chodorow suggests that Mitchell is *too* vigorous an apologist for Freud and that her uncritical stance undermines her credibility (141–42). Analyzing the blindness with which Freud approaches questions of female sexuality, and especially mothering, Chodorow nonetheless argues for the potential that lurks within the structural analysis Freud initiated: "Psychoanalysis developed out of the discovery that there was nothing inevitable in the development of sexual object choice, mode, or aim, nor was there innate masculinity or femininity. How one understands, fantasizes, symbolizes, internally represents and feels about her or his physiology is a product of developmental experience in the family, is related in many possible ways to this physiology, and perhaps is shaped by considerations completely apart from it" (154). The body, she suggests, and the sexual use to which that body is put, is a construct of the psyche, shaped by the various psychic investments, desires, and repressions instituted in the primary engine of social production, "developmental experience in the family."

Doubly concerned with production and child development, Chodorow's psychoanalytic theory benefits not only from feminism but also from the strong analytic traditions of object-relations theory and Marxism. Psychoanalytic object-relations theory shifts the focus of psychoanalysis from the father, and the determining symbolic economy of the phallus, to the mother, and the determining economy of the mother-infant relationship. When Chodorow puts object-relations theory to feminist-theoretical ends, she expands the scope of psychoanalytic feminist inquiry by means of a powerful interpretive lens for the analysis of women's cultural power. Working from an object-relations lineage that also influenced Dinnerstein, Chodorow offers insight into the processes by which social expectations and family configurations produce inchoate infants as gendered subjects. Focusing on the implication of the mother as a gendered subject in the replication of gender norms, Chodorow extends implications of Dinnerstein's understanding of the family unit as an ideological system.

In *The Reproduction of Mothering,* this effort takes place in the context of a Marxist analysis of ideology and commodity production. Chodorow's is a sociological inquiry, concerned with the implications of private psychodynamics in the material world; object-relations psychoanalysis offers a means of understanding how public and private spheres constitute one another. The family is a productive—and reproductive—institution: its psychodynamics, originating in the icon "mother," must be understood as a vital cog (perhaps the most vital cog) in the machinery of capitalism. In its continued investment in replenishing a labor force that serves capitalist production more generally, the family unit props up an economic world that in turn fosters domestic ideologies; private and public spheres, far from distinct, exist in an endlessly self-replicating loop.

Working from Rubin's argument in "The Traffic in Women," which proposes that the sex-gender system organizes economic production, and from what Chodorow calls the "psychoanalytic sociology of social reproduction" (35) developed in the Frankfurt school, Chodorow argues that "gender personalities" develop in particular ways in order to support a capitalist industrial world: "[C]apitalist accumulation and proper work habits in workers have never been purely a matter of economics. . . . Conformity to behavioral rules and external authority, predictability and dependability, the ability to take on others' values and goals as one's own, all reflect an orientation external to oneself and one's own standards, a lack of autonomous and creative self-direction. The nuclear, isolated, neolocal family in which women mother is suited to the production in children of these cross-class personality commitments and capacities" (186). Through private processes of socialization that take place within individual families, a culture invents and produces—and values, and therefore reproduces—the kind of women and the kind of men it needs.

"Women mother." Because of this, because of how it has come to be, and because of how the act of mothering has evolved, the great furnace of industrial capitalism is constantly restoked. "Exclusive mothering," Chodorow writes, is not necessarily good for infants, but it is "good for society": "Exclusive and intensive mothering, as it has been practiced in Western society, does seem to have produced more achievement-oriented men and people with psychologically monogamic tendencies" (76–77). Social institutions "create and embody conditions that require people to engage in them. People's participation further guarantees social reproduction" (35).

As Althusser also argues, the self-replicating social structures of capitalism originate with subjectivity itself, in infancy.[35] Chodorow and psychoanalytic object-relations theorists suggest that this labor occurs first and foremost within the mother-infant relationship. This is the foundational relationship of social organization, the origin of all future psychodynamics, of gender roles, and of erotic repression and desire—and it all comes back to a woman. Chodorow explains: "The reproduction of mothering begins from the earliest mother-infant relationship in the earliest period of infantile development. This early relationship is basic in three ways. Most important, the basic psychological stance for parenting is founded during this period. Second, people come out of it with the memory of a unique intimacy which they want to recreate. Finally, people's experience of their early relationship to their mother provides a foundation for expectations of women as mothers" (57). The self-replicating dynamics of human reproduction begin at the beginning, Chodorow argues, originating in the earliest moment of relating in the earliest period of human existence. Women are in on—indeed, they are—the ground floor, determining the primal psychological attitudes that perpetuate patriarchal culture and, within that culture, male and female subjectivity. Within Chodorow's framework, a mother offers its infant three templates, which the child then carries into later life and which help to condition it toward expectations of female femininity and male masculinity. First, the mother-infant relationship provides the infant with a way of understanding the abstract meaning of parenting, a how-to lesson for its future role as parent. Second, instructing the child in the terms of physical and emotional infancy, the mother is the first love of boy and girl children alike, and the model for future love relationships. And third, because mothers are usually women—and certainly in the cultural ideal they are women—the mother of infancy conditions her child into a lifetime of expectations and desires concerning women in general. By locating the origins of patriarchal culture within the psychodynamics of infancy, Chodorow suggests that patriarchy itself, past, present, and future, extends from an expectation that "women mother": "The sexual division of labor and women's responsibility for child care are linked to and generate male dominance" (214). Entrenched cultural resistance to feminism in general and to feminist challenges to domestic ideologies in particular represents an investment in the status quo: "Certainly resistance to change in the sex-gender system is often strongest around women's maternal functions" (219). Mobilizing a forceful psychological challenge, feminism causes anxiety and produces resistance and backlash.

Women's maternal function gives them a virtually limitless sphere of influence in Chodorow's account. In what has been the most influential claim to emerge from *The Reproduction of Mothering*, Chodorow argues that when women mother girl children, those girl children grow up feeling more connected to and continuous with other people, which in turn fosters personal qualities such as empathy, which in turn prepares those socialized as female for the task of mothering. In contrast, when women mother boys, mother and boy alike subtly contrast their gender roles. As a result, males learn to be boys, and later to be men, by associating that gender position with qualities such as detachment and independence. This in turn fosters an ideal of masculine achievement as competitive: "[A] girl continues to experience herself as involved in issues of merging and separation, and in an attachment characterized by primary identification and the fusion of identification and object choice. By contrast, mothers experience their sons as a male opposite. Boys are more likely to have been pushed out of the preoedipal relationship, and to have had to curtail their primary love and sense of empathic tie with their mother" (166). Maleness and femaleness come into being as "different," Chodorow suggests, not because of anatomy or biology but because mothers, themselves socialized by mothers, perceive and experience infants relative to their own gender status: "Because women are themselves mothered by women, they grow up with the relational capacities and needs, and psychological definition of self-in-relationship, which commit . . . them to mothering. Men, because they are mothered by women, do not. Women mother daughters who, when they become women, mother" (209). In the algebra by which mothering is reproduced, generations interlock, and they do so through the vehicle of female connection. Differences of gender and ideology are thus normalized and naturalized through the spiraling reiteration of mother-child dynamics generation after generation after generation.

Is there, then, a point of resistance within the reproductive cycle? Written as they are into the unconscious, are the psychodynamics that produce patriarchal power relations inevitable, and inevitably reproduced? Chodorow's book concludes where Dinnerstein's begins, with a gesture toward the need to diversify child-care arrangements in order to diversify the variously gendered persons who imprint ideological expectations on infants, and who in turn are imprinted by them: "We live in a period when the demands of the roles defined by the sex-gender system have created widespread discomfort and resistance. Aspects of this system are in crisis internally and conflict with economic tendencies. Change will certainly occur, but the outcome is far from certain. The elimination of the present organization of parenting in favor of a system of parenting in which both men and women are responsible would be a tremendous social advance" (219). But this argument is made in the last paragraph of the afterword of Chodorow's text, and it is the first such suggestion she makes; it seems, in other words, only remotely related to the feminist mission of *The Reproduction of Mothering*, which is more characteristically concerned with the oddly persistent fact of women's mothering and the cultural implications that result. Given the multigenerational history within which Chodorow situates masculine and feminine identities, and given the vested interest a capitalist economy retains in those gender conventions, it does not follow that the simple exchange of a male figure for a female figure in the role of mother will transform society. This is not least because, for Chodorow, the mother-child relationship is not a one-way emotional dynamic: the child's experience of its mother's gender is important, to be sure, but equally formative is the mother's experience of the child's gender.

Just as "mothering" is reproduced over generations, its diversification, and therefore challenges to the psychodynamic roots of the patriarchal system that mothering upholds, also demands generations of corrosive change. In a preface written for an edition of *The Reproduction of Mothering* published in 1999, Chodorow comments on the implicit weakness of her concluding call for dual-gender mothering: "If you take seriously that psychological subjectivity from within—feelings, fantasy, psychological meaning—is central to a meaningful life, then you cannot also legislate subjectivity from without or advocate a solution based on a theory of political equality and a conception of women's and children's best interests that ignores this very subjectivity" (xv). In consequence, she writes that in the first edition of the book, "the call for equal parenting, while supported by my argument linking mothering and male dominance, was contradicted in consequential ways by my accounts of maternal subjectivity and its centrality for many women and of the correspondingly distinctive character of the mother-child bond. . . . I am now more respectful of the ways in which individuals do in fact create their emotional reality and sense of personal meaning and less absolute about how they ought to create it" (xvi–xvii). Chodorow has identified a tension between politics and psychology, between the urgency of feminist demands for social change and the complexity of the claims concerning "emotional reality and . . . personal meaning" that early feminist psychoanalytic theories were at the same time unearthing. How might a feminist psychoanalytic theory concerned with the inner complexities that generate social reality provide a valuable tool in the effort for changes to that social reality? What, in the feminist struggle, can a psychoanalytically oriented theory *do*?

Mitchell, Dinnerstein, and Chodorow represent a shift in the use to which feminists put psychoanalysis. The sense in which their work is "political" involves, in each case, the feminist appropriation of the unconscious as a political force. At the very end of the afterword of *The Reproduction of Mothering,* immediately following her truncated call for male mothering, Chodorow describes the work that needs to take place in order to bring about meaningful social change: "Such advances . . . depend on the conscious organization and activity of all women and men who recognize that their interests lie in transforming the social organization of gender and eliminating sexual inequality" (219).

The transformative vision Chodorow advocates demands *conscious* organization and activity. The adjective *conscious* functions here awkwardly but powerfully. Does Chodorow mean to contrast this kind of work with *unconscious* organization and activity? Yes. And that is, in the end, the transformative potential implicit within *The Reproduction of Mothering* and other feminist psychoanalytic theories of gender, sexuality, and interpretation that propose that the unconscious is an insurgent, an activist. It is a powerful force in the creation, perpetuation, and reproduction of social conventions and power dynamics, and people committed to the resistance of such conventions must, in principle, take on the unconscious implications of, as well as resistance to, their vision. In *The Interpretation of Dreams,* Freud described the labor of psychoanalysis as making conscious the repressed, conflicted matter of the unconscious; in *Psychoanalysis and Feminism,* Juliet Mitchell writes, "Psychoanalysis makes conscious the unconscious, not only as a therapeutic technique, but also as a task of its theory."[36] Making conscious the matter of unconscious life is the descriptive task undertaken in feminist psychoanalysis. This is not necessarily for the purpose of therapy, and not only for the ends of theory, but as an intervention in the battle of social organization, the front line of which, Dinnerstein and Chodorow each argue, is motherhood, not as an identity but as a series of powerful acts that constitute a social role and determine a social order. In advance of consciousness-raising, in advance of conscious organizing, must come an understanding of the shaping powers of the unconscious mind. Chodorow's book, by defamiliarizing one of the most ordinary signposts of everyday life—"Women mother"—makes conscious unconscious dynamics that have produced and that continue to naturalize that "fact." This enables Chodorow to elucidate reasons why women, not men, take on the labor of mothering, and to explicate the "gender personalities," male and female, that originate in the fact of female mothering. This is a form of feminist analysis that accounts for the unruly activism of the unconscious and, in the process of identifying its power, begins to suggest strategies for the erosion of its entrenched position.

The Lacanian Revolution

Writing in 1982, Jane Gallop explained that psychoanalytic and feminist theories similarly seek the expansion of rigid, confining codes of individual identity. For each, this involves the detailed analysis of the social institutions—most immediately and most powerfully the family—that help to produce conventions of identity, and in each of these analyses, psychoanalytic and feminist theories can and do mutually inform one another: "Psychoanalysis . . . can unsettle feminism's tendency to accept a traditional, unified, rational, puritanical self—a self supposedly free from the violence of desire. In its turn, feminism can shake up psychoanalysis's tendency to think of itself as apolitical but in fact to be conservative by encouraging people to adapt to an unjust social structure."[37] Psychoanalysis can radicalize feminism by helping feminists to expand concepts of selfhood and desire, just as feminism can turn psychoanalysis from its observational mode into a form of radical critique. Within Gallop's analysis, the interchange between psychoanalysis and feminism is a form of seduction, in which psychoanalysis, emblematized in two powerful papa figures, Freud and Lacan, seduces and is seduced by the desiring, unruly daughter, feminism.

Gallop's representation of feminism in the role of daughter marks a major shift, both in feminist self-representation and in the U.S. feminist engagement with psychoanalysis. Beginning with Kate Millett's *Sexual Politics*, feminists objected to and resisted what they perceived as Freud's infantilization of women. In a discussion of the castration complex, Millett writes, "In formulating the theory of penis envy, Freud not only neglected the possibility of a social explanation for feminine dissatisfaction but precluded it by postulating a literal jealousy of the organ whereby the male is distinguished. As it would appear absurd to charge adult women with these values, the child, and a drastic experience situated far back in childhood, [is] invoked."[38] Infantilization, Millett argues, allows Freud to represent women as damaged goods and, accordingly, to construct them for all time as irrational, childlike beings whose concerns are not to be taken seriously. In this analysis, Millett inaugurates a feminist theoretical tradition that stakes its credibility on a construction of female subjectivity expressly within terms characterizing adult womanhood: reason, sanity, judiciousness. Thus, the American feminism most engaged with psychoanalysis is concerned with women as mothers, as adults; even as critics such as Dinnerstein and Chodorow develop a theory of the unconscious, they do so in the context of a domestic representation in which women have agency and power; in Chodorow's paradigm, the developing daughter is also a nascent mother, a person who occupies both positions at once.

Tellingly, Gallop does not engage this analytical tradition directly; although the names of Dinnerstein and Chodorow appear in the bibliography of Gallop's *The Daughter's Seduction*, neither theorist appears in the text, notes, or index. Moreover, Gallop does not engage Millett's work at all, although she does address Juliet Mitchell's critique of Millett at some length. Indeed, the only figure Gallop engages directly is Mitchell, whose title *Psychoanalysis and Feminism* Gallop cites and inverts in her own subtitle, *Feminism and Psychoanalysis* (xiii). Mitchell is a useful figure for Gallop: in her critique of a U.S. tradition fixated on "realism" and heedless of the unconscious, Mitchell has done much of the work necessary to mark off an analytical departure that Gallop then extends: "In her specific readings of the feminists, where she is at her most incisive, Mitchell is nastiest, wittiest, and most playful in her language. These chapters are characterized by a stinging informality which offers a sharp contrast to both the critical respect evident in her chapters on Reich and Laing and the objective exposition of the earliest chapters, the chapters on Freud" (4).

Within the network of family metaphors Gallop establishes in *The Daughter's Seduction*, Juliet Mitchell is the rival daughter whom Gallop construes as a failure. Gallop outs Mitchell as a closet Lacanian—but an unsuccessful one: Mitchell, Gallop suggests, fatally neglects the question of language, and it is the focus on signification that distinguishes Lacan's theoretical approach to gender and sexuality from Freud's. This neglect of language traps Mitchell herself exactly as Mitchell suggested early feminists were trapped, becoming focused on plot, on realism, on earnest superego-driven prescriptive behavior: "[A]lthough [Mitchell] wins the battle against these writers, she is contaminated by the exchange. At the end of the book, with the proposals for the use of psychoanalysis in the overthrow of patriarchy, she takes over the position of the writers she has criticized. If, after the injection of psychoanalysis into feminism, feminism remains unchanged, what is the point of that infusion?" (14). Mitchell is contaminated by feminism; feminism, though, stubbornly remains uncontaminated by the psychoanalytic injection.

Gallop's daughterly mission emerges in contrast to Mitchell's failed example and involves both decontamination and infection. To appropriate Gallop's metaphors briefly, Mitchell has been a bad daughter (of Lacan, the father she fails to acknowledge or to read carefully enough) and a bad sister (of the feminists she criticizes even as she replicates them). In her place appears Gallop, the good daughter who argues that "[f]eminism must re-examine its ends in view of Lacanian psychoanalysis," the good sister who takes Mitchell on for her careless disregard for other feminists' work. Working in Britain, Mitchell mediates between the spaces of French and American feminism; Gallop, an American claiming the subject position of a French feminist, reconstitutes Mitchell's geographical triangle as a dialectic between "the exotic space of France" and the United States, or, more precisely, between France and Gallop herself as émigré, ambassador, and insubordinate translator.

Gallop's feminism is, in the first instance, an extension of the radical feminist mission expressed by the New York Radical Women in their introduction to the annual periodical *Notes from the Second Year* (1970): a politics based on women's new opportunity "*[t]o dare to be bad.*"[39] Gallop's "badness" in *The Daughter's Seduction* is tactical. Like Valerie Solanas's method in the *S.C.U.M. Manifesto,* Gallop's method is a part of her message: her critique of feminist theoretical "realism," of feminism's rectitude, propriety, and prudery, comes not only in her analysis of seduction but also in her embrace of taboos of sexual desire and sexual language—a discourse of cunts and pussies, rape and incest. In this, Gallop locates herself in a long tradition of strategic transgression in the U.S. feminist tradition; the departure here is only that Gallop's transgression takes place within the authoritative and authorizing context of an academic book, published by an Ivy League university press, with the scandalous aim of bringing into the center of American feminist theory and politics the work of a defrocked French psychoanalyst and linguist who gave "a seminar saying 'Woman does not exist' at the moment when the impact of feminism [was] peaking and in full cognizance of that feminism" (43).

Gallop's is a theoretical argument concerned with language, with representational style, with signification. And in fine psychoanalytic style, the content of that argument is as powerfully acted out as it is described directly. Gallop's method involves a new attention to the feminist as "desiring subject," and, through Lacan's joint concern with Freudian psychoanalysis and structural linguistics, she argues that desire and subjectivity come into being together in language—and thus that their analysis can begin only in the context of the analysis of language: "Mitchell suggests that we demonstrate the contradictory nature of the cultural constructs inscribed into the unconscious. Yet those contradictions are the necessary result of the subject's place—as one who desires—within the signifying chain. Desire has a contradictory nature by being that which exceeds the bounds of the imaginary satisfaction available to the demand" (13). Desire is a paradox: it is insatiable, and it is the founding condition of subjectivity. The feminist subject is as enmeshed as any other subject within a network of desires, including, Gallop argues, the contradictory but inexorable desire for the very father figures her feminist revolutionary agenda excoriates.

It is in this sense that "the daughter's seduction" is the methodological statement of *The Daughter's Seduction.* Gallop's title can be read in at least two ways: as a description of the daughter-feminist's seduction by the big bad daddy of psychoanalysis; and as a description of the daughter-feminist's agency as a seducer—of psychoanalysis? of other feminists? of resisting readers?—in her own right. Gallop's argument involves an acknowledgment of the fact of women's necessary participation in the ideological social structures that are the target of feminist critique: "If feminism is to challenge a phallocentric world, phallocentrism must be dealt with and not denied" (18). In Lacanian psychoanalysis, the phallus is "the privileged signifier" that constructs the desiring subject in and through the insatiability of desire.[40]

Gallop's is a psychoanalysis of scandal whose insurgent methods propose that a politics of subversion replace that of revolution. The phallic father figure is powerful only in the context of consenting subjects who conceive of power only in terms of those who have and those who have not—subjects who remain unaware of the material benefits that accrue to the provocateur: "Infidelity then is a feminist practice of undermining the Name-of-the-Father. The unfaithful reading strays from the author, the authorized, produces that which does not hold as a reproduction, as a representation. Infidelity is not outside the system of marriage, the symbolic, patriarchy, but hollows it out, ruins it, from within. Unlike such infidelity, a new system, a feminist system, one constant, faithful to the tenets and dogmas of feminism would be but another Name-of-the-Father, feminism as a position and a possession" (48). Gallop endorses a politics of promiscuity—epistemological promiscuity, that is, characterized by the principled, and playful, resistance to the codifying implications of any system, phallic or feminist. Hers is a theoretical system whose method is to counter the systematic implications of theory; like Luce Irigaray, Gallop "posits a continual, analytic vigilant dissidence to any order as the necessary position for the intellectual" (119). By appearing complicit with authority figures—the Ivy League university press—but by enacting tactical "infidelity"—putting the feminist herself onstage as a sexual subject whose desires don't always conform to social expectations—authority is assailed from within. This is a very different feminist understanding of power, a very different proposal for its dismantling, than the paradigms for revolutionary overthrow produced in the women's liberation movement.

Yet the Trojan-horse strategy has risks: even the most strategic appearance of complicity is vulnerable to accusations of bolstering rather than corroding hierarchy. As Gallop herself points out, even the epistemology of scandal requires as vigilant a renewal as other "ethical discourses" generated by feminism, especially those generated in the context of the resistance to the prescriptive implications of theory. Gallop's book ends with a reading of two French feminists, Hélène Cixous and Catherine Clément, and an establishment of an unusually prescriptive pedagogical position for herself:

> [W]e must learn to accept the ambiguity, learn to make "open or shut" a matter of indifference. Both Cixous and Clément use the word "bisexual" in their texts . . . to name some sort of positive goal. Bisexuality has traditionally been linked with hysteria in psychoanalytic theory. But these women writers are talking about an "other bisexuality." Neither the fantasmatic resolution of differences in the imaginary, nor the fleshless, joyless

assumption of the fact of one's lack of unity in the symbolic, but an other bisexuality, one that pursues, loves and accepts both the imaginary and the symbolic, both theory and flesh. (149–50)

"Bisexuality" here represents an embrace of both and all positions, erotic and epistemological, in a productively disruptive mode reminiscent of the tactics Gallop earlier endorsed. It also represents an unwillingness to fore-close possibilities, whether in erotic object choice or in epistemology; a rejection of the heterosexual programming of patriarchal culture; and a recuperation of "hysteria," of the omnivorous nature of infancy, of the simultaneity of "theory and flesh."

The Daughter's Seduction is, in the end, as much a seduction of the feminist mother figures whose work preceded it as it is of the father figures of psychoanalysis, Freud and Lacan. Yet the mother-daughter dynamic so central to the plot of American feminist psychoanalysis is entirely occulted within Gallop's analysis; as an object of desire and a subject of open seductive possibilities, the mother haunts this text as relentlessly as Lacan haunts Juliet Mitchell's work. Like Mitchell, her "sister" in sibling rivalry, Gallop in the end—literally, at the end—returns to the plot of the feminist tradition from which, in theory, she was engineering a dramatic departure. In 1988, Gallop published Thinking through the Body, with a cover photo of her own body in the act of giving birth to a son. In The Daughter's Seduction, the mother is object, not subject—the object of seduction, the scandalous other, unassimilated but (and) somehow foundational to flesh and to theory. Gallop's account speaks both of and to the volatile history of a feminist psychoanalysis. I have argued in this chapter for the feminist appropriation of an activist unconscious: beginning with Mitchell and Rubin, feminists take on the Freudian insight that the unconscious mind is the only site of intervention capable of providing lasting and genuine social change—although it remains by necessity an abstraction, invisible and dematerialized. Like her predecessors, Gallop, too, routes her political intervention through the unconscious, again by figuring the mother as a site of gendered power—an object of desire and a desiring subject—and as a body that bears meaning far in excess of corporeal matter alone.

3

The Feminist Body Politic
Sexuality's Domestic Incarnation

> The tale of the clitoris is a parable of culture.
> —Thomas Laqueur, *Making Sex: Body and Gender from the Greeks to Freud*

Before Gayle Rubin's 1975 argument for a "sex/gender system," before Audre Lorde's 1978 endorsement of "the uses of the erotic,"[1] before French feminists' appropriation of the discourse of bodily semiotics, there existed a vocabulary of feminist erotic empowerment that had and retains implications for theories of gender and power. Debates in the early 1970s concerning the status of the clitoral orgasm pitted the symbolically good clitoris against the symbolically bad vagina. These discussions shaped the interpretive possibilities credited to the female body in the contexts of feminist theory and practice, affected the fragmenting of feminist theorists into cultural and sex-radical factions, and helped to construct erotic politics as a field of interpretive inquiry.

The canonization of the clitoris served as a means of situating pleasure in its relationship to politics. Feminists represented the female body as the material ground—quite literally—from which both political abstractions and political activisms originated. As they so often did, these arguments extended from a critique of Freud; feminists appropriated psychoanalytic arguments to model a vision of womanhood as equally sensitive and powerful. The arguments emerged as well from the discourses of experience and affect so central to the consciousness-raising movement. If consciousness-raising grounds women's political emancipation first in their experiences and their emotions, theories of feminist clitoral pleasure invest similarly in a politics

of feeling: the physical sensations that accompany the achievement of a clitoral orgasm are a metaphor for, and thus a first step toward, liberation in
political as well as sexual spheres.

These are debates about the meaning and social significance of sexual
pleasure. In encouraging women to seize a particular means of production—
the production of sexual emancipation through pleasure—they suggest that
eroticism is a core component of revolution. They propose a fundamentally
performative politics of feminism, suggesting that feminists are what feminists do. In the unalienated labor economy of this feminist ideal, the sex act
can be appropriated as political because pleasure is of and from the body;
bodies and the private spheres in which they interact frame a new interpretive politics of natural, normal desire. The newly feminist female body tells a
fresh story about women's capacities: self-sufficiency emblematized by clitoral
autonomy frees women from a sexual dependence on men. The empowered
clitoris initiates a narrative of female autonomy that envisions the sexually
emancipated woman as capable of providing for herself in more ways than
one; if she doesn't require a man in bed, this freedom will pertain in other
areas as well.

In this chapter, I argue that discourses of an empowered sexual body work
in two important, and not always complementary, ways for feminism. First
and most obviously, they provide a vocabulary for political empowerment
that is grounded in the bodily pleasure of clitoral orgasm, putting pressures of the sexual revolution to work for the women's movement. This
vocabulary originates in the popular scientific studies of Kinsey and Masters
and Johnson, which feminists use to make claims about the transparent
truth, and indeed the universality, of female sexual responses. In the ongoing
feminist critique of abstraction and in the effort to produce feminist theories that are populist, effective, and material, the clitoris stands for a series
of material facts or material truths that, in their unalienated state, serve to
ground abstract theoretical claims.

The evident transparency of a self-sufficient feminist body proves more
complicated with scrutiny, however.[2] I suggest that the "facts" of female
sexual response, described as universal because they are upheld by scientific
evidence, actually describe and protect a highly particularized notion of
empowerment and emancipation for women. Far from serving as a universal theory for women's liberation, these discourses help to produce a new
brand of radical married heterosexuality that leaves the middle-class domestic sphere safely intact. Through discourses of the orgasm, and particularly
through the terms by which feminists appropriate scientific evidence to bolster their arguments for orgasm, feminists produce a "natural" female body
that gradually reveals its normatively heterosexual contours. In turn, the

consolidation of that body as a natural ideal constructs unnatural, aberrant others of subjects who diverge from the standard.

Feminist normative heterosexuality is secured through two modes of identification, two ways of describing entities to which the universal feminist body is similar but not identical. The first of these identifications involves the phallus: feminist discourses of the clitoris almost always explain themselves through recourse to the phallus, which resembles the clitoris in its sensitivity, its massive number of nerve endings, its status as the origin of gendered erotic pleasure, and, most important, its use as a symbol of power. Although the clitoris is quite like a phallus both physically and symbolically, it is not in fact a phallus; attached to a female body, it serves feminist ends.

The second and related site of identification—and resistance—is the lesbian. Women emancipated into clitoral sensitivity resemble lesbians in their presumed independence from phallic sexuality; in their elevation of clitoral eroticism to a new centrality and a new ideal; and in their expertise in the matter of producing orgasms, and thus empowerment, for themselves. Although the feminist body is quite like the lesbian body both physically and symbolically, it is not necessarily a lesbian body. Like phallic male subjects, women empowered toward discovery of the clitoris find that they have equipment for sexual pleasure that leads to psychological as well as material gains. Like lesbians, women empowered toward discovery of the clitoris find that they are the experts on the achievement of their erotic fulfillment. In these identifications, a normative feminist subjectivity is born in a normatively "female" body. Though that subject and her body might have something in common with phallic male subjects and their bodies, and with lesbian subjects and their bodies, she is neither male nor, more troubling for feminism, lesbian.

The Back-Story

The sexological studies of Alfred Kinsey and William Masters and Virginia Johnson, published in 1953 and 1966 respectively, helped to establish lesbian sexuality in particular as an ideal that haunted later feminist discourses of sex and power, the personal and the political, eros and empowerment. Kinsey first worked to construct lesbianism as a form of sexual knowledge from which heterosexual women could learn; he considered lesbianism to be a conduit to women's emancipation from heterosexuality, not in terms of its practice per se but because of the insights lesbians could offer heterosexual women and men about women's pleasure. For sexologists and for the feminists who appropriated their conclusions, the implications of lesbian eroticism could extend beneficially into expectations for heterosexual domestic relations.

In 1953, the landmark publication of Kinsey's study of women's sexuality, *Sexual Behavior in the Human Female,* introduced, under the authority of empirical scientific data, a newly popular discourse of human sexuality. Constructed from surveys and interviews of "5,940 white, non-prison females,"[3] the Kinsey report on female sexuality significantly advanced both public and scientific discourses on the topic of sex. "For the first time," wrote Ruth Brecher and Edward Brecher in 1966, "millions of Americans took an open-eyed look into the yawning chasm separating the accepted myths of human sexual behavior and the actual behavior of men and women as they themselves reported it to the Kinsey Institute researchers."[4] Kinsey excluded nonwhite women and women in prison from his sample for fear of overgeneralizing their respective demographic distinctions and because those distinctions "would have seriously distorted the calculations on the total sample" (22). Despite the evenhandedness represented in Kinsey's stated desire to respect differences among sociological and racial subgroups, however, the effect of this exclusion was to normalize white middle-class women's experience as universally representative: the subjects of the study are simply described as "women."

Kinsey's analysis of female sexuality is composed equally of psychosocial and more purely scientific data, and he invokes scientific objectivity as the source of his authority to combat cultural taboos against sexual discussion (10). The ground of Kinsey's "scientific materialism" is the female erotic body, and his study represents an attempt to read the signifiers of that body outside cultural codes of propriety. Linking heterosexual conventions with property rights and questioning the equation of sexuality with reproduction, Kinsey represents bodily response as the empirical ground on which negotiations of social justice might occur. He concludes that, as it existed in contemporary American society, heterosexual, marital coitus was highly ineffective as a means of generating pleasure for the majority of women. Kinsey's intervention into the physiological background of this fact, in the context of his explicit critique of the culture of shame that surrounds discussions of sexuality, offered feminist writers two decades later the central vocabulary for their own critique of the politics of heterosexuality.

Distinguishing erotic pleasure in general from penile pleasure in particular, Kinsey writes, "The effects of any direct stimulation of the penis are so obvious that the organ has assumed a significance which probably exceeds its real importance. This overemphasis on genital action has served, more than anything else, to divert attention from the activities which go on in other parts of the body during sexual response" (573). Psychoanalytic emphases on the importance of penis and vagina to sexual satisfaction fail to get past the obvious, Kinsey argues.[5] The clitoris, however, which Kinsey

dubs the "phallus of the female" (574), is the center of female sexual response, the anatomical homologue to the fetal penis and the central location
of the nerve endings that localize sexual pleasure in women. Kinsey argues
that the vagina is relatively unimportant in women's masturbation (580)
and indeed in female homosexual relations, a fact that is significant because
"the partners in such contacts often know more about female genital function than either of the partners in a heterosexual relation" (575).

Thus, the sexual understanding of women is clear to lesbians, and the
sexologist's task is to mediate the transmission of this knowledge from lesbian culture to women more generally. This larger cultural context, however,
devalues the lessons to be learned from female homoeroticism, because "normal" heterosexual practice is oriented toward penile pleasure. In contrast to
the "widespread opinion that the female is slower than the male in her sexual
responses," Kinsey reports that "the masturbatory data do not support that
opinion. . . . It is true that the average female responds more slowly than the
average male in coitus, but this seems to be due to the ineffectiveness of the
usual coital techniques" (164). The ineffectiveness of heterosexual coitus for
women is largely attributable to the fact that "[m]ost males are likely to approach females as they, the males, would like to be approached by a sexual
partner" (468).

In contrast to the unknowing male partner, however,

[f]emales in their heterosexual relationships are actually more likely to prefer
techniques which are closer to those which are commonly utilized in homosexual relationships. . . . It is, of course, quite possible for males to learn
enough about female sexual response to make their heterosexual contacts as
effective as females make most homosexual contacts. With the additional
possibilities which a union of male and female genitalia may offer in a
heterosexual contact, and with public opinion and the mores encouraging
heterosexual contacts and disapproving of homosexual contacts, relationships between females and males will seem, to most persons, to be more
satisfactory than homosexual relationships can ever be. Heterosexual relationships could, however, become more satisfactory if they more often utilized the sort of knowledge which most homosexual females have of female
sexual anatomy and female psychology. (468)

In this, Kinsey essentially argues that lesbians have better sex because they
focus on the clitoris rather than the vagina, and that this is an insight from
which heterosexuals might profit. Feminists in particular took him at his
word in their development of the political implications of this argument.
Kinsey's construction of an incipient "lesbian mystique" has to do with
women's expertise about women's bodies, a form of knowledge devalued

within erotic contexts devoted to the culture of the phallus. Kinsey is careful to underscore the fact that the teleology of orgasm is not the only aim of sexual activity, but he also emphasizes the fact that the commonplace myth of female "sexual frigidity" is a product of education about modesty and decorous femininity rather than an index of physiological disjunction (372–73). Implicitly justifying the logic that later underscores theories of lesbian separatism, Kinsey represents female homosexuality as both the central site of erotic fulfillment for women and their source of sexual knowledge; one might imagine lesbians as erotic savants, serving the women's movement as its in-house sexologists.

Kinsey contends that the cultural perception of female sexual fulfillment has generally displaced "pleasure" from physiology to psychology and emotion: "Whether or not she herself reaches orgasm, many a female finds satisfaction in knowing that her husband or other sexual partner has enjoyed the contact, and in realizing that she has contributed to the male's pleasure. We have histories of persons who have been married for a great many years, in the course of which the wife never responded to the point of orgasm, but the marriage has been maintained because of the high quality of the other adjustments in the home" (371). This is the juncture at which feminists will intervene, with the goal of overturning the assumption that the martyrdom of vicarious erotic pleasure is sufficient for women. The tendency, however, to equate sexuality and domesticity turns on the question of normative reproductivity.

Enabled by technologies such as birth control, the sexologists of the mid-twentieth century initiated a refocusing of sexual expectations from the realm of reproductive normativity to the realm of sexual pleasure, a shift that underscores the central importance of the clitoris to feminist theories of sexuality. "The clitoris," argued Masters and Johnson in 1966, "is a unique organ in the total of human anatomy. Its express purpose is to serve both as a receptor and transformer of sensual stimuli. Thus, the human female has an organ system which is totally limited in the physiologic function to initiating or elevating levels of sexual tension. No such organ exists within the anatomic structure of the human male."[6] The significance of the physiological fact of the clitoris would be central for the women's movement; detaching female sexuality firmly from reproduction and thus normative phallocentricity, the logical but unclaimed implications of this fact extend clearly to the problematic status of normative heterosexuality as well. For Masters and Johnson, following in Kinsey's wake, the physiology of female erotic response reinforces the sense of women's sexual power emerging from the new focus on clitoral stimulation. In 1966, Daniel G. Brown wrote, "The human race could have survived, of course, without a single female having an orgasm."[7] Thus, contemporary reproductive ideologies have devalued female orgasm as a frivolous luxury.[8]

Responding against this assumption, Masters and Johnson emphasized the importance of clitoral stimulation and suggested, in the tradition of Kinsey, that conventional positions of male-female sexual intercourse fail to provide sufficient stimulation to insure female orgasm reliably. Masters and Johnson cite empirical data to counter the popular Freudian argument that clitoral and vaginal orgasms are separate entities, much less that the vaginal orgasm is somehow more "mature" and thus superior to the clitoral climax: "There may be great variation in duration and intensity of orgasmic experience, varying from individual to individual and within the same woman from time to time. However, when any woman experiences orgasmic response to effective sexual stimulation, the vagina and clitoris react in consistent physiologic patterns. Thus, clitoral and vaginal orgasms are not separate biologic entities."[9] Like Kinsey, Masters and Johnson encourage male heterosexual partners to look to women themselves as the source of sexual knowledge about women, and they cite "automanipulation," or masturbation, as the prime instance of that knowledge in practice: "Rather than following any preconceived plan for stimulating his sexual partner, the male will be infinitely more effective if he encourages vocalization on her part. The individual woman knows best the areas of her strongest sensual focus and the rapidity and intensity of manipulative technique that provides her with the greatest degree of sexual stimulation."[10] Interestingly, the lesbian erotic and epistemological ideal drops out of sight here in favor of women's knowledgeable autoeroticism. The empirical data for Masters and Johnson's study, unlike that of Kinsey, was generated from a sample that included no homosexual population; the frame of reference for their theory of female erotic fulfillment is the heterosexual marriage relationship.[11] By this means, an implicit homoerotic ideal in Kinsey turns into an implicit autoerotic ideal in Masters and Johnson. The logic in both cases, however, is identical in its suggestion that sexual knowledge about women belongs to women, and the sexologist's medical and cultural authority is constructed through his or her appropriation of—and homage to—this fact.[12]

Like Kinsey, Masters and Johnson were important to feminists because they popularized an understanding of sexuality as a manipulable, learned, conditioned, and thus changeable behavior; and because, in their focus on the clitoris as the source of women's erotic empowerment, they offered a means of debunking the cultural authority of Freud even while providing a vocabulary for feminist self-determination within the sexual revolution. By locating female sexuality outside the realm of reproduction, theories of clitoral stimulation called for a newly egalitarian approach to eroticism, for the revision of "normal" sexual positions and assumptions to correspond with female bodies newly dedicated to the radical possibilities of pleasure. The clitoral orgasm provided a potent political metaphor to the women's movement, representing the marriage relationship as a vestige (happily curable) of patriarchal oppression and the expectation of women's erotic fulfillment as a basic right. Feminist writers during this period attempted to update the concept of "normal" female sexuality to correspond more symmetrically with an understanding of the body that was newly enhanced by science; what they didn't do, however, was interrogate ideological underpinnings of the scientific forms of knowledge they represented as the bedrock of truth. This discourse, therefore, created an ideology of "pleasure," but through terms that limited the feminist critique to a conscripted understanding of eroticism. The discourse of clitoral orgasm enabled a vocabulary of feminist activism grounded in behavioral adaptation. As it was appropriated to various ends, however, its limitations became clear, and the ensuing epistemological crisis prompted the foundation of several more abstract theories of feminist eroticism, theories that renegotiated the meaning and the significance of pleasure, representation, and power within the polymorphous domain of sexuality.

The Feminist Phallus

In 1971, Alix Kates Shulman published an influential essay, "Organs and Orgasms," which built on the work of Kinsey and Masters and Johnson, endorsing the clitoral orgasm as an essential material contribution to feminist practice and concluding with the following exhortation to her readers: "Think clitoris."[13] In Shulman's account, the clitoris is central to the disruption and the strategic appropriation of patriarchal power. In contrast to the phallus, the clitoris serves material ends, enabling the feminist reevaluation of standards of sexual normalcy: clitoral pleasure is an essential right belonging to all women but historically stolen from them by the conventions of patriarchal power. It serves a strategic metaphorical purpose, too, in relation to the patriarchal phallus that was granted such significance by Freud and later Lacan; the clitoris circulates as a metaphor for women's power, for the disruptive claims feminist action proposes within an entrenched patriarchal system, and for women's agency constituted in relation to the body but not limited to the body in its effects. The process of "thinking" clitoris, then, operates metonymically as the means of access to a range of feminist political issues, rewriting interlocked narratives of bedroom, home, and culture at large, a symbol of the problem as well as its solution. The clitoris is a symbol of feminist theory put into practice: women's sexuality is a vehicle for the appropriation of agency and subjectivity.

The argument originates with Anne Koedt in 1970 in an article titled

"The Myth of the Vaginal Orgasm." Koedt's frame of reference is the Freudian paradigm of female sexuality: Freud, writing in 1931, struck an equation between erotic pleasure and emotional maturity that famously relies on a peculiar interpretation of the female genitals. He writes, "A man, after all, has only one leading sexual zone, one sexual organ, whereas a woman has two: the vagina—the female organ proper—and the clitoris, which is analogous to the male organ."[14] Capitalizing on what he represents as a binary opposition contained within the female genitals, and pitting clitoris and vagina in competition with one another, Freud constructs a schedule for "normal" female development in terms of a semantic reversal to which he applies a gendered ideology. Koedt and later feminist respondents, reacting against the hierarchical assumptions behind this theory, reverse the reversal again, but without regard to the logical premises of the initial opposition. Arguing that the vagina does not acquire the capacity for sensation until puberty, Freud concludes that normal female sexual development occurs in the transfer of sensation from the clitoris, the locus of "immature" sexuality, to the vagina, the place of "mature" response. When the focus of a woman's erotic pleasure is on the clitoris, she exists in a masculine phase, but the shift to the vagina represents the advent of "proper" femininity. Freud does not claim to know why this transition happens for women, but he insists that it must; he grants that "the clitoris, with its virile character, continues to function in later female sexual life in a manner which is very variable and which is certainly not yet satisfactorily understood."[15] Yet he proposes a logic of female development in which that clitoris is an emblem of perversity, even of failure.

The embrace of authoritative, empirically based sexological concepts, and the assumption that bodily responses are essentially true and immutable, enabled feminist writers such as Shulman and Koedt to construct a focused critique of Freudian psychoanalysis and a sexual politics that could begin—and potentially end—at home. Within the Freudian paradigm, the female genitals represent the capacity for response in both male and female terms; the genital organs themselves are gendered in accordance with expectations that equate convexity with powerful masculinity, concavity with passive femininity. Working explicitly against but implicitly alongside Freud's model, early feminist theories of eroticism assume a relationship between clitoral and phallic power: in this account, the convex form still connotes power and the concave form still connotes passivity. Following in reverse the central logic of the Freudian paradigm, feminist writers reinscribe a binary logic on the female body and within the female genitals. Idealizing the clitoris as the site at which pleasure and power converge, they demonize the vagina in turn as a vessel of patriarchy and an emblem of enthralled femininity. This logic recapitulates the very hierarchies at stake in the political contest of the women's movement; the implicit opposition of good clitoris to bad vagina, empowered clitoris to disempowered vagina, equates clitoral pleasure with a masculine form of power quite explicitly. Vaginal sexuality, in turn, represents stasis within an archaic, patriarchal form of femininity in which women stay only by choice or ignorance. Thus, some forms of female sexuality were established as aberrant and unfeminist, as a signifier of a woman's internalized misogyny and thus her self-loathing.

The female genitals themselves symbolize the extent to which this logic of erotic empowerment remains locked within a series of binary frameworks that pit male against female, evil against good, empowered against oppressed. The feminist claim to power does not pretend to subvert such binary frameworks but simply inverts them. This is particularly vexed in the context of the larger critique of power that compels the women's liberation movement: the desire to eliminate power in general and hierarchical power in particular that informs so many of the theoretical texts of this period. By canonizing the clitoris, counterposing it against the passive vagina, feminists identify both a logic for and a source of usable power for women. But they do so through the recirculation of terms familiar from the most conventional of patriarchal epistemologies.

Koedt and Shulman attack the assumption that the vagina is the center of female erotic response. Through a "rejection" of the vagina, they construct terms through which to reject corresponding ideologies of femininity—specifically the assumption of female servitude to the male, which is attached first to the penis that enters the vagina and later to the children that are the product of this transaction. The penis (or, later, the phallic signifier) is the emblem of patriarchal power; the vagina, therefore, represents conscription within the patriarchal economy of that power. The twin rhetorics of theft and recuperation are a constant of the feminist counterargument: anatomy is destiny as much for women's lib as it was for Freud, but in this logic the clitoris is reclaimed as the organ of female sexuality and the symbol of a female sexual pleasure stolen from women by the ideological assertions of Freud.[16] The clitoris, as the female phallus, represents women's "natural" claim to pleasure and to the power that accompanies that claim.

Shulman joins Koedt in dismantling the equation of male genitalia with activity and female genitalia with passivity. Both writers use the clitoris against the binary logic of Freud's erotic paradigm: his formula for normative sexual functioning—penis plus vagina—is triangulated in the feminist account to encompass penis plus clitoris plus vagina. Koedt writes, "In our society only occasionally are [the penis and vagina] used to make babies. Much more often they are used to produce sexual pleasure for men, pleasure which culminates in ejaculation. The penis and the vagina together can make either babies or male orgasms; very rarely do the two together make female orgasms. Men, who have benefited greatly from both orgasms and babies, have had no reason to question the traditional definition of penis and vagina as true genital counterparts."[17] The myth of the natural, mature, vaginal orgasm, Koedt argues, is a side effect of men's vested interest in a particular model of sexual intercourse, one that reflects the Freudian opposition of masculine activity with feminine passivity. Men maintain the myth, Koedt contends, for reasons as various as their own sexual pleasure: their "inability to see women as total, separate human beings"; their understanding of masculinity based on the symbol of the penis; their desire to control women by apparently controlling their source of sexual pleasure; and the anxiety that men are "sexually expendable" and that women are sexually self-sufficient (40–41).

Within the women's liberation movement, the mechanics of women's sexual self-sufficiency presented a rhetorical complexity. Koedt explains: "The position of the penis inside the vagina, while perfect for reproduction, does not necessarily stimulate an orgasm in women because the clitoris is located externally and higher up. Women must rely upon indirect simulation in the 'normal' position. . . . Lesbian sexuality could make an excellent case, based upon anatomical data, for the extinction of the male organ. Albert Ellis says something to the effect that a man without a penis can make a woman an excellent lover" (41). Koedt represents the sexual prowess of the "man without a penis" as directly opposed to the interests of those men with penises who were threatened with devaluation as the stock of the clitoral orgasm rose. Developing some implications of this conclusion, Koedt cites lesbianism and bisexuality as the final reason men might conspire to maintain the myth of the vaginal orgasm:

> Aside from the strictly anatomical reasons why women might equally seek other women as lovers, there is a fear on men's part that women will seek the company of other women on a full, human basis. The establishment of clitoral orgasm as fact would threaten the heterosexual *institution*. For it would indicate that sexual pleasure was obtainable from either men *or* women, thus making heterosexuality not an absolute, but an option. It would thus open up the whole question of *human* sexual relationships beyond the confines of the present male-female role system. (41; emphases in original)

"The establishment of clitoral orgasm as fact would threaten the heterosexual *institution*." Koedt only hints at the political implications of her argument, developing them no further than to deliver a subjunctive blow to compulsory heterosexuality; in an essay arguing that the clitoris has been established scientifically as the site of female orgasm, she suddenly slips into a more conciliatory mode by way of conclusion: "it would indicate that sexual pleasure was obtainable from either men *or* women." Koedt's rhetoric grows tentative when the argument approaches a challenge to the heterosexual norm. The implication not developed is perhaps the most radical of all.

In its translation of the scientific languages of psychoanalysis and sexology for a lay public, Koedt's argument remains resolutely, even defensively, phallocentric. Koedt first introduces the notion of the clitoral orgasm thus: "It is the clitoris which is the center of sexual sensitivity and which is the female equivalent of the penis" (37). She later reiterates the metaphor: "*The Clitoris* is a small equivalent of the penis, except for the fact that the urethra does not go through it as in the man's penis. Its erection is similar to the male erection, and the head of the clitoris has the same type of structure and function as the head of the penis" (39; emphasis in original). It is hardly an escape from a phallocentric hegemony to represent the clitoris as a small penis, suggesting to women who "know little about their anatomy" (40) that the female body is a smaller copy of the male.

Notably, too, the language of penile analogy belongs to Koedt. She is translating a "scientific expert" here, but the quotation in question contains no reference to the penis, describing the clitoris only as a sensitive organ of sexual pleasure: "'The head of the clitoris is also composed of erectile tissue, and it possesses a very sensitive epithelium or surface covering, supplied with special nerve endings called genital corpuscles, which are peculiarly adapted for sensory stimulation that under proper mental conditions terminates in the sexual orgasm. No other part of the female generative tract has such corpuscles.'"[18] In this light, Koedt's concluding ambivalence about the implications of her argument for heterosexuality is clarified. "The clitoris has no other function than that of sexual pleasure," she writes, locating in the clitoris a lack of practicality that sets it up in direct contrast to the more pragmatic vagina, the functions of which "are related to the reproductive function. Principally, (1) menstruation, (2) receive penis, (3) hold semen, and (4) birth passage" (39). Koedt's reproductive, indeed phallocentric, interpretation of the vagina focuses on its functionality, a concept she opposes diametrically to pleasure; in this equation pleasure represents a form of unalienated and inalienable bodily experience, whereas vaginal functionality symbolizes women's alienated labor within a patriarchal sexual economy. For Koedt, a more general social purposiveness to the vagina is inescapable: women believe they have vaginal orgasms and even fake them while understanding that orgasms derive anatomically from the clitoris, to insure that they will "catch a man" (40). The conventionally idealized vagina is just a ploy of the heterosexual traffic in women.

Alix Kates Shulman responds to the sexual and political implications of the clitoral orgasm with a more polemical edge. Shulman is forthright in her equation of the penis and the clitoris as the organs of sexual difference: "If people considered that the purpose of the female sex organs is to bring pleasure to *women,* then female sex would be defined by, and focus on, a different organ. Everyone would be taught from infancy that, as the primary male sex organ is the penis, so the primary female sex organ is the clitoris."[19] After fantasizing a dialogue between a little boy and his mother ("Do girls pee through their clitorises?"), Shulman addresses the analogy of penis and clitoris, granting the clitoris a degree of supremacy in the contest of organs: "It has long been known that the clitoris is endlessly more sensitive than the vagina, more sensitive than the penis too, if one judges by the number of nerve endings in the organs" (293–94). In contrast to Koedt's model of the clitoris as little penis, Shulman represents the clitoris as central to a complex system of sexual response: "Women know from personal experience that there is only one kind of orgasm, no matter what name it is given, vaginal, clitoral, psychological. It is a sexual orgasm. . . . Though it is produced through the clitoris, the orgasm occurs as well in the vagina, the anus, the heart, the lungs, the skin, the head" (295). Women's tentativeness about orgasm stems from the cult of vaginal intercourse, even though for most women, "intercourse by itself rarely results in orgasm" (295).

Shulman pursues this fact to political conclusions: "Now that women, the only real experts on female sexuality, are beginning to talk together and compare notes, they are discovering that their experiences are remarkably similar and that they are not freaks. In the process of exposing the myths and lies, women are discovering that it is not they who have individual sex problems; it is society that has one great big political problem" (301). Shulman protests laws that criminalize oral sex, homosexuality, and acts of sexual intercourse in which the woman is on top—that criminalize, in other words, sex outside the norm of missionary-style, penis-centered intercourse. "The word about the clitoris has been out for a long time," she writes, going on to note that, in this context, women who continue to believe that their vaginal pleasures are orgasmic are deluded by overwhelming cultural misogyny: "The sensations of a penis in a vagina are indeed different from other sensations; accompanied by the right emotions they may be so pleasurable as to tempt a woman to hope that they can somehow qualify for that mysterious, desirable thing that has been touted as vaginal orgasm, even though they may not at all resemble the sensations she knows as orgasm. . . .

The truth is, there is only *one* kind of orgasm, one set of physiological responses constituting orgasm, all those Freudians to the contrary" (296; emphasis in original). But despite its emphatic rejection of the phallocentric norm,
Shulman's essay, too, concludes firmly within the framework of heterosexual
eroticism:

> The pressures that have long made so many women forgo orgasm during
> love-making and fake orgasm during intercourse are real social pressures. . . .
> But with women getting together, the day may soon be approaching when
> they will exert enough counterpressure to define female sexuality in their
> own way, and to insist that, just as male sexuality is centered not in the
> scrotum but in the penis, female sexuality is centered not in the vagina but
> in the clitoris. When that happens, perhaps it will seem as perverse for a
> man to ejaculate without stimulating a woman to orgasm as it is now for a
> woman to reach climax outside intercourse. . . . Think clitoris. (302)

Shulman's model of female community, united through the theory of "thinking clitoris," proposes a nonphallocentric understanding of female sexual
pleasure. The final vision of this model leaves the heteronormative framework uninterrogated, however. Shulman's emphasis on the sociopolitical
implications of female sexuality represents an attempt to theorize the cultural context that constructs the "facts" of female anatomy in ideological
terms.[20]

Women's sexual responsiveness emerges here as one of the guiding epistemological codes of the women's liberation movement. It serves both as
an intervention into the sexual practices of individual women and, more
metaphorically, as a signifier of women's political agency within the erotic
economy of patriarchal culture. Deriving a vocabulary from sexology, the
feminist deployment of clitoral sexuality was quite democratic in its concern
for the possibilities of achievement inherent in every female body. Orgasm
is something that each woman can achieve, though this pleasure may evade
her because of the unconsciously internalized imperatives of patriarchal
heterosexuality.

Rhetorically, however, feminists located pleasure even more in achievement than in orgasm, achievement elevated by the fact that it has foiled
patriarchy's theft of female bodily pleasures. They have represented orgasm
here through the vocabulary of acquisition, as something women have or
don't have or should have. The commodification takes on aspects of social
regulation: notwithstanding Shulman's argument for "*one* kind of orgasm,"
there was now a particular form of bodily response that distinguished
emancipated feminist women from the rest. In their replacement of patriarchal facts with feminist facts, feminist discourses of orgasmic empowerment

began to institute a new orthodoxy. With not only orgasm but a particular kind of orgasm as the goal, many feminists found the new sexual norm just as constraining as the old.

The commodification of the orgasm suggested by such a vocabulary of achievement only underscores a limitation of the undisturbed central framework, that is, a presumption that sex will occur in some relationship of service to heterosexual marriage. Although Koedt and Shulman emphasize the asymmetrical equation of penis and clitoris, each limits herself, like Freud, to an interpretive paradigm in which penis and clitoris (or vagina) are linked to one another and are thus mutually dependent on one another for the generation of physical pleasure. Male and female sexual pleasure, they seem to argue, are mutually incompatible when considered outside the context of reproductive sex; men and women alike must learn to reconfigure "normal" sex in order to respond to female sexual pleasure as necessary. From this reconfiguration, analogous issues of political equality will present themselves and demand attention. But the domestic logic here is strained in the context of the full argument for female pleasure, as Koedt acknowledges marginally when she grants that a mainstream investment in clitoral orgasm might signify the potential obsolescence of male lovers for women; sex is not usually linked to reproductive ends, and men are not really efficient for the purposes of female pleasure. In this context, lesbian sexuality, because it further symbolizes women's erotic independence from men, emerges as a kind of epistemological ideal that, in a short-term analysis, challenges heterosexual convention. The feminist discourse of clitoral orgasm implicitly posits a logic of radical polymorphous perversity in which domestic conventions have little to do with erotic pleasure. Yet it leaves those polymorphous implications, by and large, untouched.

Pleasure and Power

From the example set by Shulman and Koedt, popular feminism appropriated the argument for the feminist clitoris in many different ways. *Our Bodies, Ourselves,* for example, first published in 1971, represents the trend toward a process of reclamation, for the book's purpose, expressed in explicitly feminist terms, equates bodily knowledge with power. (In this section, I will quote from the second edition, published in 1976.) *Our Bodies, Ourselves* mixes the discourses of medical authority and personal experience to conduct a critique of the institutions designed to meet women's health needs, because "[f]or women throughout the centuries, ignorance about our bodies has had one major consequence—pregnancy. Until very recently pregnancies were all but inevitable, biology was our destiny—that is, because our bodies are designed to get pregnant and give birth and lactate, that is what most people did."[21] The demystification of the female body is, for the collective voice of this text, central to feminist activism:

> For us, body education is core education. Our bodies are the physical bases from which we move out into the world; ignorance, uncertainty—even, at worst, shame—about our physical selves create in us an alienation from ourselves that keeps us from being the whole people that we could be. . . . Learning to understand, accept, and be responsible for our physical selves, we are freed . . . and can start to use our untapped energies. Our image of ourselves is on a firmer base, we can be better friends and better lovers, better *people,* more self-confident, more autonomous, stronger and more whole. (13; emphasis in original)

The core of knowledge consolidated in *Our Bodies, Ourselves,* as in Shulman and Koedt, concerns female sexuality, as feminists continued to strive toward the mainstreaming of the impression that women's bodies do not exist exclusively for impregnation. The logic of this text is largely visual, as the disconcertingly plural voice makes clear: "We realized we were doing a lot of talking about our sexual organs but that we were not as familiar with their appearance as we were with other parts of our bodies. We found that with just a mirror we could see how we look on the outside. We have been encouraged to look inside at our vaginal walls and cervix (lower part of the uterus) by the women's self-help movement" (26). Beginning with basic instructions for the visual inspection of the interior and exterior of the vulva, the chapter continues into a colloquial tour of the female body, guided by the collective "we" and addressed to the constructed reader as "you."

Jane Gallop has described the "oculocentrism" of theory, its reliance on actual or metaphorical tropes of the visible.[22] This underscores an important aspect of the project of *Our Bodies, Ourselves* in particular and discourses of female orgasm more generally. The putative "invisibility," mystery, and unknowability of the female genitals obscure their theorizability. By making them visible, they become knowable. In becoming knowable, they're abstracted to provide the matter of theory and the metaphors of empowerment that enfranchise women's eroticism in the name of feminist action. Theorists of female sexuality from the women's movement embrace a new knowability of the female body, a knowability that they link directly both to materiality and to the prospect of social change. It is as if to this point the female body, unknown, has been merely an abstract idea detached from feminist consequences. Now, to see it, to know it, to understand its materiality is to be able to put it to use. Ironically, the use to which it is put is largely symbolic, largely abstract—the clitoris as a signifier of women's self-sufficiency and political power.

Within the argument of *Our Bodies, Ourselves*, male and female adults alike have been damaged by social conditioning that segregates human characteristics according to anatomical sex; ideological programming begins in childhood, and the means to combat that ideology is through the body, which remains distant only in the socialized mind: "What did we really learn about sex in a positive way in our teens? We had to wait until our twenties, or thirties, to learn at last that we have the only uniquely non-reproductive human sexual organ, the clitoris. Almost none of us ever heard about that as we were growing up. In spite of all the experiences that taught us to repress our sexuality, we are learning to be proud of it" (41). The collective voice of *Our Bodies, Ourselves* is highly diplomatic when it comes to the question of the heterosexual politics of clitoral orgasm, not necessarily presenting the penile man as an enemy to female sexual enjoyment but focusing on the penis as one of several possible sexual instruments for intercourse. Underscoring—without explanation, justification, critique, or bibliographic citation—that *"[t]he distinction between vaginal and clitoral orgasm is a myth"* (45; emphasis in original), the book's writers focus on strategies for accommodating the clitoris within heterosex: "For most of us it is quicker, physiologically, to reach orgasm with direct clitoral stimulation by hand or mouth or vibrator than solely with the indirect stimulation of intercourse. Yet many of us also feel that orgasm with a penis in our vagina is pleasurable and emotionally satisfying. Since many of us find it difficult to get sufficient stimulation with a penis in our vagina but want orgasms through intercourse, we have included some suggestions that have helped us reach orgasm with intercourse" (52).

There is a rhetorical awkwardness to this argument that indicates a telling subtext of early feminist writing. The description of "orgasm with a penis in our vagina" pairs a single penis with a collective feminist vagina; in the grammar of this sentence, all women are one in their erotic responses, but all those erotic responses are oriented in a phallic direction. The stimulation of this collective vagina by that singular penis reveals a subtle awkwardness about the collective politics of feminist activism when it is deployed within a heterosexual framework: women's homosociality, or even the lurking possibly of their homoeroticism, is put to use only in the context of practical heterosexuality. Even as feminists consolidate a unified and collective identity, a feminist homosocial ideal, that homosocial ideal is pitted against a heterosexual real. This requires a disjunction of theory and practice, a severing of the individual from the collective as a prerequisite for putting feminism into practice. This paradox constitutes feminist collective identity as an abstraction in its own right, as something that exists more powerfully in theory than in practice.

Later editions of *Our Bodies, Ourselves,* which focus broadly on social, legal, and cultural as well as medical issues affecting women, acknowledge the internalized homophobia that contributes to such ambivalent representations of female sociality and sexuality, the various female homo- and hetero-relations that get constructed as a foundational opposition. Returning to Koedt's concluding implication about heterosexuality as a choice rather than a compulsion, Wendy Sandford, with Paula Brown Doress, writes in *The New Our Bodies, Ourselves* (1984), "Some lesbians today are asking their heterosexual sisters to reconsider the 'naturalness' of heterosexual preference. Can heterosexuality be a free choice when we are taught such a deep fear of loving women? Can we comfortably assume that women are 'naturally' drawn to men when we consider the many cruelties which drive us to seek protection from men and punish us for being alone?"[23]

The chapter titled "Sexuality" in *The New Our Bodies, Ourselves* begins to shift the terms of feminist discussion of power and sexual pleasure. In a section titled "Who Defines the Orgasm? The Politics of the Great Orgasm Debate," the writers critique the professionalization of clinical sexological material. Returning to Masters and Johnson's claim to exclusively clitoral orgasm, they present evidence from women who argue for a more polymorphous theory of orgasm, raising questions about the scientific institutions from which sexual knowledge is dispensed: "We are wary of these new 'experts.' Are they trying to tame our sexuality by making it respectable? To make themselves a professional reputation? Might male or male-oriented researchers, threatened by women's new sexual autonomy and assertiveness, have a bias toward reasserting women's dependence on men for sexual satisfaction?"[24] Sexual knowledge, the authors contend, is most powerfully and reliably experiential knowledge. The evidence of experience becomes a lens for women to use to interpret the personal politics of sexuality: "There is no one 'right' pattern of sexual response. What works, what feels good, what makes us feel more alive in ourselves and connected with our partners is what counts."[25]

The question of feeling good, alive, and connected is political, however. Within the vocabulary of this feminist discourse, orgasm is the signifier of successful self-realization and the first step on the path toward a utopian future. Such a commodified discourse of clitoral orgasm assumes a series of power dynamics whose contradictions are readily apparent within popular books that follow in the tradition of *Our Bodies, Ourselves.* Nancy Friday, for example, in the introduction to her best-selling collection of women's sexual fantasies, *My Secret Garden,* associates women's sexuality with hegemonic expectations of submission and docility, expectations that this text thwarts: "What women needed and were waiting for was some kind of yardstick against which to measure ourselves, a sexual rule of thumb equivalent to that with which men have always provided one another. But women were the silent sex. In our desire to please our men, we had placed the sexual constraints and secrecy upon one another which men had thought necessary for their own happiness and freedom. . . . But the same culture that gave men this freedom sternly barred it to women, leaving us sexually mistrustful of each other, forcing us into patterns of deception, shame, and above all, silence."[26] Males and females are divided ideologically on the question of sexuality, but not imaginatively. Kate Millett addresses a similar claim in her representational theory of sexual politics: "And when Henry Miller, D. H. Lawrence and Norman Mailer—to say nothing of Genet—put their fantasies on paper, they are recognized for what they can be: art. The sexual fantasies of men like these are called novels. Why then . . . can't the sexual fantasies of women be called the same?"[27]

Friday suggests that the fear of being accused of unwomanly behavior, of unfemininity and the rejection of men, conditions female reticence. The anxiety here is similar to Koedt's rhetorical unwillingness to see sex other than in heteronormative terms even when discussing the emancipating implications of clitoral orgasm. In Friday's terms, the women's movement does not offer a safe haven for the frank discussion of female sexual experience:

> Oddly enough, I think the naked power cry of Women's Lib itself was not helpful to a lot of women, certainly not to me in the work that became this book. It put too many women off. The sheer stridency of it, instead of drawing us closer together, drove us into opposing camps; those who were defying men, denying them, drew themselves up in militant ranks against those who were suddenly more afraid than ever that in sounding aggressive they would be risking rejection by their men. If sex is reduced to a test of power, what woman wants to be left all alone, all powerful, playing with herself? (7)

Friday, locating herself outside "the naked power cry of Women's Lib," articulates the fear that subtly inflects discussions of sexuality even within the "naked power cry" itself: "If sex is reduced to a test of power, what woman wants to be left all alone, all powerful, playing with herself?" The fearsome spectacle Friday invokes here of a woman all alone, playing with herself, is peculiarly counter to the express agenda of a text that endorses the normalcy, richness, and productivity of solitary sexual fantasy. Its implicit threat makes clear the more subversive implications of Masters and Johnson's emphasis on "automanipulation": as threatening as the lesbian to whom she is epistemologically linked through the ability to give pleasure to a female body, the solitary masturbating woman is a danger to conventional heterosexual expectations, and, perhaps more powerfully to the mass-market imagination, she will be punished for her violation of those domestic conventions. This suggests that the equation of sex with power has cataclysmic implications for the vulnerable woman: to reject men is to be rejected by them in turn. In the terms of this logic, you're either doing it conventionally or doing it by yourself. Although *My Secret Garden* contains dozens of fantasies of lesbian sex, most of which are contributed by straight women (the brief "lesbian chapter" is dominated by fantasies of sex with dogs), Friday's introduction represents women's sexual alternatives only in terms of heterosex or masturbation—and only heterosexual activity is part of the powerful lure of social normalcy.

This hegemonic structure is not one that Friday wants to challenge. The liberation that enabled her commercial publication of a book of female sexual fantasies is a form of sexual liberation unlike that of *Our Bodies, Ourselves,* in which the text itself serves as a road map through which women can discover their own bodies. Rather, *My Secret Garden* presents itself as a window into previously hidden realms of the female erotic imagination, offering new access for men and, through this new form of female sexual liberation, improved male sexual experience. Friday writes of her experience of the publishing world in the era of sexual revolution: "Women *were* writing about sex, but it was from their point of view (women seen only as male sex fantasies no more), and it was a whole new bedroom. The realization was suddenly obvious, that with the liberation of women, men would be liberated too from all the stereotypes that made them think of women as burdens, prudes, and necessary evils, even at best something less than a man. Imagine! Talking to a woman might be more fun than a night out with the boys!" (8; emphasis in original). Friday's argument here implies that the fantasies presented in her book are, at least in part, ultimately for the use of men. "[N]o man can be really free in bed with a woman who is not," she writes (11), constructing a larger itinerary for the sexual emancipation represented in the fantasies of *My Secret Garden*. Writing this book "became a serious and meaningful effort when I realized what it could mean, not only to all the sometimes lonely, sometimes joyful, usually anonymous women who were writing to me, but to the thousands and thousands who, though they were too embarrassed, isolated, or ashamed to write, might perhaps have the solitary courage to read" (11). Friday approaches those with "solitary courage" in order to bring them into the social realm of feminist (hetero)sexuality—for "what woman wants to be left all alone, all powerful, playing with herself?" Seeking the emancipation of the female sexual spirit for the greater good of improved heterosex, Friday combats sexual shame through the production of fantasies that, in the end, bolster erotic convention.

From a different perspective, Shere Hite's 1976 *The Hite Report* represents a provocatively hybrid approach to the question of sexual politics. Like Friday's book, *The Hite Report* was a best-seller, but unlike Friday's, Hite's volume claims scientific and feminist reputability. Hite uses a statistical apparatus that presents detailed information about the demographics of the women who answered a questionnaire distributed, in part, under the auspices of the National Organization for Women. This apparatus frames her presentation of the women's responses to questions about their own sexual experience. With its explicit discussion of the sexual experiences of women, *The Hite Report* reads at moments much like Friday's collation of women's fantasies, albeit presented in a feminist interpretive framework. Indeed, *The Hite Report* is the methodological heir of both Friday and Kinsey, for its combination of scientific apparatus and first-person narrative invests it with the twin authority of the empirical and the experiential.

Unlike Friday's, Hite's agenda is explicitly aligned with the goals of the women's movement: "This book presents what the women who answered said—in their own words and in their own way. The intention is to get acquainted, to share how we have experienced our sexuality, how we feel about it—and to see our personal lives more clearly, thus redefining our sexuality and strengthening our identities as women."[28] The survey's results reflect the view that the feminist politicization of orgasm has instituted newly "normal" ideals of sexuality for women. These new ideals replicate instead of solve the problem of female sexual subjection, because they are perceived as dictating a very narrow range of appropriate feminist sexual feelings: "It does seem clear that women should have a right to orgasms during sex as part of the natural course of things. However, now that the idea has become popular that women should enjoy sex 'too,' this new 'right' has sometimes turned into an oppression. Women are made to feel that they must have orgasms more to please the man than to please themselves" (58).

Like the theorists of the consciousness-raising movement, Hite strives to consolidate a unified populace of women, in this instance through their shared occupation of a female erotic body. Although her survey locates that erotic body within a generally heterosexual economy—women have orgasms "to please the man," for example—the body erotic also constitutes a body *politic*, a homosocial world of female sameness. Again, the conjoined norms of heterosexual homosociality sit awkwardly together; the book's language reflects a more general discomfort about priorities of erotic allegiance for women. Note, for example, Hite's rhetorically awkward use of the first-person plural pronoun to constitute her female readership, both as a collective and as empowered individuals: "[W]e can take control over our own orgasms. We know how to have orgasms in masturbation. . . . But why can't we touch ourselves? Why can't we do whatever we need to make orgasm happen?" (252). Hite's peroration deploys the collective and the individual in tandem with one another and both rhetorically and thematically conjures the "apparitional lesbian" as an implicit erotic model for all women:[29]

> We have the power to make our own orgasms, if we want. You can get control of your own stimulation by moving against the other person, or by stimulating yourself directly in the same way as you do during masturbation. Although this suggestion might sound strange at first, it is important to be able to masturbate with another person, because it will give you power over your own orgasms. . . . The taboo against touching yourself says essentially that you should not use your own body for your own pleasure, that your body is not your own to enjoy. But we have a right to our own bodies. Controlling your own stimulation symbolizes owning your own body, and is a very important step toward freedom. (253)

Hite's grammatical vacillation here from singular to plural, and between first- and second-person pronouns—from "we" to "your own" to "our own"—suggests the logic by which feminist theories extrapolate from the individual erotic gesture to more radical claims of the feminist collective.[30] It also suggests the tensions that lurk among "we," "your," and "our"— between self as a unique, individual body with privileged desires and experiences; self as a body that exists in contrast to an other, "your"; and the plural collective "our," a body that subsumes all individual selves under the presumption of unity. To make a feminist body speak for and of feminist politics requires women to inhabit all three pronouns simultaneously. From this formula for feminist identity crisis, the feminist body, clitoris and all, emerges as the ultimate abstraction.

Power and control, rights and ownership: "We have the power to make our own orgasms, if we want." A woman's emancipation, for Hite, is available at the touch of her finger; this suggests that a woman's property rights in her own person—indeed, her own self-possession—unwrite the patriarchal erotic economy that has alienated women historically not only from their own bodies and the pleasures of those bodies but also from the franchise of property rights more generally. The theory of feminist orgasm is a theory of unalienated labor. Orgasmic pleasure can be the privileged site of that labor; it has not been in the past because patriarchy has inscribed alienation onto the female body in its very construction of the mechanics of normative sexuality. The feminist reinterpretation of female anatomy introduces an entirely new sexual economy and thus a new means of describing female experience.

Against the Compulsory Orgasm

Discourses of clitoral empowerment from the women's liberation movement developed in two very different directions in the late 1970s. Each of these constitutes a backlash against the constitutive arguments initially formulated by Shulman and Koedt, and each turns on questions of power, individual choice, and, crucially, on the availability of the body as a source of metaphors for women's political condition more generally.

In the antipornography discourses of cultural feminism, the female genitals were reinterpreted—again, still within a binary that counterposed power and passivity—as a site of women's victimization. This shift relied on the emergence of a newly subordinated vision of female agency and pleasure, as well as a new interpretation of heterosexual imperatives as totalizing and inescapable. What began in the women's movement as a political act of reclamation, in which feminist theorists claimed possession of the female body through their articulation of the poetics of its pleasure, shifted gradually into a focus on the body as a site of oppression rather than liberation, victimization rather than empowerment. Focusing on theories of representation as violence, particularly in pornography, Andrea Dworkin, in 1979, recalled the semiotic power politics of genitalia but refocused emphasis on vaginal victimization. Her analysis of the symbolism of human anatomy is far less optimistic than that of her predecessors:

> Sex, a word potentially so inclusive and evocative, is whittled down by the male so that, in fact, it means penile intromission. Commonly referred to as "it," sex is defined in action only by what the male does with his penis. Fucking—the penis thrusting—is the magical, hidden meaning of "it," the reason for sex, the expansive experience through which the male realizes his sexual power. In practice, fucking is an act of possession—simultaneously an act of ownership, taking, force; it is conquering; it expresses in intimacy power over and against, body to body, person to thing. . . . The woman is acted on; the man acts and through action expresses sexual power, the power of masculinity.[31]

In analytical terms identical to those of early feminists, Dworkin wants to read the physics of heterosexual intercourse in terms symbolic of hegemonic oppression. However, the terms are inverted once again in her argument: rather than employing revisionary strategies that identify female orgasm or eroticism as a pathway to political empowerment, Dworkin reads heterosex as a symptom of patriarchal violence that invariably reifies women's objectification. Recalling Shulman's equation of heterosex with rape, "fucking,"

for Dworkin, strips women of personhood in a form of "taking" that recapitulates Freud's theft of the clitoris.

It was through the afterlife of discourses of the clitoral orgasm that mainstream feminism gained its reputation as prudish—ironically, because writers
such as Shulman and Koedt were attempting a kind of radical speech-act in
their equation of emancipated sexuality with feminist politics. In the work of
Dworkin, Susan Griffin, Kathleen Barry, Catharine MacKinnon, and other
"cultural feminists" of this period, eroticism is a trap best emblematized
by "fucking" as a dirty, shameful, and violent endeavor; women are prey
to the degradations and humiliations of eroticism; and representations of
sexuality, especially in pornography, further secure women's entrapment. In
this account, sexuality is still suffused with power, but that power belongs
to men—regardless of race, class, age, or cultural context—who have it and
use it against the women who are their victims.[32] This logic is relentlessly
heterosexual, assuming that all erotic relationships follow a male-female,
oppressor-victim structure that is both capitalist and totalizing. The analysis of sexuality that emerges with antiporn feminism distinguishes strictly
between power and desire, and this is a feminist critique that concerns itself
far more directly with the constitution of men's agency than women's.

The radical-sex feminists whose work emerged in powerful opposition to
the antiporn position provided the second branch of development from the
original discourse of clitoral empowerment. Radical-sex feminists argued
for a renewed focus on desire, and, even more important, they situated the
female erotic body not in the abstract but in a web of social connections that
implicated sexuality in power politics concerning race, class, and cultural
location, as well as concerning concepts of gender and sexuality that include
the heterosexual gender binary but are not limited to it.[33] Amber Hollibaugh
and Cherríe Moraga, in a published dialogue, respond to the implications
of this logic as subjects who do not construct their erotic lives—or their
feminism—through such terms:

> AMBER HOLLIBAUGH: I feel like I have been forced to give up some of my
> richest potential sexually in the way feminism has defined what is, and what's
> not, "politically correct" in the sexual sphere.
> CHERRÍE MORAGA: Oh, of course when feminists talk about sexuality,
> including lesbianism, they're not talkin' about Desire. It is significant to
> me that I came out only when I met a good feminist, although I knew I was
> queer since eight or nine. That's only when I'd risk it because I wouldn't
> have to say it's because I want her. I didn't have to say that when she travels
> by me, my whole body starts throbbing.
> AMBER HOLLIBAUGH: Yes, it's just *correct*.[34]

The discrepancy underscored by Moraga, between talking about sexuality and talking about "Desire," goes to the heart of the problem that fragmented feminism into a range of theoretical factions by the end of the 1970s, including the academic feminist embrace of Lacanian psychoanalysis, a model that attempts to make use of the inchoate implications of "desire." Meanwhile, the emphasis on the mechanics of women's sexual response turns into an attempt to capitalize on a codified, homogenized understanding of women's bodies through a vocabulary of pleasure authorized by a lesbian ideal of women's sexual knowledge. Moraga suggests that the concern with the commodity value of orgasm, with the mechanics of its production, has enabled the displacement of attention from gothic, uncontrollable, or disturbing implications of women's sexuality; lesbian feminism enabled Moraga herself to displace attention from desire for women to the female political allegiance that Hollibaugh dismisses as "correct." Hollibaugh identifies richness of sexual potential far in excess of the parameters feminists have established for women's sexuality. In return, Moraga articulates a theory of "Desire" that is about the perversity of wanting that inhabits each individual, a desire that is both unschematized and unable to be schematized.

The feminist fusion of erotic and political interests begs the question of boundaries, particularly concerning issues of individual sexual autonomy and sexual choices that don't necessarily conform with the feminist ideal. Carole Vance describes some of the more invasive aspects of the slogan "the personal is political":

> The ubiquity of the slogan . . . led toward unintended and problematic extremes which proved particularly damaging for sexuality. If personal life had a political dimension, did that mean that sexual life was singularly and entirely political? If so, it was perhaps logical to expect that feminists who shared the same politics should have identical or highly similar sexual lives, and that there should be a close conformity between political goals and personal behavior. If the personal was political, then perhaps the political was personal, converting efforts to change and reform sexual life and elations into substitutes for political action and organizing. If so, scrutiny, criticism, and policing of peers' sexual lives, if not fantasies, may become a necessary political obligation.[35]

Feminist discourses of orgasm equate pleasure with power. In this sense, knowledge about pleasure constitutes the heart of the movement, its most personal and most radical implications. What began as an embrace of scientific knowledge in service of women's greater sexual pleasure—and, through that pleasure, their political emancipation—turned, eventually, into a debate about the problematics of interpretation, about the deployment of that knowledge toward particular "feminist" ends. Vance writes, "There is a very fine line between talking about sex and setting norms; we err very easily given our ignorance of diversity, our fear of difference, and our naïve expectation that all like the same sexual food as we. Although we need open discussion to expand theory, we are especially vulnerable to transforming statements of personal preference that inevitably appear in honest discussion ('I like oral sex') into statements that may be probabilistically true ('Women like clitoral stimulation more than penetration') into statements that are truly prescriptive ('Women should avoid penetration')."[36] The discourse of pleasure is a powerful weapon with which to combat hegemonic oppression, Vance suggests. In the women's movement, the claim to an apparent anatomical universality of the female body—heretofore concealed by the workings of patriarchy—was a potent metaphor for the claims to other forms of political power. When the metaphor becomes a prescription for behavior or identity, however, Vance argues that feminists have shifted from the production of new theory to the invention of new ways to regulate women's sexual lives.

For Hollibaugh and Moraga, the feminist analysis of pornography as victimization in particular, and of female sexuality in general, misses the point for a large percentage of feminism's constituency. They suggest that these analyses are not only heterosexist but also marked by the normalizing implications of white middle-class abstraction from urgent issues in the erotic lives of many women:

> In our involvement in a movement largely controlled by white middle-class women, we feel that the values of their cultures (which may be more closely tied to an American-assimilated puritanism) have been pushed down our throats. . . . [W]hy is it that it is largely white middle-class women who form the visible leadership in the anti-porn movement? . . . More working-class and Third World women can be seen actively engaging in sex-related issues that directly affect the life-and-death concerns of women (abortion, sterilization abuse, health care, welfare, etc.). It's not like we choose this kind of activism because it's an "ideologically correct" position, but because we are the ones pregnant at sixteen (straight *and* lesbian), whose daughters get pregnant at sixteen, who get left by men without child care, who are self-supporting lesbian mothers with no child care, and who sign forms to have our tubes tied because we can't read English. But these kinds of distinctions between classes and colors of women are seldom absorbed by the feminist movement as it stands to date.[37]

Hollibaugh and Moraga here identify against feminism but with women. The terms of their resistance come as an ad hoc challenge to the implicit identification, in feminist theories, with middle-class white heterosexual femininity. Shifting the discourse of "sex-related issues" from the antiporn movement's focus on women's victimization in representational contexts, they give voice to a coalition of women whose bodies and experiences are "seldom absorbed" in contemporary feminist discourses for which compulsory sexuality remains a matter of choice. Feminist theories of sexuality, argue Hollibaugh and Moraga, are implicitly classed and raced, and feminists' blindness to this fact indicates the ever widening gap between feminist theories and the material circumstances of the women to, for, and of whom those theories are intended to speak.

The feminist body, constructed in the abstract as a metaphor to describe a path out of gender subordination for middle-class women, fails in the concrete. "[T]he rush to reject personal subordination left intact many taken for granted assumptions about the nature of sexuality," writes Elizabeth Wilson of discourses of the orgasm in 1970s feminism. "Many bourgeois theories remained embedded and invisible in the feminist debate; and feminism took over from established revolutionary movements a moralism about the meaning of sexual behavior in relation to politics."[38] The rejection of feminism's normative body enabled later feminists to expose the lurking "bourgeois theories" Wilson describes. That body was originally asked to tell a story, written on the genitals, of a dialectic between power and passivity—a dialectic written figuratively into the being of every female subject simply by virtue of the bodily form she inhabits. Koedt and Shulman emphasize the powerful end of that dialectic, and they use discourses of phallic power, lesbianism, and autoeroticism to construct the clitoris as a site of identification for women; whereas Dworkin shifts the emphasis back to the site of disempowerment, to the vagina in its conscription to phallic invasion. For Hollibaugh and Moraga, however, the story feminists tell of the body is partial, in every sense of the term. The theory of "sexuality" produced from that body is simply an abstraction, a displacement, from issues that challenge the core complacencies of feminism itself.

4

The Feminist Abject
Death, Fiction, and Theory

> The corpse (or cadaver: *cadere*, to fall), that which has ir-
> remediably come a cropper, is cesspool, and death; it upsets
> even more violently the one who confronts it as fragile and
> fallacious chance.
>
> —Julia Kristeva, *The Powers of Horror: An Essay on Abjection*

When Ginny Babcock, the wealthy, white, Southern protagonist of Lisa
Alther's novel *Kinflicks* (1976), moves from Cambridge to Vermont to live in
a women's collective with her lesbian lover, Eddie, she soon grows impatient
with the pieties of her liberationist friends. That impatience swiftly yields
poetic justice, however, as Ginny's irritants are hoisted, jointly and sever-
ally, with their own petards. First falls Laverne, best known for her close
relationship with an enormous vibrator. Ginny narrates: "Just then there
was a scream and a sizzling sound from upstairs, and all the lights went
out."[1] Putting out the electrical fire, Ginny and her friends find Laverne,
charred and apparently dead, lying under a sleeping bag. They resuscitate
her, and when the ambulance arrives, the driver inspects Laverne's prostrate
body: "Folding down the sleeping bag another turn, he rolled out one of her
knees and discovered raw burned patches on the insides of her thighs. With
a frown, he noticed an electrical cord. As he pulled on it, Laverne's vibrator
popped out of her. . . . The doctor held the phallus-shaped vibrator, turned
it over, sniffed it, scratched his head. It had a big crack all the way up it.
Laverne had apparently achieved her goal of the Ultimate Orgasm" (332).

Laverne survives the trauma but leaves the commune for life in a convent; this is either a retirement or a retreat, depending on one's perspective on her pursuit of "the Ultimate Orgasm." The next victim is not so lucky, however. Ginny's lover, Eddie, seeks revenge on freewheeling snowmobilers who trespass on the commune's property. In defense of that property, and hoping to entrap the trespassers, she erects a thin, nearly invisible piece of wire along the property line. But in a hysterical rage against Ginny, Eddie herself steals a snowmobile and shoots across the snowy meadow. Ginny is watching: "[J]ust before Eddie reached the pond, Ira's Sno Cat appeared to hesitate slightly. The next instant, Eddie's head flew off her shoulders and bounced and spun across the ice like a crazed basketball. I watched with utter appalled disbelief: What I had just seen couldn't possibly have happened! Ira's Sno Cat coasted to a stop, and Eddie's headless body rolled off the seat and onto the ice with a dull plunk" (335). Most shocking for Ginny about this death is its cleanness: no blood is spilled as Eddie's head and body are severed far more precisely than even the adjective *surgical* might suggest. And if Eddie's decapitation underscores the flimsy logic of her feminist commitment, dying as she does in defense of private property, Laverne's self-inflicted injury suggests the dangers inherent in appropriating the phallus, especially when that phallus comes equipped with an electrical cord.

Soon after Eddie's death, Ginny leaves the commune to marry Ira Bliss, the owner of the snowmobile on which Eddie met her demise. Thus ends Ginny's radical feminist phase and, with the death of Eddie and the cloistering of Laverne, thus ends the novel's engagement with nonheterosexual eroticism of any sort. Eddie's wire boundary in the end proves brutally efficient as the commune becomes its own structure of feminist containment, securely detached from the world at large.

Episodes of violent death such as Eddie's serve a constitutive, boundary-establishing function within feminist popular novels produced in the United States during the late 1970s and early 1980s. The invisible wire that kills Eddie marks off violent borderlines of class and erotic difference, borderlines that produce distinctions between feminist survivors and feminist scapegoats, between the feminist mind and the feminist body. Indeed, as Eddie's death most gruesomely suggests, the mind-body divide is a core concern for feminist fictions of this period; and in the novels on which I will focus, Marilyn French's *The Women's Room* (1977) and Amanda Cross's *Death in a Tenured Position* (1981), it is thematized through the negotiation of protagonists' academic careers and their complex, often contradictory personal lives.

In this chapter, I argue that these novels are instrumental to the construction of "feminist theory" in U.S. popular culture. This argument reverses the expected priorities of literary text and literary theory; though several generations of feminist critics have suggested ways in which theoretical paradigms illuminate important aspects of novels and poetry, it is more unusual to think about how literary texts contribute to the constitution of theoretical paradigms. Yet a consideration of fiction's shaping power, particularly in the context of second-wave feminism, represents a return to the importance granted the literary by Kate Millett and other theorists of women's liberation. Just as important, too, it reflects the ongoing history of feminist challenges to the theory-practice relationship. At the same moment in which feminist work was beginning to become absorbed into academic institutions, disciplines, and methodologies, feminist novelists took up the issue of academic feminism as a problem, and they did so through a return to the familiar terms of theory and practice, abstraction and materiality. In these novels, which are themselves instances of a feminist fictional practice, possibilities for any feminist practice at all are limited, radically, in what the novelists render as the abstracted and disengaged world of the academy. Taken collectively as a site of and a voice for activism, feminist fictions mobilize a forceful skepticism toward a mode of feminist detachment newly associated with the academic institution.

Representations of academic feminists abound in feminist popular fiction of this period. The academic trope presents an image of feminist theory as an arcane, abstracted pursuit in explicit contrast to the material engagements of feminist praxis. Like the feminist discourse of orgasm, this is a discourse about bodies in their relationship to private erotic and domestic concerns. Rather than locating power in female embodiment, however, these novels concern themselves with bodily filth and degradation, with the scathing humiliations that accompany femininity in a misogynist world. In this context, the academy offers the consolation of retreat into abstraction and thus into the clean, orderly world of the mind. Ultimately, the pressing claims of feminist principle reveal this solution as, at best, an ambivalent compromise with and, at worst, a fresh imprisonment to, patriarchal prerogatives. These novels foster a vision of academic feminism as a pursuit fatally abstracted from the contingencies of everyday life. In this, they suggest that academic idealisms are abstracted from the nitty-gritty of the feminist real.[2]

Indebted to *The Group*, Mary McCarthy's 1963 novel that follows a group of Vassar undergraduates into the world, feminist novels of the late 1970s and early 1980s exploit a university context in an attempt to fathom the intersection of the feminist mind and the feminist body and, in the process, to develop a critique of the misogyny endemic within institutions. Among the many novels featuring university settings are *Kinflicks*, *The Women's Room*, *Death in a Tenured Position*, Rita Mae Brown's *Rubyfruit Jungle* (1973), Marge Piercy's *Small Changes* (1973), Erica Jong's *Fear of Flying* (1973), and Alice Walker's *Meridian* (1976).[3] My particular interest in *The Wom-*

en's Room and *Death in a Tenured Position* involves their setting in English departments and thus their engagement with intersections, however tenuous, between aesthetics and feminist social action. Characters' intellectual concern with literature—with instabilities of meaning, the construction of women's literary ancestry, and the far reaches of aesthetic sublimity—exists in marked contrast with the "here and now" of their own fictional lives, the painful compromises that they strike in order to survive, and the bodies that they inhabit and encounter, and for which they clean.

The deployment of tropes of indeterminacy, ambiguity, and compromise is markedly different from the literary-theoretical investment in linguistic indeterminacy invoked but marginalized within each text. These novels emphasize the blurry boundaries of their protagonists' complex lives, privileging the determinacy, the fixedness, of women's plots over the indeterminacy, and thus the potential for subversion, built into the linguistic regimes that organize those plots and give them social meaning. Although each protagonist is at one moment or another engaged in the study of literature and language, and although each is acutely attuned to the gender politics that inflects her work, her academic undertaking is cloistered within, and subordinated to, the far more urgent demands of existence in a female body in a misogynist world. Through that gesture of subordination, the novels themselves privilege formal imperatives—the protagonists' ambivalence toward conventions of romantic love, for example, constituting at once a critique and a reification of realist fictional forms—over language, aesthetics, literary tradition, and other signifiers of abstraction. In the context of plot, then, the contrast of mind and body, of academy and "real life," represents a standoff between feminism in theory—that is, feminism as an idealized, abstracted, oftentimes academic pursuit—and feminism in practice, which involves difficult demands of the body, of dirt, of pleasure, of the daily degradations and humiliations that put theory to the test, find it wanting, and work to fine-tune its generalizing assumptions.[4]

In 1981, Carolyn Heilbrun, a professor of English at Columbia University who writes detective novels under the name Amanda Cross, published *Death in a Tenured Position*. This novel is part of a series that features the protagonist Kate Fansler, an independently wealthy, Waspish, feminist English professor at a major university in New York City, who happens to solve murder mysteries in her spare time.[5] I emphasize the categories of identity that Cross/Heilbrun rather aggressively attaches to her detective not simply to suggest that Fansler is a surrogate for Heilbrun but rather to emphasize the fact that Fansler, by virtue of her identity, symbolizes a series of bourgeois feminist values: like many of her counterparts, including Isadora Wing in Jong's *Fear of Flying*, Fansler is a New Yorker who is financially invulnerable on account of her possession of a trust fund; heterosexual; white; well educated; and, because of her own personal experiences, concerned with sexual chauvinism. Kate Fansler's feminist politics run deep but not radical; early in *Death in a Tenured Position*, she encounters the lesbian separatist Joan Theresa and becomes painfully conscious of the legibility of her own appearance: "The raincoat Kate had hung up was a fashionable raincoat. Her shoes, though flat, were fashionable shoes. Her panty hose covered shaved legs. Her suit, ultra-suede, was worn over a turtleneck knit, and on her jacket was a pin: a gold pin. Kate was dressed for the patriarchy."[6] "My clothes," says Kate to Joan Theresa, "make my life easier, as yours make your life easier" (10). Upper-class, educated, and feminist, Kate Fansler's very liminality enables her to achieve the symbolic translations necessary to accommodate both feminist and "patriarchal" agendas. She is intelligent, attractive, and desirable, and, in fictional worlds, the material and especially sartorial tokens of middle-class respectability are a central mechanism through which feminist agendas are transmitted to a mass-market readership. Later in the novel, Kate jokingly accuses her friend Sylvia of becoming "one of those awful women's libbers." Sylvia's response: "You betcha. I eat bras; my favorite is 34B, pink, lightly sizzled. I will eat one soon if the waiter doesn't come. Shall we have it with white wine or red?" (26).

This novel's lightly satirical detachment from radical politics belies the fact that it presents the spectrum of feminist possibilities in characters that range from commune-dwelling lesbian separatists, to the gentler feminism of Kate and Sylvia, to the brutal misogyny of its villains and its victim. Indeed, as both a detective and, suggestively, an academic, Kate needs the protective coloring of her wealth and conventional style, for the novel's mystery goes right to questions of institutional authority: *Death in a Tenured Position* concerns first the career crisis, then the death, of Janet Mandelbaum, the first female professor of English at Harvard University.

If Columbia University's English department was symbolically central to the women's movement because of the scandal surrounding Kate Millett's publication of *Sexual Politics* in 1969,[7] Harvard's English department emerges even more powerfully as an emblem of patriarchal privilege paradoxically surrounded by Cambridge, the heart of youth culture and a center of the antiwar movement. The juxtaposition of Harvard's backwardness and the progressiveness of Cambridge is fruitful within popular literature of the women's movement, a dichotomy deployed not only by Cross but also by Alther in *Kinflicks,* Piercy in *Small Changes,* and most famously by French in *The Women's Room.* Cross and French alike frame their fictions through the observation that there is almost literally no place for women at Harvard, using an architectural critique that symbolizes implicit institutional misogyny. Both novels focus on what Lacan calls "urinary segregation," borrowing on bathroom politics to make a point about gendered ideologies that follow from entrenched social conventions of sexual difference.[8] But whereas Lacan's argument is focused on the twinned functions of language and desire in the construction of sexual difference, the novels' politics of gendered place emphasizes the arbitrary violence of sexual difference as a system engineered to deny some, but not others, access to resources and opportunities.

French's novel opens with Mira peering into the mirror in an obscure Harvard "ladies' room"—"She called it that, even though someone had scratched out the word *ladies'* in the sign on the door, and written *women's* underneath"[9]—whereas at the beginning of Cross's novel, Janet Mandelbaum is found dead in the English department men's room. True to the larger lavatory motif, the professional politics of misogyny represented through these women's encounters with the university focuses on bodily implications; the insistence on women's bodies suggests that the body is inescapable, untranscendable even in the loftiest of contexts. In Cross's novel, a young Harvard English professor writes to a friend about his department's mandate to hire and tenure a woman, implicitly equating the male-separatist enclave of the academy with the politics of the old-boys' room: "Of course, they are all worried about menopause—it is absolutely all they can think of when a woman threatens to penetrate their masculine precincts—how revealing language is" (1). Kate Fansler has been summoned by Janet Mandelbaum, her friend from their graduate school days, to help her through a career crisis. When Kate first considers coming to Janet's assistance at Harvard, she recalls Henry James, who "wrote a novel in the 1890s in which a young woman shows an admirer around Harvard, pointing out each of the buildings and remarking that there is no place for women in them; Harvard hasn't changed much since. Little more than ten years ago, women could not use many of the libraries" (14). Kate responds to Janet's call and heads to Cambridge.

For French, too, the architectural exclusion of women from Harvard underscores a more widespread pattern of exclusion justified by the putative uncontainability of the female body. Linking the scatological implications of bathrooms with libraries, Val, the most radical of Mira's graduate-student friends (and the one who is ultimately punished for her radicalism, with death), argues that Harvard discriminates against women for "sanitary" considerations: "You let women through the front doors and what will they do? Splat splat, a big clot of menstrual blood right on the threshold. Every place women go they do it: splat splat. There are little piles of clotty blood all over Lamont Library now. There are special crews hired just to keep the place decently mopped down" (304). Val's fantasy of the library's contamination caricatures misogynist fears about the uncontainability of women's bodies even as it suggests that patriarchal institutions—the library, the university—are insufficiently fortified to effect that containment at all.

Emily Martin argues that women have used sex-segregated bathrooms as "backstage areas" and spaces in which they could constitute their own "solidarity and resistance" to the containment of their bodies in the public sphere of the workplace.[10] *The Women's Room,* from its title to its conclusion, registers the possibilities and the dangers of such resistance. Although bathrooms themselves in this novel tend to be spaces of women's isolation, anxiety, and panic, the collegial community that the women in Mira's circle succeed in constructing serves as the kind of "women's room" Virginia Woolf imagines in *A Room of One's Own,* its own site of subversion from within. But, for some, the inescapable, visceral embodiedness of women is the stuff of the most treacherous anxiety dreams, presenting a conundrum that is as frightening as it is liberating. Reflecting Val's imagery, the graduate student Kyla has the following dream prior to an oral exam:

> She dreamt she was in the room where orals were held, a wood-paneled room with small paned windows and a broad shining table. The three men who were to examine her were sitting at one end of the table quarreling as she walked in. She had just stepped inside the door when she spied the pile in the corner. Instantly she knew what it was, but she was incredulous, she was so ashamed, she moved nearer to check it out. It was what she thought. She was horrified. Those stained sanitary napkins, those bloody underpants were hers, she knew they were hers, and she knew the men would know it too. She tried to stand in front of them, but there was no way she could conceal them. The men had stopped quarreling, they had turned to face her, they were peering at her . . . (410; ellipsis in original)

In a startling moment of unconscious identification, Kyla aligns herself, and her fears for and about herself, with the misogynist establishment: she, like her examiners, fears the uncontainable bloody excesses of the female body, and such a fear of bodily betrayal is at once embarrassing and professionally disabling. Her body's secrets refuse to remain contained in the other space of the women's room. In Kyla's deepest anxiety, her body refuses to collude with "the men" over the open secret of its femaleness; the dream simply reiterates the fear that her examiners will fail to perceive her mind within the insistent context of her uncontrollable body.

"Menstrual blood," writes Julia Kristeva, ". . . stands for the danger issuing from within identity (social or sexual); it threatens the relationship between the sexes within a social aggregate and, through internalization, the identity of each sex in the face of sexual difference."[11] For Val, for Kyla, and for Janet Mandelbaum, their bodies signify sexual difference even as their vocational ambitions lay claim to a pretense of gender neutrality; the well-trained mind should, in theory anyway, neutralize the ideological effects of a binary-sex model. Like Cross, French deploys the ostensibly abstract intellectual politics of the university to undercut the ascetic assumptions of disembodiedness implicit within the life of the mind, foregrounding instead the painful struggle that 1970s feminists faced in the effort to reconcile the body politics of academic labor with more abstract claims of aesthetics and the intellectual sphere. By forcing the reconciliation of the abstract and the material, such bodily degradations help to constitute the border-lines of the feminist subject, even as they expose the very vulnerability of that subject position by modeling the most spectacular, even mortal, implications of its failure.

Kristeva suggests that the degradations of the abject help to serve a constitutive function: mediating within the binary pair "subject" and "object," the abject becomes recognizable through the act of expulsion, through the putting out that, in one stroke, constitutes and maps the boundary line between "in" and "out." The bodies in these novels, especially the corpses, are very different feminist bodies from those found in psychoanalytic discourses of the period, particularly discourses that focus synecdochically on the empowering potential of the clitoris. To be sure, the abject body here serves a similarly constitutive and also potentially empowering function. Bodily humiliation signifies the risks feminists take and accounts for the psychological costs of patriarchy as it is experienced by subjects trapped within a female body. Social systems reason from the body outward, these realist texts suggest. And in their exposé of the arbitrary nature of the violence that ensues, they map and mobilize modes of resistance, not as claims to clitoral power do by reinterpreting the female body's meaning and thus the terms of the heterosexual contract, but by presenting models of female resourcefulness, resilience, and community that short-circuit the totalitarian regimes of patriarchy.

"As in true theater, without makeup or masks, refuse and corpses *show me* what I permanently thrust aside in order to live," writes Kristeva.

> These body fluids, this defilement, this shit are what life withstands, hardly and with difficulty, on the part of death. There, I am at the border of my condition as a living being. My body extricates itself, as being alive, from that border. Such wastes drop so that I might live, until, from loss to loss, nothing remains in me and my entire body falls beyond the limit—*cadere,*

cadaver. If dung signifies the other side of the border, the place where I am not and which permits me to be, the corpse, the most sickening of wastes, is a border that has encroached upon everything.[12]

Within Kristeva's theoretical model, produced in 1980, at the very transitional moment negotiated within these novels, the crisis of categories staged in the expulsion of the abject involves the psychic processes through which not only subjectivity but subjectivity as a gendered category is constituted: "The abject confronts us . . . with our earliest attempts to release the hold of *maternal* entity even before ex-isting outside of her, thanks to the autonomy of language. It is a violent, clumsy breaking away, with the constant risk of falling back under the sway of a power as securing as it is stifling."[13] As Kristeva suggests, the process of boundary formation is delicate: the nascent subject, shuttling between the predicament of maternal claustration and its patriarchal obverse, autonomy, finds herself called upon to reconcile the irreconcilable in a context in which her very survival is on the line.

The double bind that characterizes Kristeva's emerging subject recapitulates the predicament of the mature, would-be feminist subjects of Cross's and French's novels, and in all three cases the subject formation at stake involves the conundrum of femininity: how might female, and indeed *feminist*, subjectivity come into being, caught as it is between the annihilating codes of maternity on one side and the equally dangerous patriarchal sphere on the other? The corpses of Janet Mandelbaum and, in *The Women's Room*, of Val, Mira's heartiest, most joyously embodied feminist friend, exist in these novels as abjectified objects against which a feminist subject expresses the extremes of her own enterprise. In one sense, and paradoxically perhaps, such feminist corpses act the role of good mother: they play dead, accordingly constituting themselves as unresistant objects to be inscribed with meaning from the outside by those who profit from their loss. But more disturbingly, perhaps, they also serve the function of scapegoat: because the abject have been punished so brutally for their failings, the feminist subjects constituted in their wake are damaged goods, made timid and conciliatory by their awareness of the thin line they walk, by the mortal dangers implicit within the apparently paradoxical construct "autonomous woman."[14]

The result is a form of bodily self-loathing, which these novelists associate with the academy, a misogynist institution that stands in the way of women's access to the life of the mind, to aesthetic worlds, and to the professional prestige and livelihood that are presumed to follow upon academic success. Hence *Death in a Tenured Position,* a novel that presents its own ambivalence about the first woman to achieve the professional success that universities—and the culture for which they stand—would deny to the general population of women. Janet Mandelbaum has been selected strate-gically to join the Harvard faculty, more perhaps because of her antipathy toward feminism than for the excellence of her scholarship. Janet rails against the expectation that she, as the token woman, will lobby for the greater good of women: "[A]ll the women—students, assistant professors, administrators—seem to think I should rally to some woman's cause: wom-en's studies, the problems of women at Harvard, welcoming women to the graduate program, to Radcliffe—as though there were only one sex in the universe. Why should I be more interested in the women than the men? I'm interested in good seventeenth-century scholars; the sex is irrelevant" (45). She continues later: "I honestly do think that if women have the ability and are willing to pay the price they can make it. I did" (46). Along those lines, Joan Theresa, lesbian separatist and radical feminist, argues that not only was Janet never a feminist, "[s]he was never a *woman*, professionally speak-ing," and Kate Fansler agrees: "I assumed that was why Harvard had taken her. She had also had a hysterectomy, when young, and therefore could be guaranteed not to have a menopause, during which all women go mad, as everyone knows" (12; emphasis in original).

Stripped of her "woman" credentials explicitly because she does not iden-tify with woman-centered political causes and implicitly because she lacks that fundamental equipment for hysteria, the womb, Janet Mandelbaum is nonetheless punished—by misogynists, by feminists, by herself—because she is a professional woman. The first instance of this punishment occurs in the context of a rather improbable crisis, in which a graduate student slips Janet a drugged cocktail; when she passes out, he places her limp body in the ornamental bathtub located in the Harvard English department men's bath-room. He then telephones Joan Theresa's commune and warns the residents that one of the "sisters" is in trouble. The idea, apparently, is to suggest that Janet, who appears to know the lesbian separatists who come to her rescue, will be tarred with the same brush, will be taken for a lesbian herself; this produces crisis not only for Janet but also for the rescuing lesbian, Luellen, who is in a custody battle for her children. Kate's friend Sylvia muses on the illogic of this plot: "The point however, is that *they* [misogynists in the Harvard English department] thought they could discredit Janet by getting her involved with that all-women commune in Cambridge. Perhaps add an-other suspicion to her deteriorating reputation. But they were fools. They united two groups who would never, otherwise, have anything to do with each other: the woman-identified and the male-identified" (30; emphasis in original).

Kate Fansler is initially called to Harvard to intervene informally on Janet's behalf, and the women's commune has something at stake in her presence in Cambridge: Luellen hopes Kate will testify in her custody battle, and Kate realizes that "a judge would take my word about whom to give the children to because of the way I dress" (87). As Sylvia suggests, the commune women are the polar opposite of antifeminist Janet Mandelbaum, but, as the novel's plot suggests, they remain united in two concerns common to them as women: both parties need the help of mainstream feminist Kate Fansler; and they are similarly degraded and publicly humiliated in an intellectual (and homophobic and misogynist) context because of their bodies and what their bodies suggest about their sexuality. But although Kate suspects that the entire Harvard faculty is capable of murdering its first tenured woman professor to "scotch the whole scheme" of female faculty (106), in the end, quite chillingly, it is not one of the suspects but rather Mandelbaum herself who acted in violence.

Kate Fansler's investigation into Janet's murder represents an attempt to locate violent hatred of Janet either in the radical feminist fringe or in the misogynist Harvard faculty, each of which has something to gain by her death. But it is ultimately revealed that Janet died by her own hand and, in the course of the investigation, that everyone is guilty—the Harvard English department for its close-minded loathing of her; her friends Kate and Sylvia for isolating her, for giving her "no community" (187); her lesbian feminist "sisters" for turning their back on a woman in need: "She belonged nowhere, poor Janet" (181). Janet's chosen symbolic gesture was to commit suicide in the office of the English department chairman; her colleague Allen Adam Clarkville, on discovering the body, moved it from the office to the men's room (where it had already been discovered, unconscious, once before) in a misguided attempt at concealment. Because Janet's body "was in a position with the legs drawn up," putting it "on the toilet in the stall may have seemed, under the circumstances, the logical thing" (166), and Clarkville, chivalrous to the end, chooses the men's room in order to spare the English department's secretaries the shock of discovering Janet dead.

The circumstances of Janet's death, the ensuing cover-up, and its discovery decisively reiterate the scatological motif. But this time, Janet herself, although a prominent scholar, is responsible for placing her own body in a suggestive position. The novel ultimately punishes Janet, exchanging her embrace of scholarly asceticism for a conclusive gesture toward her body's status as material and as grotesque. Why, though, despite its indictment of everyone from radical feminists to vicious misogynists for failing to accept Janet's person and politics, must this novel conclude with a revelation of her suicide? Despite the belated regrets of most of the novel's characters, they initially direct tremendous hostility toward Janet Mandelbaum, some because she is female and others because she is not a feminist. The message implicit in a text whose protagonist speaks for a feminist bourgeoisie is that, although there might be no room for women at Harvard now, there will be eventually; but there is no room for women such as Janet Mandelbaum within the women's movement. Kate Fansler represents a new feminist orthodoxy here, a middle ground available to women who fall somewhere between the radical feminism of Joan Theresa and the borderline misogyny of Janet Mandelbaum; vaguely skeptical of both, Kate looks on more in sorrow than in anger as both are punished for their respective locations on the fringes.

Death in a Tenured Position is set in an English department. It exploits its setting in order to foreground not only questions of professionalism, politics, and sexuality relevant to the women's movement but also questions of aesthetics. In this it is paradigmatic of popular feminist fictions from this period, which consistently emphasize the importance of beauty, pleasure, creativity, and, in that vein, education as fundamental to feminist social action. In the context of the consciousness-raising movement, Kathie Sarachild of the Redstockings collective was among many feminists arguing for women's right to study, suggesting a new awareness of analysis as a form of radical praxis: "In the beginning we had set out to do our studying in order to take better action. We hadn't realized that just studying this subject and naming the problem or problems would be a radical action in itself, action so radical as to engender tremendous and persistent opposition."[15] Cross's novel, like French's, extrapolates from Sarachild's argument, building on the suggestion that the liberal feminist egalitarian impulse can be addressed through a cultivation of the analytical tools of academic work, and suggesting further that the study of literature and history is itself a form of feminist action. Indeed, the cultivation of the mind, as Cross's novel suggests, offers a means to circumvent the gross bodily implications of femininity. As fictional texts, these novels clearly have much at stake in underscoring the importance of fictional and literary works to a larger feminist project. But the consistent representation of aesthetic concerns within the aggressively professional context of the academy—Janet Mandelbaum's investment in George Herbert, for instance, concerns her labor, not her pleasure—equates the cultural valuation of the sublime with a kind of bourgeois careerism. An academic career is potentially feminist and also quite democratically accessible to smart women with the proper training. The university, paradoxically, symbolizes both the most rigidly entrenched of patriarchal institutions and a context in which feminist political interventions might take hold. In this it stands somewhat optimistically for the potential of bourgeois feminism to transform the world.

Feminist fictions emphasize the profound importance of class issues to the women's movement through their concern not only with the class status of women but also with the fluid class boundaries available through education. The sense in which they remain conventional narratives underscores the nature of the fictional intervention into feminist practice, addressing central questions of the women's movement while putting a premium on the human cost of the difficult decisions these central questions require. These are novels in which female characters agonize over the double binds that characterize their lives and in which every decision, one way or another, has negative implications. Just as Kate Fansler serves a crucial mediating function between the extremes of radical lesbian feminism and rigid misogyny, these narratives, too, operate in terms of mediation. They construct an implicit readerly identification for white middle-class heterosexual women, and, through the trials of their white middle-class, usually heterosexual protagonists, they model strategies for the accommodation of feminist principles of equality within essentially conventional lives.[16] In the context of such narratives of identification, the topos of violent death persists as a sign of abjection that, through the purifying, even excretory, function, exposes the outermost limits—and the frightening risks—of the feminist project.

Marilyn French's *The Women's Room* is the most fully realized of various attempts to work through the conflicts created by cultural expectations for women. As in most feminist novels, feminism here is a positive possibility within otherwise annihilating choices. French follows her protagonist, Mira, through girlhood, adolescence, marriage, life as a suburban housewife and mother, divorce, and graduate school, and ultimately—though not optimistically—to a lonely existence as a junior-college instructor of English literature in an isolated town on the coast of Maine. This is not a happy ending, but Mira is introspective and intact at the novel's conclusion—no mean feat considering the extent to which her ostensibly normal and certainly conventional life experiences are represented in their ability to inflict psychic and even physical damage despite Mira's reasonably protected status as an open-minded, intelligent, middle-class, well-educated white woman. She is not a woman living in poverty, like the lesbians in *Death in a Tenured Position* and Piercy's *Small Changes,* who must fight the system that would take away their children; nor does she experience overt misogyny, and certainly nothing like racial prejudice. Rather, Mira is a woman who suffers because she is a member of the cultural mainstream, even the cultural ideal, an intelligent, thinking, sensitive woman living in the postwar United States; her suffering is acute and its damage genuine.

Mira's predicament leaves her split, more knowingly than in Janet Mandelbaum's case, between body and mind, between the grotesque implications of her material existence and the possibilities held forth in the act of intellection. It is not possible for Mira to reconcile these claims. Accordingly, her feminism, however abstract it gets, never fully escapes the most degraded bodily implications of patriarchy, in terms ranging from the cleaning of toilets to rape at knifepoint. *The Women's Room* is a novel set largely in a university context, but it opens in the bathroom of that university, and French is meticulous in situating the more abstract ideological concerns of the women's movement within the material context of women's lived experience: university, bathroom.

Mira, an acutely intelligent child, first finds that intelligence disrupted by menstruation: "The problem was sex. . . . At the end of her fourteenth year, Mira began to menstruate and was finally let in on the secret of sanitary napkins. Soon afterward, she began to experience strange fluidities in her body, and her mind, she was convinced, had begun to rot. She could feel the increasing corruption, but couldn't seem to do anything to counter it" (14). With menstruation comes the beginning of sexual desire and Mira's introduction to the entire consumer economy of womanhood: she is "finally let in on the secret of sanitary napkins." Suddenly the intellectual emphases of her private life give way to ideas of romantic love, but as a teenager she swiftly learns that her participation in romance means that she must forsake not only physical but also mental independence: left alone one night in a bar, she drinks too much, dances with a number of teenage boys, and comes dangerously close to being gang-raped by them: "Other girls went to bars, other girls danced. The difference was she had appeared to be alone. That a woman was not marked as the property of some man made her a bitch in heat to be attacked by any male, or even by all of them at once. . . . She was a woman and that alone was enough to deprive her of freedom no matter how much the history books pretended that women's suffrage had ended inequality, or that women's feet had been bound only in an ancient and outmoded and foreign place like China. She was constitutionally unfree" (35). Having been introduced to the consumer culture of womanhood, Mira soon learns, violently, that she is its chattel. Significantly, as this quotation should demonstrate, the feminist praxis modeled by *The Women's Room,* with the allusion of its title to Woolf's peroration for women's intellectual freedom in *A Room of One's Own,* is more concerned with the subtle sexism of white middle-class heterosexual culture than with interventions at the level of formal law.

Like the women in Woolf's text, Mira discovers that her intelligence, her private life of the mind, is her only path of escape from the insidious degradations of middle-class femininity. But mind is inextricable from body, and Mira's body, as she so rapidly learns, represents a problem in a culture that would see it only in terms of a man's ownership: "Mira understood—what young woman does not?—that to choose a husband is to choose a life. She had not needed Jane Austen to teach her that. It is, in a sense, a woman's first, last, and only choice. Marriage and a child make her totally dependent on the man, on whether he is rich or poor, responsible or not, where he chooses to live, what work he chooses to do" (26). As Woolf suggests and French reiterates repeatedly, women are a social class, and as a class they are generally poor. This point is represented particularly acutely given the novel's normative middle-class context and its version of heterosexual marital convention, for Mira's perception that her future physical well-being depends on her choice of husband presupposes certain assumptions about that husband's earning power. In contrast, in *Rubyfruit Jungle,* Rita Mae Brown's lesbian protagonist, Molly Bolt, working outside the presumption that her life is coextensive with her marriage, tells a story of economic self-sufficiency that originates in a childhood of constant poverty.[17]

For the women of Mira's suburban adult lifestyle, "work" is tied to the body and detached from the monetary economy of wages; they are in a secondary relationship to earning power, and the power relations of their marriages reflect the equation of money and control: "Women see men as oppressors, as tyrants, as an enemy with superior strength to be outwitted. Men see women as underminers, slaves who rattle their chains threateningly, constantly reminding the men that if they wanted to, they could poison his food: just watch out" (68). Women's work involves the bearing of and caring for children, tasks that further alienate them from "ownership" of their bodies and that impose a form of exhaustion that drains their intelligent minds. When Mira first gets pregnant, "[s]he saw the situation as the end of her personal life. Her life, from pregnancy on, was owned by another creature" (48). The narrator interposes here with a commentary on Mira's "unnatural" response to her predicament: "What is wrong with this woman? you ask. It is Nature, there is no recourse, she must submit and make the best of what she cannot change. But the mind is not easily subdued. Resentment and rebellion grow in it—resentment and rebellion against Nature itself. Some wills are crushed, but those that are not contain within them, for the rest of their days, seeds of hate. All of the women I know feel a little like outlaws" (48). Feminism, for Mira, represents the fomenting of rebellion in her mind against the captivity and ownership registered on her body. Because of the differences between male and female bodies, "[t]hey played by different rules because the rules applied to them were different. It was very simple. It was the women who got pregnant and the women who ended up with the kids" (216). The material implications of women's lack of access to money and men's access to freedom are dire for women and children; after Mira's divorce and the midlife divorces of several of her

friends, the narrator comments, "If you want to find out who all the welfare mothers are, ask your divorced male friends. It sounds easy, you know,
going on welfare. But apart from the humiliation and resentment, you don't
really live very well. In case you didn't know. Which is unpleasant for a
woman, but sends her into fits when she looks at her kids" (230).

The indignities, petty humiliations, and injustices represented in *The
Women's Room* are the by-product of "normal" American life, and in her
exposé of the quotidian, French locates women's liberation at and as the
heart of middle-class concerns. French's critique of marriage represents a
logical progression from material degradation to larger epistemological
questions, and, as theorists of the consciousness-raising movement noted,
the novel's more esoteric academic analyses of inequality suggest that experience and epistemology are inextricable. Feminist praxis begins, for
French and for Mira, at home: "But for women especially, the new washing
machine or dryer or freezer really was a little release from slavery. Without
them, and without the pill, there would not be a woman's revolution now"
(72). Indeed, the liberating implications of labor-saving devices have been
central to bourgeois feminism, from Friedan's *The Feminine Mystique* (1963),
with its analysis of affluent women's boredom, through more contemporary
debates about day care.[18] In *The Women's Room,* labor-saving devices represent an avenue out of the endlessly self-replicating implications of dirt
generated by human bodies. "All my life," the narrator comments, "I've
read that the life of the mind is preeminent, and that it can transcend all
bodily degradation. But that's just not my experience. When your body
has to deal all day with shit and string beans, your mind does too" (46).
From this point on, the phrase "shit and string beans" is the novel's refrain,
representing the physical and mental captivity entailed in housewifery, particularly in the raising of small children and the maintenance of the affluent
suburban household. Mira, living the "American Dream" and trying to "get
her mask on straight" (151), is explicit about the most hideous aspects of
middle-class womanhood: "Down on her hands and knees in one of the
endless bathrooms, she would tell herself that in a way she was fortunate.
Washing the toilet used by three males, and the floor and walls around it, is,
Mira thought, coming face to face with necessity. And that was why women
were saner than men, did not come up with the mad, absurd schemes men
developed: they were in touch with necessity, they had to wash the toilet
bowl and floor" (150).

For Mira and women like her, the "necessity" of dealing with "shit and
string beans" is a universal among women; this novel suggests a related
universality of female oppression, even if the presence of options in this
context, such as cleaning help, appliances, and even access to birth control,

locates this iteration of oppressive circumstances firmly in the middle of the middle class. "Everybody should clean up their own vomit," Mira thinks. "Everybody should clean up the toilet they use" (227). But in Mira's world, everybody doesn't—women do. And even in the most openly feminist contexts, behavioral expectations based on gender roles are stubborn; theory and practice remain at odds with one another. In response to the idea of universal "selflessness," to men and women equally bearing the expectations of the other, Mira contemplates the limits of her friends' compromises:

> It was a rhetorical solution. Because the fact is that everyone doesn't act in both roles and probably can't and not everyone would be willing to accept that and so the whole thing seemed to me as if we'd been talking about the street plan and architecture of heaven. In fact, it didn't make much sense even for us to insist that men and women both should be selfless, because although we were all in graduate school, all of us took the female role at home. . . . And we were supposed to be "liberated." . . . I mentioned this, and Isolde sighed. "I hate discussions of feminism that end up with who does the dishes," she said. So do I. But at the end, there are always the damned dishes. (60)

Someone is always stuck doing the dishes, and the question of cleaning up afterward is allegorized in this novel to suggest its centrality for both feminist practice and theory. "Women always have to clean up their own messes," thinks Mira (246); the rage provoked by such debasement is the fire behind feminist theoretical passions. After a theoretical argument, Kyla, Mira's graduate-school colleague, bursts out, "'Oh, Mira! . . . Why do you always have to bring us down to the level of the mundane, the ordinary, the stinking, fucking refrigerator? I was talking about ideals, nobility, principles. . . .' And she leaped up and charged across the room and threw herself on Mira and hugged her, kept hugging her, saying, 'Thank you, oh, thank you, Mira, for being so wonderful, so awful, for always remembering the stinking, filthy refrigerator!'" (241).

As Kyla's outburst indicates, the "evidence of experience" proves to be a powerful polemical tool within *The Women's Room*.[19] In contrast to similar claims to the primacy of experience found in feminist discourses of consciousness-raising, however, in which experience is the evidence from which theories of social change are produced, "experience" in *The Women's Room* stands as a phenomenon of embodiment directly antithetical to the linked realms of theory and the analytical abstractions that characterize academic labor: "For here, underneath all the intellect, the abstraction, the disconnection, were the same old salt tears and sperm, the same sweet blood and sweat she'd wiped up for years. More shit and string beans" (304). Mira's return to school following her divorce occurs as an attempt to transcend the "real" implications of everyday existence: "It was a new life, it was supposed to revitalize you, to send you radiant to new planes of experience where you would get tight with Beatrice Portinari and be led to an earthly paradise. In literature, new lives, second chances, lead to visions of the City of God" (147). But, typically within the genre of feminist realism, Mira quickly realizes that the formal conventions of representation fail to accommodate her own lived experience, with the re-sult that "shit and string beans" continue to preoccupy her daily life. The narrator comments: "The problem with the great literature of the past is that it doesn't tell you how to live with real endings. In the great literature of the past you either get married and live happily ever after, or you die. But the fact is, neither is what actually happens. Oh, you do die, but never at the right time, never with great language floating all around you, and a whole theater full of witnesses to your agony. What actually happens is that you do get married or you don't, and you don't live happily ever after, but you do live. And that's the problem" (148–49).

Marriage in French's novel rarely guarantees happiness, and life without happiness is, in effect, a living death. This novel, consistent with its dark aesthetic vision, is pragmatic about the implications of Mira's feminist struggle. She gets her Ph.D., true, from the same Harvard English depart-ment that witnessed the death of Janet Mandelbaum, but she does not turn into Janet, much less Kate Fansler, reaping the material and intellectual benefits of a scholarly life. Mira, an older graduate, settles into a job at a very isolated small college in Maine. So, despite the fact that she opts out of marriage and more children with her lover Ben in favor of her intellectual freedom, she winds up a solitary eccentric wandering the rocky shores of Maine all winter long.

But, employed and living on her own terms, Mira is alive. She is friends with her adolescent sons and occasionally even enjoys her life as a teacher. If Mira represents the feminist mainstream, French paints a bleak picture of the implications of acting on a commitment to personal freedom; typically pragmatic, French underscores the sense in which every decision carries its price, and Mira's integrity costs her human relationships. This novel, like so many others of this historical moment, articulates a feminist mainstream through sharp contrast with the feminist radical fringe—and occupation of that radical fringe is lethal.

In French's novel, Mira's most radical friend is Val. Val and her daugh-ter, Chris, constitute a family unit that is presented as idyllic: it is open, fluid, accepting, political, welcoming, a household of women who practice a utopian, user-friendly version of the feminism with which the novel's more conventional women struggle. Chris, however, goes off to college and is raped, and Chris and Val's ensuing trip through the justice system brings them down to the level of degradation, humiliation, and debasement that is the more common experience of women in patriarchal culture. This radicalizes Val to a degree that the novel represents as understandable but untenable; Chris and Val conclude that any male attention is rape, that the legal system is complicit with the rapist, and that Chris must fight for her very right to exist in a world of men. Representing an extreme version of separatism, Val declares, "Whatever they may be in public life, whatever their relations with men, in their relations with women, all men are rapists, and that's all they are. They rape us with their eyes, their laws, and their codes" (462).

The novel rejects this position implicitly.[20] Mira is the mother of two sons and thus typifies the feminist struggle for equality without separatism. She feels "liberated" through her pursuit of her scholarly work: scholarship, she believes, "did not seem slavery to her but freedom. For the first time, she understood what graduate school had been all about: it was designed to free her for this. She did not have to worry over every detail; she had enough knowledge to make certain statements, and enough awareness of how to get knowledge to find out how to make others. That was liberating. She was free to be as methodical as she chose, in a work that seemed significant. What more could she ask?" (475). If knowledge is Mira's ticket to liberation, then political action is Val's, for Val becomes a political activist—indeed, an extremely radical feminist—as a result of her daughter's rape.[21] And for this decision she pays the price of death. Hers is no mere poisoning, as in Janet Mandelbaum's case, but a brutally graphic and public destruction of her body and all that it stands for: while participating in a protest, police shoot so many bullets into Val's body that it explodes.

"There are no words," someone says at Val's funeral (496). Unlike Mira, whose choice in the mind-body binary places her on the side of the mind, Val surpasses the contingencies of materiality; because she explodes, she is containable neither in body nor in words: "No words to wrap her body in like a shroud, like clean white sanitized bandages, around and around and around until she was all clean and white and sanitized and pure, her blood dried, her mass of exploded flesh covered, her stink deodorized, and she sanitary, polite, acceptable for public notice, a mummy propped on a table for public ceremony, its very presence a promise, a guarantee that she will not rise up in rage with hair wild on her head, a knife in her hand, screaming, 'No! No! Kill before you accept!'" (496). The novel does not deal with Val's death with any real explicitness, nor does it pursue the implications of the cause in which she died: Val and her group were protesting the arrest and trial of a young black woman, Anita Morrow, who had been raped and had stabbed her rapist in self-defense. The rapist, "from a respectable white family," died, and Anita was charged with murder. The prosecution claimed she was a prostitute and the media represented her as uneducable, but, like most of the female characters in this novel, she was a university student who "wanted to be an English teacher" (492). Eventually, "Anita Morrow was found guilty of murder on grounds of illiteracy" (493)—as if illiteracy were a crime.

This murder case introduces an important new tension late in the novel; the suggestion that education and the upward mobility that it purchases are the prerogative of middle-class white women alone underscores a certain complacency within Mira's analysis of the class politics of gender difference. Anita, Val, and Chris are punished for declarations of rage and selfhood that are significantly more extreme than the world, including the world of protagonist Mira, is willing to handle. And in the context of the novel's dark representation of feminist life choices, the injustice of these concluding events is clear, their overarching message still more clear: there is an ineradicable danger to life as a radical feminist, and in the bourgeois world of feminism, radical life choices are conventionally punished either by humiliating ridicule or by death. To put theory into real-life practice, in other words, is to put the body on the line. To practice feminism is to realize the danger ever present within women's resistance. The protections afforded within this equation are various, for some lives—Anita Morrow's, for example—are always already in danger; the concept of "choice" for Anita involves only the degree to which she might dare to resist a system that is implicitly constructed to resist her. Mira's place on the scale of privilege is quite high, but even her choices, reasonably moderate though they are, strand her on the rugged coast of Maine. And Val is forced by circumstance and by violence to choose a life for which there is no place at all in the world. This causes her body to be shattered to bits all over the street in the name of legal justice.

The fictional texts of the mainstream women's movement are decidedly anxious about feminist rage and feminist activism, and they represent an ideal of bourgeois feminism as a cerebral endeavor. Characters such as Alther's Ginny or Jong's Isadora Wing, whose trust funds enable them to try on roles, jobs, and sexualities without material consequences, enable a parody of the double bind that French represents as agonizing and inextricable: more abstract theoretical approaches to sexual discrimination emerge subtly as the property of the "straight," of the white heterosexual middle classes.[22] Amanda Cross's series detective Kate Fansler is certainly represented as a feminist, but, short of coming to the rescue of a colleague in crisis at Harvard, her more conventional mode of feminist action is her eternal presence as "The Token Woman" on university committees (5). The ubiquitousness with which feminist novelists in the late 1970s and early 1980s situate their characters' political activities within universities is symptomatic of a larger set of agendas pertaining to the brand of feminist action they represent: feminism is an individual concern, a movement connected with the achievement of personal career and intellectual goals facilitated by education, and relies on a logic of metonymy, suggesting that what is good for one woman will be good for women more generally. In this context, radical individualism becomes its own form of activist intervention; Ginny Babcock leaves the commune to marry Ira Bliss, and later still she leaves him, rolling her "Sisterhood Is Powerful" T-shirt into a knapsack and striking out after new adventures.

Serving the practical aims of consolidation in death, the feminist abject is occasionally recapitulated in further service to the feminist subject. At the end of Jong's *Fear of Flying*, in a moment of crisis, the protagonist and first-person narrator, Isadora Wing, who is separated from her current husband, reads a notebook she kept in the early days of her marriage: "I sat very quietly looking at the pages I had written. I knew I did not want to be trapped in my own book."[23] Isadora then falls asleep and into an anxiety dream that is at once liberating and anomalous, rupturing the terminologies of psychological, intellectual, narrative, and sexual entrapment that constitute Isadora's "own book"—her diary as well as the novel *Fear of Flying*. Isadora dreams of walking up the steps of Columbia's Low Library to receive her college diploma, her three successive husbands watching from the audience, and encountering lesbian novelist Colette at the lectern, "only she was a black woman with frizzy reddish hair glinting around her head like a halo." Colette speaks to Isadora, who narrates:

> "There is only one way to graduate, . . . and it has nothing to do with the number of husbands."
>
> "What do I have to do?" I asked desperately, feeling I'd do anything.
>
> She handed me a book with my name on the cover. "That was only a very shaky beginning," she said, "but at least you *made* a beginning."
>
> I took this to mean I still had years to go.
>
> "Wait," she said, undoing her blouse. Suddenly I understood that making love to her in public was the real graduation, and at that moment it seemed like the most natural thing in the world. Very aroused, I moved toward her. Then the dream faded. (290; emphasis in original)

Jong's novel continues for two more chapters of denouement, in which Isadora considers a reunion with her husband. But despite the structural centrality and psychological importance accorded to this dream, the novel never refers back to it or attempts to elucidate its implications.

Why does *Fear of Flying* reach its climax in and through these terms? Somehow Colette is a useful, if alien, object of desire to the rampantly heterosexual, white New Yorker Isadora Wing.[24] Interracial, transnational, exhibitionist lesbian sex is tied up here with the goal of successful authorship, both registering in the realm of "academic" achievement: Isadora's book represents a form of ongoing coursework, whereas "making love to [Colette] in public was the real graduation." The novel that begins with the notorious fantasy of the "Zipless Fuck" (11) concludes with a commencement that reestablishes the boundaries of sexual transgression: "Very aroused, I moved toward her. Then the dream faded." In the end, the erotic encounter between Isadora and Colette is relegated, again, to the realm of the unsaid.

The love that dare not speak its name speaks volumes for Isadora Wing, whose Colette fantasy consolidates a number of crucial—and troublesome— identity categories within the women's movement. Colette is a white Frenchwoman turned into a red-haired African American; she is a lesbian and a theoretician; she is a literary figure, access to whose fictions, in practical terms, presupposes a certain degree of literacy; and "making love to her in public was the real graduation," for Isadora the key to escaping the conventional narrative of her life thus far, the "graduation ceremony" that leads Isadora to the brink of an independent, self-determined identity.

In her deployment of Colette, Jong, like other feminist novelists of this period, forges a strategic connection between pleasure and knowledge, linking women's unleashed eroticism both to the concept of their intellectual freedom and to formal institutional structures of the academy—Columbia's Low Library, a graduation ceremony. Knowledge is not only power, it is power rooted in pleasure, the realization of the creative and the beautiful, the construction of a feminist countercultural utopia right in the belly of the patriarchal beast. But perhaps the most common critique of the women's liberation movement in the late 1970s and early 1980s focuses on what feminism leaves out. The argument that feminists, and feminist theories, construct white middle-class heterosexual women's experiences as normative recapitulates the politics of abjectification modeled by fictional deaths. In both cases, the mainstream constitutes itself through an act of violent expulsion, through a philosophical decapitation symbolically rendered, like Eddie's, through self-contradiction, through the failure to perceive the invisible boundaries that feminists have established.

"Here it is not only a question," writes Judith Butler, "of how discourse injures bodies, but how certain injuries establish certain bodies at the limits of available ontologies, available schemes of intelligibility. . . . [H]ow is it that the abjected come to make their claim through and against the discourses that have sought their repudiation?"[25] How, in other words, do the dead reawaken? Or, more appropriately perhaps, how do they expose themselves as the always already there, as the ghosts on whose very animating alterity feminist theories of animation, and of alterity, rely? In this context, Isadora Wing's transformative dream is as efficient as it is revealing of the undead feminist's formative role. Colette, ghost, is the token black woman, lesbian, feminist literary ancestor, import from the prestigious context of French high culture. This leads to a new form of liberation: Isadora, intensely aroused, responds sexually to Colette. Then she and her novel together walk away from this encounter; in the last scene Isadora is contemplating reunion with her husband. By reawakening the dead Colette and apostrophizing her in the name of identities under erasure in *Fear of Flying*, Jong reveals the contingencies to which Isadora Wing's ultimate liberation, her release from entrapment within the generic confines of the fictional real, are indebted. Literally, figuratively, and politically, Colette's outrageously overdetermined alterity serves an authorizing, even constitutive, function for Isadora, for this novel, and for the witty, urbane feminist subject canonized in its graduation ceremony. Isadora forgets, but the novel reminds us, that it is Colette who confers the degree. And then she is gone.

5

Obstructive Behavior
Dykes in the Mainstream of Feminist Theory

DYKE: *a person or animal . . . that leaps over fences; . . . a transgressor of the laws of morality*
—*Oxford English Dictionary,* 2d ed. (1989)

Novels of the women's liberation movement present the intellectual labor of the academy as marked by both the abstraction from and the abjection of a material, female body that stands for the urgencies of a material feminism. Feminism's theoretical texts, during as well as since the women's movement, are similarly concerned to mark distinctions between the usefully abstract and the excessively detached. By doing so, they constitute a feminist episte-mology that legitimizes some forms of feminist critical authority even as it delegitimizes others.

In this chapter I suggest that "lesbian" serves not only as a category of feminist analysis, not only as a formation of female identity linked with a set of material practices, but also as a trope for feminist critical authority. It is a trope, furthermore, with a peculiarly volatile history in the context of that critical discourse. A study of its itinerary marks divergent visions of what feminism is meant to do, what problems it is meant to solve, what opportu-nities it affords, and what and who feminists are meant to be. By tracking the oscillations of "lesbian" through a range of critical discourses, I return to questions of abstraction and materiality, arguing that the "dyke," as a metaphor and as a signifier of issues insistently embodied, and through pat-terns of alternating appropriation and abjectification, constitutes feminist theory as an authoritative mode of practice.

Thus, the "obstructive behavior" I analyze here involves the consideration of those "dykes" as a form of obstruction that impedes or redirects a current or flow. I want to argue that feminist theory in the United States has come into being in relation to a set of dykes, through contact with critical obstructions that shape, divert, and otherwise help to define the mainstream. The function of these dykes is an ambiguous one; they are at once necessary and problematic, central yet diversionary. Dykes are not of the mainstream, but the mainstream necessarily shapes itself in response to them.

At its most literal level, the metaphorical "dyke" signifies a concern with the tendentious shape shifting that has characterized feminist theory, producing new and innovative theoretical concerns and applications. At another level, however, it signifies its concern with the discourse of obstruction, with impudent behaviors and political impediments that have confronted and shaped academic discourses of the feminist. At still another level, I am concerned with the discourses of sexuality in feminism and the sense in which the issue of sexuality itself operates as a dyke, as a shaping impediment, for colloquially *dyke* itself signifies—sometimes rudely, sometimes not—a way of being named or self-identifying as lesbian.[1] And the question of lesbians in feminist criticism has been the single most powerful dyke in the evolution of this critical discourse.

In the second edition of the *Oxford English Dictionary* (1989), the definition of *dyke,* or *dike* (the "more conventional" spelling), depends on an interestingly redoubled sense of ambiguity. The *OED* traces the etymology of *dyke* through a series of exchanges of masculine and feminine cases, evolving, perhaps ironically, from versions of the word *dick* in the masculine to versions of the word *dyke* in the feminine, pausing only in Icelandic at the neuter. Its history of etymological indeterminacy notwithstanding, "dyke" consistently signifies a form of diversionary obstruction, whether ditch, trench, mound, embankment, or dam: "The application thus varies between 'ditch, dug out place,' and 'mound formed by throwing up the earth,' and may include both." Under its first definition, a dyke is "an excavation narrow in proportion to its length, a long and narrow hollow dug out of the ground; a DITCH, trench, or fosse," or "such a hollow dug out to hold or conduct water." Under its second, it is "[a]n embankment, wall, causeway," and, still more specifically, "'A bank formed by throwing the earth out of the ditch' (Bosworth)" or "[a] wall or fence . . . [t]he wall of a city, a fortification."

Dyke is a word that presupposes the complication, conflation, even the collapse of binary categories. Confounding notions of masculinity and femininity in the case of etymology and of structure in the architectural significance of a barrier, conflicting definitions of *dyke* exploit an ambiguity at the heart of the concept itself. In its first definition, a "narrow hollow dug out of the ground," the function of the dyke is to enable another activity, such as the holding or the conducting of water, but is essentially passive: it exists primarily not as a presence but as an absence, a negative space sculpted from the positive surface of the earth. Yet, in its alternate definition, the dyke exceeds that positive surface, existing as the highly visible surplus of earth in fortifying relation to the populace whose existence it protects and enables. Whether the dyke is a canal permitting transport from one place to another or a protective wall impeding that transport, the well-being of its architects depends on the dyke's structural integrity. In either incarnation, the transformative capacity of the dyke remains its most powerful capital: articulating a space that is, by definition, both marginal and central, the dyke demarcates difference, transition, liminality, and vulnerability. That vulnerability inheres in the status of the dyke as a protective structure: without the need to guard against difference, against the threat of difference to destroy, the dyke would be completely unnecessary.

A slang definition, listed after and separated from the nearly three columns of preceding definitions in the *OED*, reads as follows: "DIKE, DYKE . . . *slang*. [Of obscure origin.] A lesbian; a masculine woman." Citing as its earliest usage a 1942 entry in the *American Thesaurus of Slang*, this "dyke," "of obscure origin," remains distinct from the *OED*'s other "dykes" yet shares with them certain implications of liminality. Not only a lesbian but also a "masculine woman," the "dyke" in this definition blurs the borderline between masculinity and femininity. In her appearance, and presumably in her affective alliances, she, like her fellow "dykes," marks, embodies, and deconstructs that borderline by disrupting conventional practices of self-presentation and desire. Like the other "dykes," this "dyke" offers a limiting case and a liminal space, enabling definitions of inside and outside, enabling, through her location of and as a border, binary systems of logic that exploit fixed notions of identity and identifiability.

Feminist critical discourses, I argue, articulate themselves both through and against a relationship to dykes, depending precisely on the dyke's function as a borderline to mark the parameters of feminist theory and practice. In an important essay about feminism's "origin between 1968 and 1972," Katie King argues that the term "lesbian" has served as a "magical sign," a privileged signifier, and as the term over which contests for meaning have occurred: "Lesbianism stands as a sign of something 'entirely new' for both lesbians and non-lesbians. Knowing about lesbians, being in association with lesbians, having control of the arguments about lesbianism, these are all accesses to lesbianism that one doesn't have to practice lesbianism to have."[2] Lesbians serve as a site of identificatory practice for feminists, suggests King. By expanding on the historical scope of this inquiry and focusing broadly on a twenty-five-year history of feminist discourse, I suggest that, over time, "lesbian" came to serve more as a marker of feminist ambivalence and less as a marker of feminist identification, however hypothetical. At once needing and abhorring the dykes that exist at and as the shaping margins of its discourse, feminist theory has struggled to accommodate competing desires for popular acceptance and individual sexual diversity. Catalyzing questions about sex, sexuality, eroticism, pleasure, identity, politics, and power, the dyke has always been the site of contention, the source of troubling questions, both for and within feminism.

> DYKE: *A ridge, embankment, long mound, or dam, thrown up*
> *to resist the encroachments of the sea, or to prevent low-lying*
> *lands from being flooded by seas, rivers, or streams*

From the vocabulary of lesbian separatism in the 1970s through queer theory's emergence in the 1990s, feminists have always engaged questions of sexuality. But although the vantage point of history often associates the early women's movement with the political enthusiasms of the sexual revolution, in fact the very personal politics of sexual difference has historically marked the most dramatic fault lines among feminists. In 1970, at the Second Congress to Unite Women, twenty women stormed the meeting's plenary session with the words "Lavender Menace" emblazoned on their chests. Prompted to act by Betty Friedan's notorious, and perhaps apocryphal, remark that lesbians in the women's movement were a "lavender menace" who would ultimately impede cultural acceptance of feminist sympathies, the women calling themselves the Lavender Menace challenged conference members to confront homophobia in the women's movement. Later renaming themselves the Radicalesbians, this group soon produced an essay titled "The Woman-Identified Woman," which argued that all sexualities exist in the service of patriarchy and that a challenge to rigid notions of sexuality must accompany feminist critiques of patriarchy. Women who fail to consider the erotic potential of other women are trapped in a patriarchal web, living their lives and setting their expectations only in terms of their relationships to men; thus, feminists fail to confront their full investment in patriarchal power until they confront the personal politics of their bedrooms. "Real" women, "feminine" women, the Radicalesbians suggested, "are authentic, legitimate, real to the extent that we are the property of some man whose name we bear. To be a woman who belongs to no man is to be invisible, pathetic, inauthentic, unreal. He confirms his image of us—of what we have to be in order to be acceptable by him—but not our real selves; he confirms our womanhood—as he defines it, in relation to him—but cannot confirm our personhood, our own selves as absolutes. As long as we are dependent on the male culture for this definition, for this approval, we cannot be free."[3]

The Radicalesbians identified female homosexuality as a political choice. Lesbianism, within their rubric, is a political mandate, as it were, more than an erotic one; the utopian vision of a lesbian-separatist community, often figured as the return of the Amazons, is frequently constructed as the only plausible alternative within a radical and thoroughgoing critique of patriarchy. And indeed, this is a notion that has loomed large over the culture of feminist discourse to this day, for, as lesbian separatists throughout the early days of the women's movement insisted, separatism remains a logical extreme of feminist critiques of patriarchy, a logical solution to often painfully paradoxical attempts to live a "feminist life." Catharine MacKinnon writes, "Feminism is the epistemology of which lesbianism is an ontology," in an explanation that reinscribes a theory-practice divide through the distinction between feminism and lesbianism.[4]

Lesbian separatism was one of the greatest challenges to and anxieties of early feminists. Ti-Grace Atkinson presents a summary of the theory informing political lesbianism in the collection *Amazon Odyssey*: "It is the commitment of individuals to common goals, and to the death if necessary, that determines the strength of the army"; "[l]esbianism is to feminism what the Communist Party was to the trade-union movement. Tactically, any feminist should fight to the death for lesbianism because of its strategic importance."[5] Invoking metaphors ranging from the martial to the economic, Atkinson emphasizes the importance of linking feminist theory and feminist practice: "I'm enormously less interested in whom you sleep with than I am in with whom you're prepared to die."[6] Atkinson interrogates the inherently political nature of lesbianism, suggesting that affective and erotic object choices themselves do not necessarily make a politics, but that lesbianism has occupied a politically significant structural position within feminism: "[B]ecause of their particularly unique attempt at revolt, the lesbian role within the male/female class system becomes critical. Lesbianism is the 'criminal' zone, what I call the 'buffer' zone, between the two major classes comprising the sex class system. The 'buffer' has both a unique nature and function within the system. And it is crucial that both lesbians and feminists understand the strategical significance of lesbianism to feminism."[7] In Atkinson's analysis, the liminal lesbian position, the "buffer," becomes strategic turf: it is the battlefield of actual feminist practice, the space intervening between "oppressor" and "oppressed," men and women. Semantically, however, within the discursive structure of Atkinson's vision, lesbians are not women, nor are they men, feminists, oppressors, or oppressed; they exist, as dykes so often have, as the mark of the difference between feminists and their oppressors. Significantly, lesbians themselves manage to elude definition, categorization, political importance, even inclusion in this framework. That both "lesbians" and "feminists" must understand the crucial significance of lesbianism to feminism sacrifices lesbian interests to a larger feminist cause. Nowhere are lesbians supposed to consider the significance of feminists; they are simply assumed to *be* feminists. Despite Atkinson's comment that feminists should fight to the death for lesbians, she more frequently assumes the opposite logic: she sees lesbians as the front line of the feminist army. Feminism, for Atkinson, regardless of its radical politics, is a heterosexual movement; dykes exist merely to facilitate, protect, and maintain the larger movement. Unlike the Radicalesbians, for whom lesbianism is feminist theory in its purest form, for Atkinson lesbianism is a means to an end, a strategic position on a much larger battleground.

Atkinson's interest in the concept of lesbianism originates in the persistence of homophobic invective against feminists: "[F]rom the outset of the Movement, most men automatically called all feminists 'lesbians.' This connection was so widespread and consistent that I began to wonder myself if maybe men didn't perceive some connection the Movement was overlooking."[8] Atkinson, like the Radicalesbians, wonders why feminism engenders this response: "Generally speaking, the Movement has reacted defensively to the charge of lesbianism: 'No, I'm not!' 'Yes, you are!' 'No, I'm not!' 'Prove it.' For myself I was so puzzled about the connection that I became curious. . . . Whenever the enemy keeps lobbing bombs into some area you consider unrelated to your defense, it's always worth investigating."[9] As Miriam Schnier points out in a recent discussion of the Radicalesbians, "The lesbian issue continued to generate personal and ideological splits among feminists—including among radical feminists—that sisterhood could not always surmount. Lesbians and straights both played a part in this unfortunate turn of events: Some straight feminists were afraid of being labeled dykes and wished to dissociate both the movement and themselves from lesbianism, while some lesbians claimed that lesbianism was an example of feminism in action and preached that the only true feminists were those who renounced relations with the opposite sex entirely."[10] Rather than disavow the label "dyke," Atkinson attempts to appropriate it as "buffer": within her theoretical paradigm, lesbians exist on the front line of the gender wars. The logic here is that of a speech act: the men lobbing the explosive word *dyke* succeed in labeling all practicing feminists as dykes. Atkinson assumes that those who are called dykes necessarily become dykes, whether in theory or in practice. And within her vision of feminist activism, these dykes will be sacrificed, in theory or in practice, for a feminist utopian vision.

DYKE: *The application thus varies between "ditch, dug out place," and "mound formed by throwing up the earth," and may include both.*

Split between defensive responses to internalized homophobia and the political logic of separatism, feminist definitions of *lesbian* during the early 1980s were marked by a noteworthy ambivalence toward questions of sexual practice and erotic pleasure: lesbianism, when it entered into definitions of *feminism* at all, entered almost exclusively as a political ideal, undistinguished by any real erotic significance. In Adrienne Rich's landmark essay "Compulsory Heterosexuality and Lesbian Existence," which appeared in the journal *Signs* in 1980, Rich's articulation of a "lesbian continuum" indicated a significant development in popular feminist attempts at self-definition. Interrogating heterosexuality as a vestigial structure of patriarchal power, Rich argued, in the tradition of early political lesbians, that "the denial of reality and visibility to women's passion for women, women's choice of women as allies, life companions, and community, the forcing of such relationships into dissimulation and their disintegration under intense pressure have meant an incalculable loss to the power of all women *to change the social relations of the sexes, to liberate ourselves and each other.*"[11] In the terms of Rich's argument, feminists historically have been their own worst enemies, thwarting their own political agendas through their failure to truly challenge "the social relations of the sexes." Rich suggests that homophobia informs feminists' unwillingness to ally themselves fully—politically, personally, or intellectually—with lesbians, duplicating the oppression of women more generally under patriarchal power structures and undermining the viability of all feminist theory. Recalling the Radicalesbians' argument about the need to theorize heterosexuality rigorously, not as a "natural" category but as a complex and problematic construct, Rich modifies their concluding exhortation of lesbianism as the feminist political ideal through the development of two strategic arguments.

The first, which encompasses the mission statement of Rich's essay, calls for a more comprehensive and rigorous feminist theory that takes into consideration all forms of erotic, political, and intellectual individuality; extending a critique of Dorothy Dinnerstein to feminist theory as a whole, Rich writes: "[Dinnerstein] ignores, specifically, the history of women who—as witches, *femmes seules,* marriage resisters, spinsters, autonomous widows, and/or lesbians—have managed on various levels *not* to collaborate. It is this history, precisely, from which feminists have so much to learn and on which there is overall such blanketing silence" (230). Rich's form of feminist theory would have at its center the interrogation of "compulsory heterosexuality":

"The assumption that 'most women are innately heterosexual' stands as a theoretical and political stumbling block for feminism. . . . [T]he failure to examine heterosexuality as an institution is like failing to admit that the economic system called capitalism or the caste system of racism is maintained by a variety of forces, including both physical violence and false consciousness" (238–39). Calling for a rigorous analysis of the power dynamics at stake in compulsory heterosexuality, Rich is sharply critical of feminist unwillingness to consider the full range of sexual diversity. Her suggestion that this analysis would be anxiety-producing because feminists themselves have something at stake in the institution of heterosexuality recalls the Radicalesbians' arguments about the political inconsistencies in most attempts to combine feminist theory with a bourgeois, heterosexual life. But Rich stops short of calling for political lesbianism, insisting instead on a feminist theoretical analysis of issues previously hidden by assumptions of normative heterosexuality.

In fact, Rich's second argument represents a neat appropriation of the anxieties that inevitably seem to accompany discussions of political lesbianism. She argues, through a radical expansion of the term "lesbian," that all feminists—in fact, all women—are already lesbians; "feminist" thus becomes a subset of "lesbian," rather than the other way around:

> I mean the term *lesbian continuum* to include a range—through each woman's life and throughout history—of woman-identified experience, not simply the fact that a woman has had or consciously desired genital sexual experience with another woman. If we expand it to embrace many more forms of primary intensity between and among women, including the sharing of a rich inner life, the bonding against male tyranny, the giving and receiving of practical and political support, if we can also hear it in such associations as *marriage resistance* and the "haggard" behavior identified by Mary Daly (obsolete meanings: "intractable," "willful," "wanton," and "unchaste," "a woman reluctant to yield to wooing"), we begin to grasp breadths of female history and psychology which have lain out of reach as a consequence of limited, mostly clinical, definitions of *lesbianism*. (239; emphases in original)[12]

Rich's identification of the "lesbian continuum" is the logical yield of her interrogation of compulsory heterosexuality. She emphasizes the fact that the deconstruction of the assumptions and dynamics informing compulsory heterosexuality will bring into view many forms of profound interconnection among women, connections that have always existed but that have been obscured from view by assumptions of normative heterosexuality. In naming these relationships "lesbian," Rich accommodates and thus begins to value women's relationships with one another across a wide range of be-haviors that presumably includes, but is not limited to, the erotic: "As the term *lesbian* has been held to limiting, clinical associations in its patriarchal definition, female friendship and comradeship have been set apart from the erotic, thus limiting the erotic itself" (240).

In addition to the notion of the lesbian continuum and the critique of compulsory heterosexuality, the other significant innovation of Rich's argu-ment is its shift in the locus of activism. Identifying her task as a primarily critical one, Rich targets an audience composed principally of feminist aca-demics. She identifies literary criticism, as well as related modes of historical and social-scientific research, as central to feminist praxis and instrumen-tal to the process of locating the lesbian continuum; literary critics and other academics possess the ability to produce a more accurate version of women's history. Significantly, however, even as Rich empowers academ-ics within feminist activism, academics are also a target of her critique: she condemns "the virtual or total neglect of lesbian existence in a wide range of writings, including feminist scholarship" (229). By the early 1980s, liter-ary criticism was ground zero in what was previously a grassroots political movement, as academic work, especially in the humanities, was increasingly claimed as a form of activist intervention. Rich's focus on literary criticism constructs feminist politics as a battleground of metacriticism; the issues at stake concern not only the practicalities of feminist critique in the world at large but also the novels of Colette, Charlotte Brontë, and Toni Morrison, and the theoretical paradigms of Mary Daly, Catharine MacKinnon, and Nancy Chodorow. Focusing on the historical period from which Rich's essay emerged, Jane Gallop, in the book *Around 1981: Academic Feminist Literary Theory*, argues that, in the early 1980s, feminism "entered the heart of a contradiction": "It became secure and prospered in the academy while feminism as a social movement was encountering major setbacks in a climate of new conservatism. The Reagan-Bush years began; the ERA was defeated. In the American academy feminism gets more and more respect while in the larger society women cannot call themselves feminist."[13] Under-scoring Gallop's argument regarding the yawning divide between academic feminism and the lives of women "in the larger society," bell hooks, writing in *Feminist Theory from Margin to Center* (1984), saw academic discourse as part of the problem, alienating mainstream women from feminist activ-ism: "The ability to 'translate' ideas to an audience that varies in age, sex, ethnicity, degree of literacy is a skill feminist educators need to develop. Concentration of feminist educators in universities encourages habitual use of an academic style that may make it impossible for teachers to communi-cate effectively with individuals who are not familiar with either academic style or jargon."[14] Hooks's critique of self-conscious academic language extends from the same metacritical impulse as Rich's critical rereading of feminist texts for their prescriptions of compulsory heterosexuality. But hooks's target audience is somewhat different from Rich's; hooks sees the exclusionary language of academic feminism as part of a problematic system of oppressive power relationships relating to race, class, and gender. Hooks argues that feminists, far from escaping the pernicious implications of these power relations, consistently duplicate those power relations in their blindness to and exclusion of women of color and poor women. Whereas Rich's critique focuses on assumptions of normative heterosexuality, hooks's focuses on assumptions of normative white middle-class status:

> White women who dominate feminist discourse today rarely question whether or not their perspective on women's reality is true to the lived experiences of women as a collective group. Nor are they aware of the extent to which their perspectives reflect race and class biases, although there has been a greater awareness of biases in recent years. Racism abounds in the writings of white feminists, reinforcing white supremacy and negating the possibility that women will bond politically across ethnic and racial boundaries. Past feminist refusal to draw attention to and attack racial hierarchies suppressed the link between race and class. (3)

Given hooks's useful insistence on sex, race, and class discrimination as symptoms of larger systemic problems, it is noteworthy that discrimination based on sexuality drops out of her larger structure of critique. Hooks is deeply concerned that feminist theory address issues across lines of race and class, but to do so, she argues, feminism must begin to disassociate itself from its image as a movement consisting primarily of lesbians; she sees feminism as a movement dominated by dykes at the expense of diversity. Hooks is sharply critical of what she perceives as the facile equation of lesbian sexuality with political correctness: "[W]omen who are not lesbians, who may or may not be in relationships with men, feel that they are not 'real' feminists. This is especially true of women who may support feminism but who do not publicly support lesbian rights" (151).

Unwilling to apply the same critique to homophobia that she does to racism, hooks exhorts feminists to "diversify" the public face of feminism by making clear that feminists are not necessarily lesbians or man haters. In hooks's view, the failure of feminism to become a truly massive social movement inheres in its anxiety-producing association with nonhetero sexualities:

> My point is that feminism will never appeal to a mass-based group of women in our society who are heterosexual if they think that they will be

looked down upon or seen as doing something wrong. . . . Just as feminist movement to end sexual oppression should create a social climate in which lesbians and gay men are no longer oppressed, a climate in which their sexual choices are affirmed, it should also create a climate in which heterosexual practice is freed from the constraints of heterosexism and can also be affirmed. One of the practical reasons for doing this is the recognition that the advancement of feminism as a political movement depends on the involvement of masses of women, a vast majority of whom are heterosexual. As long as feminist women (be they celibate, lesbian, heterosexual, etc.) condemn male sexuality, and by extension women who are involved sexually with men, feminist movement is undermined. (153)

The rhetoric of comprehensive, systemic analysis of power relations has shifted by this point to a more coercive rhetoric of marketing: "feminism will never appeal to a mass-based group of women in our society who are heterosexual *if* . . ." Although hooks claims concern here for the discriminatory assumptions of heterosexism, nowhere else does she suggest that feminist theory pander to the comfort of the "vast majority" in exchange for a rigorous consideration of the rights and the existence of an endangered minority.

My critique of hooks's position is not a new one; in fact, the preceding quotation is part of hooks's response to "lesbian feminist Cheryl Clarke," whose remarks in an essay titled "The Failure to Transform: Homophobia in the Black Community" hooks herself quotes: "Hooks delivers a backhanded slap at lesbian feminists, a considerable number of whom are black. Hooks would have done well to attack the institution of heterosexuality as it is a prime cause of black women's oppression in America."[15] Hooks replies, "Clearly Clarke misunderstands and misinterprets my point. I made no reference to heterosexism and it is the equation of heterosexual practice with heterosexism that makes it appear that Clarke is attacking the practice itself and not only heterosexism" (153). Clarke's point, reminiscent of Rich, that hooks should examine "the institution of heterosexuality" is revealingly translated by hooks directly into "heterosexism": it is not Clarke but hooks who makes the equation of heterosexual practice with heterosexism.[16] The question of the problematic institutional dynamics of heterosexuality is neatly subsumed under this equation; hooks's discussion continues on into a critique of feminist heterophobic impulses, in defense of "the choice women make to be heterosexual" (154). Heterosexuality, not normally seen as an endangered category, makes a strange bedfellow with the other forms of oppression and exclusion hooks treats in this text, including racial and class prejudice. Hooks's heterosexuality is vulnerable, defensive, embattled, but ironically her need to defend heterosexual practice duplicates a function of the "dyke": she is eager to set up protective walls around heterosexuality, thus liberating women everywhere into the radical freedom of heterosexual object choice. In another twist of irony, hooks begins to set up dykes to defend against dykes.

Hooks's logic at this point is complicated, for several reasons. In her larger argument, her desire to ensure that feminists are consistent in their critique of any form of compulsory sexuality, whether gay or straight, is a direct extension of powerful early feminist critiques of limiting patriarchal roles for women. However, in a book critiquing feminist marginalizations of women of color, it is strange that hooks's analysis of phobic exclusionary practices should fail to extend to her discussion of sexuality. The apparent suggestion that feminists should disassociate themselves—at least publicly—from the issue of lesbian sexuality seems linked to another paradigm of the 1970s: the antifeminist rhetoric that labeled feminists, often arbitrarily, as "dykes," intimidating through the invocation of internalized homophobia. Instead of reading "mass-based" anxiety about lesbianism as a need for "mass-based" education about forms of prejudice that are as pernicious in the case of sexuality as in the case of race, hooks seems to suggest that feminists need only change the window dressing in order to appeal to a wider range of women; her feminist paradigm seems to sacrifice sexual diversity in the cause of racial diversity, and she bars altogether the possibility that lesbians of color might exist. This platform clearly returns to the scene of the "lavender menace" and the backlash against the suggestion that the marketing of the feminist movement must occur under the aegis of a normative sexuality.

Although Barbara Smith echoes hooks's sharp criticism of white middle-class feminist narcissism in "Toward a Black Feminist Criticism," she does not see the interests of black women and lesbians as mutually exclusive or even competitive, insisting on the importance of a feminist discourse that considers race and sexuality together: "Long before I tried to write this I realized that I was attempting something unprecedented, something dangerous, merely by writing about Black women writers from a feminist perspective and about Black lesbian writers from any perspective at all. . . . All segments of the literary world—whether establishment, progressive, Black, female, or lesbian—do not know, or at least act as if they do not know, that Black women writers and Black lesbian writers exist."[17] Jane Gallop claims, in a discussion of *The New Feminist Criticism* (the anthology in which Smith's essay is reprinted), that feminist criticism of the early and mid-1980s struggled explicitly with problems of self-definition and with issues of inclusion and exclusion.[18] Judith Roof has argued that in feminist anthologies published in the mid-1980s, "the myriad differences among women are often reduced to the formula 'black and lesbian.' . . . I suspect that this . . . critical reliance upon black and lesbian is symptomatic of some underlying critical difficulty with multiplicity."[19] Roof suggests, usefully, that feminists read such tropes of association by analogy as the sign of efforts to address feminist pluralism: "For feminist critics, the decade of the 1980s has been occupied with the attempt to recognize and comprehend the multiple differences that exist among women and to work these different perspectives into a feminist methodology that can allow and theorize multiplicity while remaining politically and intellectually effective."[20] There's a flip side to this logic, too, Roof suggests. The "black and lesbian" analogy proliferates so conspicuously in literary-critical anthologies from the mid-1980s that it demarcates just as much a feminist resistance or defensiveness to the new demands of multiplicity as it does an attempt to theorize the implications of that multiplicity. Within the discourses of feminist theory and criticism of the mid-1980s, the categories "black" and "lesbian" demarcate similar modes of "difference," both existing, in most cases, as "other than" a norm. The white middle-class heterosexual assumptions of that norm are made visible only through the tension produced by the defining presence of the other.

> DYKE: *A mass of mineral matter, usually igneous rock, filling up a fissure in the original strata, and sometimes rising from these like a mound or wall, when they have been worn down by denudation*

Roof's productive focus on the historical epoch of 1985 isolates an extremely sensitive moment in feminist history, when the articulation of "difference" presented multiple, and at times apparently competing, claims on the category "woman." Such discourses of difference developed rapidly as the 1980s progressed, to the extent that terms of race and sexuality were equated less persistently. But the contentious question of dykes continued, throughout this period, to serve a uniquely definitional function for feminist theory. In the early 1980s, feminism was faced with a central division: some critics argued that feminism was all about—too much about—lesbianism and lesbian sexuality; others argued that the heterosexist bias in feminist discourse betrayed itself constantly in the marginalization and the silencing of lesbians and lesbian writers. This particular dyke shaped the peculiar path of feminist discourse in the second half of the 1980s.

Literary theory more generally was reinfused with a politics of activism in the mid-1980s; as the AIDS epidemic ravaged the gay male community, many critics turned to the complexities, discourses, and representation of male homoeroticism with a sense of political urgency unseen since the early days of the women's movement. Using the tools of feminist theory, literary theorists began to focus on homosexuality through the newly repoliticized discourses of masculinity. Interestingly and ironically, this development created yet another dyke in the world of literary criticism: although lesbians belonged to the gay rights movement and the feminist movement, suddenly they were centrally implicated in neither. Although questions of homosexuality were central to both feminist and gay male discourses, they were primarily questions of male homosexuality. Lesbians existed at the discursive margins, in and as the space between these two newly prominent theoretical positions.

Through the middle 1980s, the central terms of feminist literary theory underwent a significant paradigm shift, refocusing from a concern with the politics of female sex and sexuality to a theoretically broader concern with the notion of gender. As Elaine Showalter points out in the introduction to the anthology *Speaking of Gender*, which appeared in 1989, "[T]alking about gender means talking about both women and men": "The introduction of gender into the field of literary studies marks a new phase in feminist criticism, an investigation of the ways that all reading and writing, by men as well as by women, is marked by gender. Talking about gender, moreover, is a constant reminder of the other categories of difference, such as race and class, that structure our lives and texts, just as theorizing gender emphasizes the parallels between feminist criticism and other forms of minority discourse."[21] The rise of gender studies during the 1980s served practical as well as theoretical functions. Among other things, it opened the doors of feminist theory unambiguously to male practitioners and, as Showalter points out, presented a more sophisticated notion of the ways in which language and power converge to shape a speaking subject, whether "male" or "female." The focus on gender further served to dismantle monolithic notions of "maleness" and "femaleness" per se, in exchange for a theory of gender as cultural construct, symptomatically reflecting larger cultural investments.

Gender theory has proved both invigorating and problematic for more conventional feminist political concerns. As Showalter notes, "[S]ome readers . . . worry that 'gender studies' could be a pallid assimilation of feminist criticism into the mainstream (or male stream) of English studies, a return to the old priorities and binary oppositions that will reinstate familiar male canons while crowding hard-won courses on women writers out of the curriculum. Others fear that talking about gender is a way for both male and female critics to avoid the political commitment of feminism. Still others raise the troubling possibility that gender will be isolated from issues of class and race."[22] As Showalter suggests, many feminists were and remain concerned that to forsake the focus on "women" in favor of a broader focus on "gender" is to retrench feminist inroads in the academy; if there is no longer any basis for a practical concern for and with women specifically, they ask, then what is the difference between the academy now and the academy before early feminist pioneers appeared on the horizon? The generalization outward of feminist political and theoretical interests reflects a different understanding of the ways in which structures of gender and sexuality are supported; in a poststructuralist theoretical universe that privileges indeterminacy, to talk about "women" alone is, in some sense, to return to an artificial and potentially simplistic means of categorization. Yet this artifice is belied by the materialist concerns of patriarchal class politics: the opening out of feminist theory into gender theory certainly risks the reinstitutionalization of male-centered concerns, even as it represents an enriched understanding of gender categories as mutually constitutive.

Feminist ventures in gender theory constantly engage this ambivalence. The important linkage of feminist and gay male theories of discourse and narrative was facilitated by several prominent feminist critics, who were necessarily prompted at every turn to theorize, even to justify, the gender politics of their methodologies. For example, Eve Kosofsky Sedgwick, in the groundbreaking study *Between Men: English Literature and Male Homosocial Desire*, both avows a feminist methodology and defends her exclusive focus on male subjectivity and male homosociality. In her introduction, Sedgwick discusses "the isolation, not to mention the absolute subordination, of women, in the structural paradigm on which this study is based": "The absence of lesbianism from the book was an early and, I think, necessary decision, since my argument is structured around the distinctive relation of the male homosocial spectrum to the transmission of unequally distributed power. Nevertheless, the exclusively heterosexual perspective of the book's attention to women is seriously impoverishing in itself."[23] Profoundly feminist in its methodology, Sedgwick's rereading of Freud, Girard, and the structure of triangulated desire does not offer a deeper understanding of the place of the woman in that structure but, instead, demonstrates implications of the vector connecting its two male subjects, in a rich analysis of the male homosocial relations previously concealed by assumptions of normative heterosexuality. The payoff to Sedgwick's work on male homosociality is an understanding of patriarchy itself as a male homosocial construct mediated through what Gayle Rubin influentially described as the "traffic in women."[24]

Sedgwick's analytical model implies a noteworthy distinction in the status of male and female homosocial and homoerotic relations in patriarchal culture. Her work on the contingencies by which patriarchy is constituted advances an important feminist project. But the lone theoretical distinction Sedgwick makes between male and female homoeroticism is a significant one; she justifies her focus on the distinction between homosociality and homosexuality in men based on the fact that it is more of a distinction for men than for women:

> The diacritical opposition between the "homosocial" and the "homosexual" seems to be much less thorough and dichotomous for women, in our society, than for men. At this particular historical moment, an intelligible continuum of aims, emotions, and valuations links lesbianism with the other forms of women's attention to women: the bond of mother and daughter, for instance, the bond of sister and sister, women's friendship, "networking," and the active struggles of feminism. The continuum is crisscrossed with deep discontinuities—with much homophobia, with conflicts of race and class—but its intelligibility seems now a matter of simple common sense.[25]

Writing off the theoretical complexity, even the specific discernibility, of lesbian erotic desire as "simple common sense," Sedgwick inaugurates an era in which feminist practitioners fixate on male homoeroticism as an interesting problematic while dismissively relegating the "dyke" to the outer reaches of feminist discourse. Implicitly accepting Rich's notion of the "lesbian continuum" as theoretically exhaustive, Sedgwick ironically reinscribes the very problem Rich was hoping to dismantle, for Rich was concerned with precisely "how and why women's choice of women as passionate comrades, life partners, co-workers, lovers, community has been crushed, invalidated, forced into hiding and disguise," as well as with "the virtual or total neglect of lesbian existence in a wide range of writings, including feminist scholarship." Rich startlingly predicted a predicament redescribed a decade later: "I believe that much feminist theory and criticism is stranded on this shoal."[26]

In *The Apparitional Lesbian: Female Homosexuality and Modern Culture*, Terry Castle explores Sedgwick's resistance to, or "blockage" against, any form of rigorous consideration of female homosexuality:

> Lesbians, defined . . . with telling vagueness only as "women who love women," are really no different, Sedgwick seems to imply, from "women promoting the interests of other women." Their way of bonding is so "congruent" with that of other women, it turns out, that one need no longer call it homosexual. "The adjective 'homosocial' as applied to women's bonds," [Sedgwick] concludes, *"need not be pointedly dichotomized as against 'homosexual'; it can intelligibly denominate the entire continuum."* By a disarming sleight of phrase, an entire category of women—lesbians—is lost to view.[27]

Castle's objection to Sedgwick's "uncharacteristically sentimental" reliance on the continuum metaphor (71) indicates a major problem in conventional feminist analyses of homoeroticism. Castle's critique implicitly returns to and begins to trouble Rich's notion of the "lesbian continuum," which pointedly desexualizes lesbianism in favor of a more panfeminist vision of meaningful engagement among women. Castle's discomfort with the lesbian continuum betokens a new negotiation for feminist theory: a theoretical practice that interrogates the specificity of male homoerotic desire cannot rely complacently on a notion of lesbianism that is vague, deliberately broad, and explicitly detached from any form of eroticism or desire whatsoever. Rich's argument for the lesbian continuum was the product of a specific historical moment and served several important functions within the discourse of feminist theory, particularly in its defusing of the term "lesbian" and its situation of feminist methodology firmly in the center of a literary-critical disciplinary practice. However, as Castle implies, Rich's project is not the lesbian equivalent to the carefully theorized analysis of male homosociality that Sedgwick conducts in *Between Men* and elsewhere. Indeed, Rich's essay announces as its goal the more rigorous inclusion of lesbians throughout the range of academic discourses; thus, Sedgwick's appropriation of Rich in order to justify the exclusion of lesbians represents a perfect example of the phenomenon Rich hoped to counteract.

Pursuing the implications of Castle's argument, I would agree that feminists, working from the heritage of such broad definitions as Rich's lesbian continuum, are quick to assume that they already fully understand "lesbianism," most conventionally as something inherently feminist or as something having to do with (not necessarily sexual) female bonding. Accompanying this model are assumptions that lesbianism is only occasionally or tangentially related to sex and sexual pleasure. These assumptions are engendered in part by the history, within feminism, of a political lesbianism that constructs lesbianism as a separatist opting out of patriarchy rather than an erotic object choice. They are also facilitated by historical conventions of female friendship, or "Boston marriage," which again are perceived as related more to women's mutual empathy than to mutual erotic pleasure. These assumptions suggest a dramatic historical difference in cultural perceptions of female and male homosexuality. From gay liberation to queer theory, analyses of male homosexuality have rarely assumed that eroticism, sexual attraction, and sex acts, covert or explicit, are marginal or irrelevant issues. Following Sedgwick's lead, feminist and queer analyses of polymorphous sexualities ironically continue to fixate on problems of male homoeroticism because of the perception that these relations are somehow underexplored and/or more complex than female homoeroticism. In turn, lesbianism is too often dismissed as either coextensive with any sort of feminist practice or completely accessible within any conventional understanding of female friendship. "What may appear 'intelligible' or 'simple common sense' to a nonlesbian critic," writes Castle, "will hardly seem quite so simple to any female reader who has ever attempted to walk down a city street holding hands with, let alone kissing or embracing, another woman": "The homosexual panic elicited by women publicly signaling their sexual interest in one another continues, alas, even 'at this particular historical moment,' to be just as virulent as that inspired by male homosexuality, if not more so. To obscure the fact that lesbians are women who have sex with each other—and that this is not exactly the same, in the eyes of society, as voting for women or giving them jobs—is, in essence, not to acknowledge the separate peril and pleasure of lesbian existence" (71–72). Explicitly detaching lesbianism from the broader concerns of feminism in general, Castle returns to Rich again, this time replacing the term that Sedgwick appropriates, "lesbian continuum," with the term that Rich uses in her title, the far more insistent and aggressive "lesbian existence." With this gesture, Castle begins to call for an analysis of female homosexuality, not homosociality, that accounts for the sexual pleasure and personal danger that accompany living as a lesbian. In response to Sedgwick's contention that male homosociality is the figure of patriarchal power, Castle suggests the insurgent potential of a theory of lesbian desire: "To theorize about female-female desire . . . is precisely to envision the taking apart of this supposedly intractable patriarchal structure. Female bonding, at least hypothetically, destabilizes the 'canonical' triangular arrangement of male desire, is an affront to it, and ultimately—in the radical form of lesbian bonding—displaces it entirely" (72).[28]

Castle's discomfort with the feminist absorption of lesbian concerns is also reflected, albeit somewhat differently, in the initial theoretical formulation of "queer theory," which appeared in a 1991 special issue of the journal *differences* titled "Lesbian and Gay Sexualities." Again, the voice behind this formulation is that of a prominent feminist, Teresa de Lauretis. In her introduction to this issue, de Lauretis notes that whereas gay male and lesbian discourses have evolved along basically separate paths in the past, recent critical tendencies to see them as versions of one phenomenon, "lesbian and gay" (ladies first, of course), threaten to erase the specificity of that history: "[O]ur 'differences,' such as they may be, are less represented by the discursive coupling of those two terms in the politically correct phrase 'lesbian and gay,' than they are elided by most of the contexts in which the phrase is used; that is to say, differences are implied in it but then simply taken for granted or even covered over by the word 'and.'"[29] Thus occurred the birth of "queer theory," a metacritical praxis that is "intended to mark a certain critical distance" from the formulaic and reductive phrase "lesbian and gay." "Queer theory," writes de Lauretis, "conveys a double emphasis—on the conceptual and speculative work involved in discourse production, and on the necessary critical work of deconstructing our own discourses and their constructed silences."[30] By definition a self-interrogating methodology, queer theory is conditioned by a tradition of oppression, erasure, and silence to constantly examine its own "constructed silences."

De Lauretis's logic is both provocative and problematic. To replace a phrase like "lesbian and gay" with a phrase like "queer theory" is quite literally to cover over any notion of lesbian and gay difference, to subsume male and female homosexuality within the single, potentially monolithic category "queer," to depend on the self-policing integrity of queer theorists to deconstruct "our own discourses and their constructed silences." In its ideal form, queer theory would be a constantly self-interrogating practice and, through that self-interrogation, would succeed in retaining the specificity of lesbian and gay histories while also exploring the theoretical complexity of lesbian and gay difference. However, the replacement of a plural term—"lesbian and gay"—with a singular term—"queer"—appears to counteract de Lauretis's desire for increased specificity. And, as queer theory begins to articulate itself as a practice distinct from feminist theory, the question of women, and particularly the question of lesbians, is persistently sidelined.

In the introduction to *Epistemology of the Closet,* Sedgwick addresses the question of a specifically lesbian-centered theoretical practice: "It seems inevitable to me that the work of defining the circumferential boundaries, vis-à-vis lesbian experience and identity, of any gay male-centered theoretical articulation can be done only from the point of view of an alternative, feminocentric theoretical space, not from the heart of the male-centered project itself."[31] Within the context of a book that is quite explicitly at "the heart of the male-centered project itself," Sedgwick's discussion of a lesbian implication to gay male theory demonstrates ambivalence. Although this introduction gives a nod, like the introduction to *Between Men,* to the urgent necessity for "feminocentric theoretical space," the place of lesbians in *Epistemology of the Closet* is, at best, marginal. Acknowledging lesbian activists' work in the AIDS epidemic, Sedgwick writes, "The newly virulent homophobia of the 1980s, directed alike against women and men even though its medical pretext ought, if anything, logically to give a relative exemptive privilege to lesbians, reminds urgently that it is more to friends than to enemies that gay women and gay men are perceptible as distinct groups" (38). Though Sedgwick acknowledges only in a footnote that lesbians, too, are vulnerable to AIDS, she emphasizes the fact that gay and

AIDS activism are indebted to lesbian practitioners and feminist theories: "The contributions of lesbians to current gay and AIDS activism are weighty, not despite, but because of the intervening lessons of feminism. Feminist perspectives on medicine and health-care issues, on civil disobedience, and on the politics of class and race as well as of sexuality have been centrally enabling for the recent waves of AIDS activism. What this activism returns to the lesbians involved in it may include a more richly pluralized range of imaginings of lines of gender and sexual identification" (38–39). Sedgwick is significantly vague about the yield of lesbian investment; that activism "*may* include a more richly pluralized range of imaginings" seems tepid consolation within a context of "virulent homophobia." Sedgwick is cautionary about the tendency of gay male discourse to "subsume" lesbian "experience and definition":

> The "gay theory" I have been comparing with feminist theory doesn't mean exclusively gay male theory, but for the purpose of this comparison it includes lesbian theory insofar as that (a) isn't simply coextensive with feminist theory (i.e., doesn't subsume sexuality *fully* under gender) and (b) doesn't a priori deny all theoretical continuity between male homosexuality and lesbianism. But, again, the extent, construction, and meaning, and especially the history of any such theoretical continuity—not to mention its consequences for practical politics—must be open to every interrogation. (39; emphasis in original)

Sedgwick, like de Lauretis, is always careful to argue that male and female homosexuality are very different phenomena, a useful and critical point. In fact, in this passage, as Sedgwick tries to articulate a sufficiently specific and differentiated theoretical agenda for her text, she recurs to an implicit structure of triangulation: gay male theoretical concerns, lesbian theoretical concerns, and feminist theoretical concerns are all related yet distinct entities. Once again, the "dyke" operates as the border, the literal site of connection and distinction between feminist and "gay" concerns in general. But, as with all triangulated structures, as Sedgwick has demonstrated, one term is inevitably subordinated in favor of a dynamic connection between the other two. In Sedgwick's *Epistemology of the Closet,* as in *Between Men,* the coincidence of feminist methodology and gay male subject matter consistently produces lesbian concerns as that third term, emerging occasionally, marginally, and primarily in introductory matter. This is one example of a larger critical phenomenon in which, once again, the dyke demarcates the border of internal and external: she offers a frame of reference, but she herself is not in the picture.

Risking the inevitable pun, I would argue that although feminist theory engendered queer theory, the two remain distinct. By now the dualism that so profoundly shaped feminist discourse at the end of the 1970s and into the early 1980s has been literalized in the separate entities of feminist and queer scholarship. But what has been factored out, oddly enough, is the specificity of lesbian discourse: caught between the feminist and the queer, the lesbian again occupies the problematic third position in the triangle of contemporary critical discourse. And, as with the triangular structure posited in Sedgwick's early analysis, the third term is not the one that counts; the animate connection is the one between feminists and queers, and the third term, the site of connection and disjunction, marks the space between without signifying itself. Lesbians occupy the subordinated place of the woman in the structure of triangular desire in which the primary desiring relationship is constituted between feminists and queers.

Back in 1980, in "Compulsory Heterosexuality and Lesbian Existence," Rich produced what seems today a startlingly prescient commentary: "Lesbians have historically been deprived of a political existence through 'inclusion' as female versions of male homosexuality. To equate lesbian existence with male homosexuality because each is stigmatized is to erase female reality once again."[32] Equated not only with male homosexuals but with feminism in its most generalized form, lesbians remain consistently—and paradoxically—marginalized. And as a marginalized population, dykes serve a useful function within the context of feminist and queer theories alike, acting as the border against which the mainstream can define itself. The specific location of that margin, that "dyke," reveals particular, often shifting engagements within theoretical discourses as they struggle to define themselves, their constituencies, their politics, and their activisms. The dyke marks the space of margin and connection, offering at once a point of view that is and is not of the central flow.

Within the metaphorical structure I have explored throughout this chapter, I have argued that feminist theory has consistently seen the dyke as marginal, protective, and contingent, facilitating the existence of a larger whole rather than independently significant. Yet the specificity of lesbian discourses and desires has independently significant value, not only as a metacritical instrument for the analysis of a broader feminist theory but also as a historically complex cultural phenomenon it its own right. Behind the metaphorical, architectural dyke is another dyke, a figure too often marginalized, too frequently and too vaguely appropriated within larger theoretical paradigms of sexuality and politics—for listed after and separated from the nearly three columns of preceding definitions of *dyke* in the *OED* is the following slang definition: "DIKE, DYKE . . . *slang*. [Of obscure origin.] A lesbian; a masculine woman."

Conclusion
Left Justified

This is the double bind of feminist theory: the effort to locate and valorize women's voices, subject positions, identities, experiences, and desires comes up against ethical resistance to the proposition that any one voice speak for the rest. The counterargument: any single explanation or point of view inevitably homogenizes and oversimplifies, falsely stylizing the impossibly intricate nuances of human gender arrangements and the power relations that follow. In this book I have highlighted salutary effects of this conundrum, suggesting that the resistance to theoretical generalization is a site of cyclical renewal for feminist politics and feminist principles. The resistance to theory, in other words, is the powerful, if perverse, substance of theory in feminist political and intellectual contexts. In theory, as in politics, the very meaning of "feminism" is negotiated through questions of voice, of the representative and representational politics of language.

This argument is concerned with the gendering of knowledge; that is, with the association of particular modes of expression with social characteristics conventionally ascribed to the masculine and the feminine. In this context, "abstraction" is often seen as a uniquely masculine mode, representative of male psychological patterns of detachment. In contrast, more concrete, contextual, or particularized modes of thought represent conventional qualities of femininity, including attachment and empathy. Such gendered associations are eroticized, too: they are frequently inscribed within a nuclear, heterosexual domestic model in which abstraction plays papa to a good mother concerned with context and detail.

Where, then, does this leave the feminist, whose theoretical labors are directed toward the revolution, or the subversion, or the revision of just such gendered associations? How might one "do" feminist theory in a way that refuses to reify the conventional hierarchies? What are the larger implications of feminist theoretical resistance within the power politics of epistemology?

Carol Gilligan is one of the many feminists whose theoretical objective has involved a challenge to conventional epistemological categories through the representation of women's social, psychological, and interpretive "difference." Gilligan's book *In a Different Voice: Psychological Theory and Women's Development* was first published in 1982, and, like many of the major theoretical texts of feminist theory, it was republished in the 1990s as part of a burgeoning effort to map the historical implications of the women's liberation movement. In a new preface produced for the 1993 reprint, Gilligan observes the women's movement with the historical benefit of hindsight, and to this end she begins, as my project has begun, with a return to 1970.

Gilligan writes, "I began writing *In a Different Voice* in the early 1970s, at a time of resurgence in the Women's Movement. College students now are incredulous when I say that in the spring of 1970, at the height of demonstrations against the Vietnam war, after the shooting of students at Kent State University by members of the National Guard, final exams were canceled at Harvard and there was no graduation. For a moment, the university came to a stop and the foundations of knowledge were opened for reexamination."[1] Because the university stopped for a moment, its orderly spring schedule stymied by antiwar demonstrations, the "foundations of knowledge" that the university traditionally represented were newly assailable. In exchange for the final exams that they expected, students found themselves an opportunity to undertake an entirely new kind of exam: a reconsideration of the categories of social reality that the university, as the embodiment of high culture and established truth, had endorsed as "normal."

Gilligan symbolically locates the birth of feminist epistemology in the tiny gap opened by the university's unprecedented silence: as I have suggested here, feminist theory and praxis alike have had an ambivalent relationship, to say the least, to the patriarchal, institutional university. However symbolic the moment of silence offered Gilligan in May 1970, though, it enabled her to mount an analysis of the standard theories of human development, identity, and morality through their relationship to the empirical data provided by studies of women and, in the course of that analysis, to offer a method of rethinking the terms by which epistemological conventions of gender and human identity have been constructed. In the book's original introduction, Gilligan wrote, "My goal is to expand the understanding of human development by using the group left out in the construction of theory to call attention to what is missing in its account. Seen in this light, the discrepant data on women's experience provide a basis upon which to generate new theory, potentially yielding a more encompassing view of the lives of both of the sexes" (3–4).

As a corrective to "old" theory, Gilligan's analysis is concerned with subtle assumptions about gender that underwrite even the most credible scientific data: "This discovery occurs when theories formerly considered to be sexually neutral in their scientific objectivity are found instead to reflect a consistent observational and evaluative bias. Then the presumed neutrality of science, like that of language itself, gives way to the recognition that the categories of knowledge are human constructions" (6). *In a Different Voice* represents an attempt to produce theory in a different voice—indeed, in a dialectical process that disclaims pretenses to omniscience or objectivity. Gilligan endorses an interpretive mode newly focused on process, privileging theories developed from the assumption of women's difference; the radical potential of her argument involves the challenge to conventional understandings of "normal" psychological and moral development posed by the value newly found in women's unique modes of self-expression. Gilligan's argument was foundational to the theoretical tradition that became known as "difference feminism."

In this effort, Gilligan, whose book features analyses of a number of literary texts as well as interpretations of data offered by the subjects of several psychological studies, joined the widespread feminist effort in the 1980s to present the interpretation of language and voice as a crucial feminist methodology. That effort, however, confronted and continues to confront the accusation that it is insufficiently radical; that it is esoteric, abstracted from the material effort to better the lives of women in need; and even, in its more arcane incarnations, that it represents feminists getting in bed with the enemy, with patriarchal high culture. Gilligan's book is characteristically ambivalent about its epistemological authority: published by Harvard University Press and generalizing from samples of well-educated, usually white, usually affluent girls and women, *In a Different Voice* arguably reinforces much of what it appears to assail.

The struggle, for Gilligan, is one between the attempt to speak "in a different voice" and the need to speak in a voice that can be heard, that can be recognized, that can imaginably spark a prairie fire in the act of making its ideas and arguments available to a widespread audience. In contexts ranging from zap actions of the women's liberation movement to analyses of drag, camp, and parody that have exemplified queer theories of performativity, gender theorists have achieved that goal by getting inside conventions themselves—by subverting ideas of nature and truth from within, and in the process exposing those ideas as constructs with something at stake in maintaining the "normal" as the true and natural. Symptomatic of Gilligan's own effort to dismantle high culture from within its bounds is her book's unconventional format: the margins of each page of *In a Different Voice* are left-justified only. The book's ragged right margin epitomizes Gilligan's disavowal of a pretense to objectivity, if not of cultural authority. The symbolic effect of this irregularity is a valorization of the imperfect, the incomplete—of the process as much as the product.

In this context, Gilligan makes, and acts out, a case for gendered epistemology: "The moral imperative that emerges repeatedly in interviews with women is an injunction to care, a responsibility to discern and alleviate the 'real and recognizable trouble' of this world. For men, the moral imperative appears rather as an injunction to respect the rights of others and thus to protect from interference the rights to life and self-fulfillment" (100). Men, Gilligan continues, tend toward the hypothetical, toward abstraction, the divestment of "moral actors from the history and psychology of their individual lives," and the separation of "the moral problem from the social contingencies of its possible occurrence" (100). Women, motivated by an ethic of care and connection, demonstrate a tendency "to reconstruct hypothetical dilemmas in terms of the real, to request or to supply missing information about the nature of the people and the places where they live" (100–101). Abstraction and context, hypothetical and material: male voices and female voices, speaking differently.

My interest here in Gilligan's work is only indirectly concerned with the case it makes about the divergent thought patterns of male and female human beings, regardless of the compelling, disturbing implications of that argument. I am more immediately concerned with the unexpected effects of gendered epistemologies on the growing field of feminist theory. Gilligan argues powerfully against the exclusive valuation of male-identified logics of abstraction, and in favor of the equally important value of female-identified logics of contiguity. Yet *In a Different Voice* concludes with the classic gesture toward an ideal that is presented as new but is as old as the hills. Not surprisingly, perhaps, considering its representation of epistemological styles within the binary terms of male and female, and its stylistic and methodological gestures toward the synthesis of those gendered positions, Gilligan's argument in the end resolves into a conventional, heteronormative ideal of the happy marriage: "Through [the] expansion of perspective," Gilligan writes on the last page, "we can begin to envision how a marriage between adult development as it is currently portrayed and women's development as it begins to be seen could lead to a changed understanding of human development and a more generative view of human life" (174). Male and female are, in the end, the generative coupling, and their offspring offers a new "voice" that is the hybrid of the two genders, the two gendered modes of expression.

Second-wave feminists in the United States have struggled to produce theories that resist replicating the patriarchal hierarchies of abstraction. Such resistance often takes the form of an embrace of abstraction's opposite; and in some cases, like Gilligan's, it takes the familiar form, a symbolic marriage of two minds. But as long as abstraction and contiguity, indeed male and female, are construed as logically opposed to one another, tactics of resistance are limited within that oppositional structure, resulting in the tendency either to demonize abstraction or, as Gilligan does, to erect a theoretical ideal whose heterosexual imagery sits uncomfortably alongside feminist critiques of the heteronormative injunctions by which women are conventionally constrained.

Abstraction and contiguity. Male and female. Either/or.

In a 1999 review of four books written by the queer theorist and philosopher Judith Butler, Martha C. Nussbaum argues for a return to "old-style feminist politics and the material realities to which it was committed."[2] Nussbaum, a prominent classicist and legal scholar who has worked most recently on questions of women's and especially lesbian and gay rights in a global context,[3] analyzes Butler's representation of individual agency, what Butler terms the "ironic hopefulness" that any one person can hope to make inroads toward changing her violently deterministic culture. Butler, writes Nussbaum, contends that "there is no agent behind or prior to the social forces that produce the self":

> If this means only that babies are born into a gendered world that begins to replicate males and females almost immediately, the claim is plausible, but not surprising: experiments have for some time demonstrated that the way babies are held and talked to, the way their emotions are described, [is] profoundly shaped by the sex the adults in question believe the child to have. . . . Butler shows no interest in these empirical facts, but they do support her contention. . . . If she means, however, that babies enter the world completely inert, with no tendencies and no abilities that are in some sense prior to their experience in a gendered society, this is far less plausible, and difficult to support empirically. Butler offers no such support, preferring to remain on the high plane of metaphysical abstraction. (41)

Critiquing Butler on the grounds of her investment in "metaphysical abstraction," Nussbaum subtly constructs as abstraction's opposite not only the empirical but the empirical embodied in the person of an infant. Continuing, Nussbaum writes, "One would like to see [Butler] engage with the strongest forms of [empirical arguments in favor of material agency], and to say, clearly and without jargon, exactly why and where she rejects them. One would also like to hear her speak about real infants, who do appear to manifest a structure of striving that influences from the start their reception of cultural forms" (42).

Once again, infancy, the offspring born of—but also somehow prior to—cultural influence, emerges as a feminist epistemological ideal. What Nussbaum wants from Butler is clear speech—the rejection of jargon and (correspondingly?) a discussion of "babies." In some sense, Butler, on the basis of her theoretical style, stands accused of being a not-good-enough mother whose vulnerable infants are neglected in favor of a promiscuous dalliance with abstraction. Indeed, the indictment of Butler's abstract style of writing suggests a more general aberrance of gender-identification: bad theory, bad mother, bad woman, bad feminist.

In the context of Butler's influence, Nussbaum writes, "The great tragedy in the new feminist theory in America is the loss of a sense of public commitment. In this sense, Butler's self-involved feminism is extremely American, and it is not surprising that it has caught on here, where successful middle-class people prefer to focus on cultivating the self rather than thinking in a way that helps the material condition of others. Even in America, however, it is possible for theorists to be dedicated to the public good and to achieve something through that effort" (44). "The new feminist theory" is selfish and bourgeois; in its abstraction and its inability to reach beyond "the symbolic" (45), it is insufficiently "dedicated to the public good." What interests me in Nussbaum's representation of "the new feminist theory" as embodied in the person and work of Judith Butler is less Nussbaum's critique of Butler's writing style and her objections to Butler's theories of agency and identity, and more the sense in which the theoretical terms—specifically "abstraction" and its various antonyms—are *moralized*, and moralized within a framework of judgment that reinstitutes standards of acceptable, and implicitly maternal, femininity. In other words, this critique is grounded in an erotic politics that subtly aligns the queer with the abstract with the vicious, and the maternal-feminine with the material-empirical with the virtuous. Bad theory, bad mother, bad woman, bad feminist.

Describing the ethic of care, self-sacrifice, and dedication to others that constructs the bourgeois feminine ideal, Carol Gilligan writes, "The conflict between self and other thus constitutes the central moral problem for women, posing a dilemma whose resolution requires a reconciliation of femininity and adulthood. In the absence of such a reconciliation, the moral problem cannot be resolved. The 'good woman' masks assertion in evasion, denying responsibility by claiming only to meet the needs of others, while the 'bad woman' forgoes or renounces the commitments that bind her in self-deception and betrayal."[4] A woman's failure to dedicate herself sufficiently to the public good places her in violation of the moral virtues that constitute virtuous femininity: "the 'bad woman' forgoes or renounces the commitments that bind her in self-deception and betrayal." An investment in the symbolically masculine discourse of abstraction represents just such a betrayal of feminine principles. Nussbaum's review concludes with the following demonization: "Judith Butler's hip quietism is a comprehensible response to the difficulty of realizing justice in America. But it is a bad response. It collaborates with evil. Feminism demands more and women deserve better" (45).

What feminism should represent, in Nussbaum's argument, is exactly what Gilligan suggests women have always been programmed to provide: "an injunction to care, a responsibility to discern and alleviate the 'real and recognizable trouble' of this world."[5] By identifying Butler's work as "collaborat[ing] with evil" because in its abstraction it is detached from "real and recognizable trouble," Nussbaum, ironically, recycles conventions of femininity in the name of feminism: Butler is not doing theory, she suggests, in an acceptably feminine way.

Is it not a constitutive goal of feminist theory—and feminist praxis, too—to challenge the straitjackets of feminine convention? Perhaps Butler's most powerful tactical position, not only as a feminist but also as a queer, is the strategic appropriation of epistemological categories not only across lines of gender but also in terms of the heterosexual narrative conventions whose most radical vision extends only as far as the symbolic coupling of male and female.

This is to suggest the radical implications of the feminist- and queer-theoretical appropriation of abstract logic. It is also to suggest the urgent political need for continued conversations about—and resistance to—that act as potentially preserving an exclusionary and oppressive hierarchy. In an op-ed piece published in the *New York Times* shortly after Nussbaum's review of her work, and in explicit response to being awarded a "bad writer" prize by the journal *Philosophy and Literature,* Judith Butler spoke for the use of "difficult and demanding language" as part of an ethical challenge to naturalized conventions of "common sense": "If common sense sometimes preserves the social status quo, and that status quo sometimes treats unjust social hierarchies as natural, it makes good sense on such occasions to find ways of challenging common sense. Language that takes up this challenge can help point the way to a more socially just world."[6]

But, as Butler suggests later, "translations are sometimes crucial."[7] The common critique of academic feminist and queer theories involves their inaccessibility to interested readers who are not trained in the academic disciplines in question. Margaret Cruikshank, editor of the pathbreaking 1982 anthology *Lesbian Studies,* gives voice to just such a critique in her foreword to *The New Lesbian Studies,* published in 1996 and edited by Bonnie Zimmerman and Toni A. H. McNaron. Cruikshank criticizes both theoretical writing that appeals solely to cognoscenti invested in a prestigious subgenre of academic language and writers who seem unwilling—or, worse still, unable—to translate their ideas into more widely available terms or to take seriously theoretical interventions emerging from other contexts:

> One disadvantage of being out of the academic loop is that I can't understand some of the work now being published in gay and lesbian studies. It's natural for the first people in a new territory to feel baffled by newer settlers, and inevitable that the aftercomers set off on new trails. But gay and lesbian work in obscure and needlessly difficult language reminds me of priestcraft. Some scholars seem to be writing only for each other. Their language may be an emblem of power, a sign of initiation. I want lesbian and gay books to be written in language my students can understand. Some scholars have replied defensively to this observation by claiming that complex ideas require difficult language. My retort: read bell hooks, read Gloria Anzaldúa.[8]

Cruikshank makes a serious point: if scholars are limited to an exclusive and potentially exclusionary language for the communication of their most important political ideas, their theories are drastically limited as a viable political tool. In response to such language, Cruikshank cites the critics bell hooks and Gloria Anzaldúa, whose ethical commitment to producing theoretical models accessible to academic and nonacademic practitioners alike extends from a related commitment to challenging the normative, universalizing assumptions of feminism's (white) racial, (middle-) class, and (straight) erotic identity politics.

Thus, through the examples of hooks and Anzaldúa, Cruikshank suggests that the diversification of feminist discourse and the consciousness of discursive elitism will produce a more rigorous, more forceful feminist theory. What is now fostered instead, she argues, is an increasingly intimate, intra-academic conversation and an increasing divide from other theoretical models whose diversity might provide useful insights into the academic project. My point here is not to suggest anything inherently wrong with theoretical discourses that operate within the vocabularies and institutional boundaries of particular disciplines or practices. It is, however, to urge awareness of the potentially exclusionary implications of such a pattern—exclusionary implications that, depending on the cultural status of the practice in question, have potentially hierarchical effects. As Cruikshank points out, such effects might be counteracted by supplementary cooperative and coalitional work that cuts across categorical, institutional, and discursive differences.

As Gilligan suggests, the act of listening is key to the disruption of rigid epistemological categories. Historically, the strength of feminist theory has involved the inclusive spirit in which feminists have attempted to locate an expressive voice. Bonnie Zimmerman, writing in the concluding essay of

The New Lesbian Studies, calls for a newly rigorous lesbian-feminist-queer theoretical consciousness, not out of a nostalgic return to the utopian energies of liberation politics but rather out of a renewed commitment to rigorous thought: "The problem as I see it is that the discourse of lesbianism—specifically, lesbian feminism—has been all but silenced. This leads to the appropriation of our work and ideas (including feminism itself) without any recognition or citation of sources, the vilification of our values and continued existence, and the appalling misrepresentation and ahistorical construction of the past twenty years. To counter this, lesbian feminists need to reinsert ourselves into the debates in a forceful and intellectually impeccable way."[9] *The New Lesbian Studies* honors this proposition in practice. Neither sentimentalizing earlier traditions of lesbian feminism nor demonizing more recently developed theoretical voices, the collection takes on the complex entanglements, anxieties, and connections among feminist, lesbian, and queer social movements directly, in the varied context of histories, pedagogies, racial diversities, epistemologies, institutions, and futures. Assuming that there *is* a future to this discussion, Zimmerman describes what is, to her view, the most powerful means of reasserting a lesbian-feminist historical and theoretical perspective: "I believe that lesbian and/or lesbian/gay/queer/sexuality studies will develop best if each constituency maintains some healthy and skeptical distance, engages in open and critical dialogue, and acknowledges both the similarities and the differences, the congruencies and the contradictions, among our multiple points of view."[10]

There is a sobering persuasiveness to this argument, offered as it is in the spirit of "forceful and intellectually impeccable" participation in ongoing debates. Far from suggesting that any one theory or theorist should represent the sum total of available perspectives, Zimmerman argues that strength is in numbers, in the competing, potentially incoherent, certainly uncomfortable abundance of "multiple points of view." Knowledge is power, and the categories by which it is made meaningful are artifacts of culture and ideology. The feminist critique of social hierarchies necessarily encompasses structures of knowledge; but the form in which that critique is conducted also demands the invention, and the reinvention, and the reinvention still again and again, of analytical methods that remain scrupulously self-conscious of their participation in the politics of meaning making. There are no exemptions. In the rigorous consideration of this fact, the ethical objectives of feminism, in practice, coincide with the practice of feminism, in theory.

Notes

Preface

1. Fredric Jameson, *The Political Unconscious: Narrative as a Socially Symbolic Act,* 9.

Introduction

1. Millett's memoir *Flying* is, in large part, an account of her experience with *Time* magazine; see especially chapter 1, "Vertigo," 1–126. The *Time* cover story was only one of a number of prominent feature stories in the 1970s on the burgeoning women's movement, including coverage by the *Village Voice, Newsweek, Cosmopolitan,* the *New Yorker, Esquire, New York,* the *London Sunday Times Magazine,* and *Mademoiselle.* Media representations of women and the women's movement were, from the first, a concern to women's liberation activists; the issue came to a head in the March 1970 feminist occupation of the editorial offices of the *Ladies' Home Journal.* On the media, the *Ladies' Home Journal* action, and sex-discrimination lawsuits brought by female reporters at *Newsweek,* see Susan Brownmiller, *In Our Time: Memoir of a Revolution,* 136–66. On the *Ladies' Home Journal* sit-in, see Karla Jay, *Tales of the Lavender Menace: A Memoir of Liberation,* 113–20.

2. "Who's Come a Long Way, Baby?" 16.

3. "Women's Lib: A Second Look."

4. Millett wrote, "Someone from *Time* came when I talked at [Daughters of Bilitis] in August, candid, one gay to another. But they didn't pick it up" (*Flying,* 15).

5. Describing the evening of the Columbia panel event, Millett wrote, "When I came into Macmillan [Hall], Sidney [a friend] warned there'd be trouble, the place full of Radical Lesbians wanting me to clear things up, contradict the press image of the nice married lady" (ibid.).

6. Ibid., 17.

7. Barbara Christian, "The Race for Theory."

8. Deborah McDowell, "Transferences; Black Feminist Discourse: The 'Practice' of Theory," 107.

9. Ibid., 105. Nina Baym's essay "The Madwoman and Her Languages: Why I Don't Do Feminist Theory" argues differently for feminist theory's andocentric, misogynist, totalizing presumptions.

10. McDowell, "Transferences," 105.

11. My analysis here is indebted to Katie King's work in *Theory in Its Feminist Travels: Conversations in U.S. Women's Movements.* In King's introductory chapter, "What Counts as Theory: Travels through Several Histories of U.S. Feminism" (1–54), she analyzes feminism's "origin stories" for their investment in different concepts

of "theory": "Concerned with the kinds of political agencies that are deployed in the interwoven rewritings of theory in feminism, I . . . examine several 'moments' (texts/locations/historical shifts) in feminism in the last two decades, local moments defined by specific strategies and stakes in 'what counts as theory?'" (2).

12. José Esteban Muñoz, *Disidentifications: Queers of Color and the Performance of Politics*, 32–33.

13. Ibid., 33.

14. Sharon Marcus, "The Profession of the Author: Abstraction, Advertising, and *Jane Eyre*," 207.

15. Ibid.; emphasis added.

16. Ibid., 207–8. Marcus quotes Lacan's "The Signification of the Phallus," 288. See also Karl Marx, *Capital*, vol. 1, especially 46.

17. See especially Jacques Lacan, "The Mirror-Stage" and "The Signification of the Phallus."

18. David Simpson, *Romanticism, Nationalism, and the Revolt against Theory*, 3. See also Bruce Robbins, "The Politics of Theory"; Terry Eagleton, *Literary Theory: An Introduction*; and W. J. T. Mitchell, ed., *Against Theory: Literary Studies and the New Pragmatism*. On early feminist theory in its relationship to a masculinist, patriarchal theoretical tradition, see Judith Newton, "History as Usual? Feminism and the 'New Historicism,'" especially 93–106.

19. Paul de Man, "The Resistance to Theory," 5, 6. For discussions about the implications of "portability," I am indebted to John Plotz.

20. Simpson, *Romanticism*, 7; see also 183–88.

21. Judith Butler, *Gender Trouble: Feminism and the Subversion of Identity*, 13; emphasis in original. See also Butler's *Bodies That Matter: On the Discursive Limits of "Sex,"* 18. On the "epistemophilic impulse" as constitutive of the individual subject within imperialistic and strategically gendered terms, see Carolyn Dever, "Psychoanalytic Cannibalism," in *Death and the Mother from Dickens to Freud: Victorian Fiction and the Anxiety of Origins*, 39–77.

22. Gayatri Chakravorty Spivak, "Explanation and Culture: Marginalia," in *In Other Worlds: Essays in Cultural Politics*, 113; quoted in J. Butler, *Gender Trouble*, 153 n. 23.

23. J. Butler, *Gender Trouble*, 13.

24. Editorial Collective, "Variations on Common Themes," 213; emphases in original.

25. The historians of feminist theory have produced a rich archive of primary materials and analysis. In the context of this impressive body of work, see especially bell hooks, *Feminist Theory from Margin to Center*, as well as her *Ain't I a Woman: Black Women and Feminism*; Toril Moi, *Sexual/Textual Politics: Feminist Literary Theory*; Spivak, *In Other Worlds*; Diana Fuss, *Essentially Speaking: Feminism, Nature, and Difference*; Jane Gallop, *The Daughter's Seduction: Feminism and Psychoanalysis* and *Around 1981: Academic Feminist Literary Theory*; King, *Theory in Its Feminist Travels*; Judith Roof, *A Lure of Knowledge: Lesbian Sexuality and Theory*; Elaine Showalter, ed., *The New Feminist Criticism: Essays on Women, Literature,*

and Theory; Ann Snitow, Christine Stansell, and Sharon Thompson, eds., *The Powers of Desire: The Politics of Sexuality*; Josephine Donovan, *Feminist Theory: The Intellectual Traditions of American Feminism*; Alison Jaggar and Paula R. Struhl, eds., *Feminist Frameworks: Alternative Accounts of the Relations between Men and Women*; Gayle Rubin, "The Traffic in Women: Notes on the 'Political Economy' of Sex"; and Robin Morgan, ed., *Sisterhood Is Powerful: An Anthology of Writings from the Women's Liberation Movement*. For a number of the influential arguments in the particular arena of feminist political theory, see especially Brooke A. Ackerly, *Political Theory and Feminist Social Criticism*; Seyla Benhabib, *Democracy and Difference: Contesting the Boundaries of the Political*; Seyla Benhabib and Drucilla Cornell, eds., *Feminism as Critique: On the Politics of Gender*; Drucilla Cornell, *At the Heart of Freedom: Feminism, Sex, and Equality*; Nancy Fraser, *Unruly Practices: Power, Discourse, and Gender in Contemporary Social Theory*; Diana Tietjens Meyers, ed., *Feminist Social Thought: A Reader*; Chantal Mouffe, *The Return of the Political*; Linda J. Nicholson, *The Play of Reason: From the Modern to the Postmodern*; Martha C. Nussbaum, *Sex and Social Justice*; and Iris Marion Young, *Justice and the Politics of Difference*. On feminists in the academy, see Joan E. Hartman and Ellen Messer-Davidow, eds., *(En)Gendering Knowledge: Feminists in Academe*; and Ellen Messer-Davidow, *Disciplining Feminism: From Social Activism to Academic Discourse*.

26. Kate Millett, *Sexual Politics*, xiii.

27. Ann Pellegrini, *Performance Anxieties: Staging Psychoanalysis, Staging Race*, 7–8; emphasis in original.

28. Alice Echols, *Daring to Be Bad: Radical Feminism in America, 1967–1975*, 11.

29. Barbara Johnson, "The Postmodern in Feminism: A Response to Mary Jo Frug," in *The Feminist Difference: Literature, Psychoanalysis, Race, and Gender*, 194; emphases in original.

30. Ibid., 193.

31. Roof, *A Lure of Knowledge*, 216. For more on the symptomatic equation of "black and lesbian" women's agendas as a site of resistance, see Roof's chapter 5, "All Analogies Are Faulty: The Fear of Intimacy in Feminist Criticism," 216–36. On "normalization," see Jürgen Habermas, *Between Facts and Norms: Contributions to a Discourse Theory of Law and Democracy*.

32. Moi, *Sexual/Textual Politics*, xiii. Further quotations from this book in this section refer to this edition and are cited parenthetically in the text.

33. For more on French feminism, especially in its relationship to what Moi terms "Anglo-American feminist criticism," see Moi, *Sexual/Textual Politics*; Fuss, *Essentially Speaking*; J. Butler, *Gender Trouble*; Jane Gallop, *Reading Lacan*; Alice Jardine, *Gynesis: Configurations of Women and Modernity*; Juliet Flower MacCannell, *Figuring Lacan: Criticism and the Cultural Unconscious*; Ann Rosalind Jones, "Writing the Body: Toward an Understanding of *L'Écriture féminine*"; and Juliet Mitchell's and Jacqueline Rose's respective introductions to *Feminine Sexuality: Jacques Lacan and the École Freudienne*, by Jacques Lacan. The collection *New French Feminisms: An Anthology*, edited by Elaine Marks and Isabelle de Courtivron, presents excerpts

from a variety of French feminist texts, including selections from Hélène Cixous, Luce Irigaray, and Julia Kristeva, whose work has played an especially influential role in the formation of later theories of gender, signification, and power.

34. Christian, "The Race for Theory," 68.

35. Brownmiller, *In Our Time*, 329.

36. See hooks, *Feminist Theory*, 112. See also Lisa Duggan, "Scholars and Sense," in Duggan and Nan D. Hunter, *Sex Wars: Sexual Dissent and Political Culture*, 173–78.

37. Biddy Martin, *Femininity Played Straight: The Significance of Being Lesbian*, 128.

38. See also Deborah McDowell's reading of this passage in "Transferences," 97.

39. hooks, *Feminist Theory*, 30.

40. B. Martin, *Femininity Played Straight*, 127.

41. Millett, *Sexual Politics*, xiv.

42. Millett's assertion of her political agenda, and particularly her construction of this agenda in terms of "patriarchy," exclusive of any acknowledgment of strong female intellectual precursors, opened her up to critique by later feminists. See, for example, Moi, *Sexual/Textual Politics*, 26.

43. B. Martin, *Femininity Played Straight*, 43–44.

44. hooks, *Feminist Theory*, ii.

45. See especially Ann Fausto Sterling, *Sexing the Body: Gender Politics and the Construction of Sexuality*.

46. See, for example, Susan Gubar, "What Ails Feminist Criticism?" 879 n. 1. In the introduction to their anthology *Conflicts in Feminism*, editors Marianne Hirsch and Evelyn Fox Keller suggest that dissonance within feminist discourses is especially highly charged because it runs counter to the ideals of egalitarian consensus that are central to the women's movement. The 1980s, "a decade of intense mutual criticism and internal divisiveness," they write, were "a decade in which the feminist illusion of 'sisterhood' and the 'dream of a common language' gave way to the realities of fractured discourses" (1).

47. Sigmund Freud, "Observations on Transference-Love," 163.

48. Wlad Godzich, "The Tiger on the Paper Mat," xiv.

49. John Ruskin, quoted in ibid.

50. Paul Feyerabend's critique of the empirical within scientific discourses is sympathetic in method to Millett's emphasis here on the need for a feminist commitment to unstable forms of evidence. See Feyerabend's *Against Method*.

51. Godzich, "The Tiger on the Paper Mat," xiv; emphasis in original.

52. de Man, *The Resistance to Theory*, 3. Further quotations from this book in this section are cited parenthetically in the text.

53. In an analysis of this aspect of de Man's argument, John Guillory observes, "The syllabus of theory has even now conquered only minor territories in disciplines other than literary criticism, and the agency for the dissemination of theory has remained departments of literature; for that reason the emergence of theory remains indissolubly linked to the discipline of literary criticism, and thus to the literary cur-

riculum. Theory is last, if not first, *literary* theory." See Guillory's "Literature after Theory: The Lesson of Paul de Man," 177; emphasis in original.

54. For an analysis of the relationship between language and performativity, see Judith Butler, *Excitable Speech: The Politics of the Performative*; and J. L. Austin, *How to Do Things with Words*.

55. Daly's work in both feminist and religious studies has always implicated questions of language; in addition to her *Webster's First New Intergalactic Wickedary of the English Language,* see also *Gyn/Ecology: The Metaethics of Radical Feminism* and her more recent memoir, *Outercourse: The Be-dazzling Voyage: Containing Recollections from My Logbook of a Radical Feminist Philosopher (Be-ing an Account of My Time/Space Travels and Ideas—Then, Again, Now, and How)*. Alice Walker, *In Search of Our Mothers' Gardens: Womanist Prose*.

56. Donna Haraway, "A Cyborg Manifesto," 175. On the feminist implications of deconstructive methodologies, see Barbara Johnson, "Gender Theory and the Yale School," in *A World of Difference*; and Drucilla Cornell, *Beyond Accommodation: Ethical Feminism, Deconstruction, and the Law*.

57. For an analysis of the social constitution of an abstracted aggregate identity, see Mary Poovey, *Making a Social Body: British Cultural Formation, 1830–1864*.

58. Judith Butler appropriates the Nietzschean concept of the "necessary error" to argue that gender-identification can be deployed temporarily and strategically as feminist praxis; see especially "Imitation and Gender Insubordination."

59. Robbins, "The Politics of Theory," 16.

60. Ginia Bellafante, "Feminism: It's All about Me!" 57. Further quotations from this article in this section are cited parenthetically in the text.

61. Bellafante credits the invention of the popular phrase "duh feminism" to "some wags" (ibid., 58). For a reading of Bellafante's story, see Jennifer Baumgardner and Amy Richards, *Manifesta: Young Women, Feminism, and the Future*, 119–25.

62. Bellafante refers to Susan Brownmiller's *Against Our Will: Men, Women, and Rape*.

63. Gubar, "What Ails Feminist Criticism?" 878. Further quotations from this article in this section are cited parenthetically in the text.

64. See also Robyn Wiegman's response, "What Ails Feminist Criticism? A Second Opinion."

65. Gubar quotes Marianne Hirsch and Evelyn Fox Keller, eds., *Conflicts in Feminism*, 382.

66. Gubar refers here to hooks, *Ain't I a Woman,* and also singles out Audre Lord, Michele Wallace, Hazel V. Carby, and Chandra Talpade Mohanty. See also Christian, "The Race for Theory," as well as Nancy Miller, *Getting Personal: Feminist Occasions and Other Autobiographical Acts*.

1. The Future of an Ideal

1. Flora Davis, *Moving the Mountain: The Women's Movement in America since 1960*; Alice Echols, *Daring to Be Bad: Radical Feminism in America, 1967–1975*; Karla Jay, *Tales of the Lavender Menace: A Memoir of Liberation*; Susan Brownmiller,

In Our Time: Memoir of a Revolution; Ruth Rosen, *The World Split Open: How the Modern Women's Movement Changed America.* Several recent anthologies also participate in this historiographical project; see especially Rachel Blau DuPlessis and Ann Snitow, eds., *The Feminist Memoir Project: Voices from Women's Liberation,* which features the memoirs of a range of participants in women's lib; and also Rosalyn Baxandall and Linda Gordon, eds., *Dear Sisters: Dispatches from the Women's Liberation Movement,* a documentary history of the women's liberation movement.

2. For an analysis of this particular aspect of consciousness-raising discourse, and for an argument about the innovations and failings of the consciousness-raising movement more generally, see Carla Kaplan, *The Erotics of Talk: Women's Writing and Feminist Paradigms,* especially 155.

3. Kathie Sarachild, "Consciousness-Raising: A Radical Weapon," 144.

4. Ibid., 145.

5. Juliet Mitchell, *Woman's Estate,* 62. Empirical information about the number, tenure, procedures, and constituencies of consciousness-raising groups is minimal, due to the informal, private nature of the organizations themselves. What is certain, however, is that in the late 1960s and early 1970s in the United States, they flourished as an idealized form of feminist populist practice. Echols situates feminist consciousness-raising methodologies within the larger historical context of civil rights and workers' rights movements: "The proponents of consciousness-raising took their inspiration from the civil rights movement where the slogan was 'tell it like it is,' the Chinese revolution when peasants were urged 'to speak pains to recall pains,' and from the revolutionary struggle in Guatemala where guerillas used similar techniques" (*Daring to Be Bad,* 84). Echols and Kaplan both emphasize that the consensus-driven methods of c-r "not only reflected radical feminists' discomfort with difference, it also contributed to the muting of differences," as Echols writes (91), and thus to the marking of second-wave feminism in terms of white middle-class and, I would add, heterosexual identity. See also Kaplan, *The Erotics of Talk,* 155.

6. Gerda Lerner, *The Creation of Feminist Consciousness: From the Middle Ages to Eighteen-Seventy,* 14.

7. Esther Newton and Shirley Walton, "The Personal Is Political: Consciousness-Raising and Personal Change in the Women's Liberation Movement," 122. On religious conversion, see especially 115–16.

8. Ibid., 114–15.

9. Mary Daly, "The Spiritual Dimension of Women's Liberation," 74, 79.

10. Kathie Amatniek, "Funeral Oration for the Burial of Traditional Womanhood," n.p.

11. Betty Friedan, *The Feminine Mystique*; Alice S. Rossi, "Equality between the Sexes: An Immodest Proposal." Friedan implicitly and Rossi more explicitly construct their analyses of women's domestic circumstances through the lens of white middle-class women's experience.

12. For a reading of the familial rhetorics informing the French Revolution, see Lynn Hunt, *The Family Romance of the French Revolution.*

13. For an analysis of both sides of the "sisterhood" question, see Helena Michie, *Sororophobia: Differences among Women in Literature and Culture.*

14. Jo Freeman, "The Building of the Gilded Cage," 50.

15. Adrienne Rich, "Compulsory Heterosexuality and Lesbian Existence."

16. Dana Densmore, "On Sisterhood," in *Sex Roles and Female Oppression: A Collection of Articles,* 29.

17. Newton and Walton, "The Personal Is Political," 134–35.

18. Pamela Allen, "Building a Movement: Free Space," 97–98.

19. Kathie Sarachild, "The Power of History," 19.

20. Rita Mae Brown, *Rita Will: Memoir of a Literary Rabble-Rouser,* 233.

21. Sarachild, "The Power of History," 19.

22. Ti-Grace Atkinson, "Radical Feminism," 33; emphasis in original.

23. Allen, "Building a Movement," 98.

24. See Marie Moyer, "The Female Studies as Joke Syndrome," 34.

25. Dana Densmore, "Our Place in the Universe," in *Sex Roles and Female Oppression,* 1.

26. Valerie Solanas, *S.C.U.M. Manifesto,* 25.

27. Nancy Hartsock, "Fundamental Feminism: Process and Perspective," 68–69. Further quotations from this article in this section are cited parenthetically in the text.

28. Hartsock quotes Antonio Gramsci, *Selections from the Prison Notebooks,* 344.

29. Kaplan, *The Erotics of Talk,* 155.

30. Ibid. Kaplan also suggests that consciousness-raising, with its emphasis on nonconfrontational self-revelation, was frustrating to many potential feminists who found it doctrinaire, excessively homogeneous, or resistant to exploring challenging or uncomfortable feelings.

31. J. Mitchell, *Woman's Estate,* 61; emphasis in original.

32. "Ain't I a Woman?" Collective, "More Thoughts on Structuring a Revolution," 2. The anonymous article "Liberate Women to Liberate Society," also from 1972, uses virtually identical language to describe this radical educational process.

33. Joan W. Scott, "The Evidence of Experience," 400. In response to Scott's argument, see Lisa Duggan, "The Discipline Problem: Queer Theory Meets Lesbian and Gay History," in *Sex Wars: Sexual Dissent and Political Culture,* by Lisa Duggan and Nan D. Hunter. Scott and Duggan each argue for the need to historicize "experience" as a means of articulating a politics of the local, of location, and of historical particularity.

34. See especially Michel Foucault, *The Archaeology of Knowledge* and *The Order of Things: An Archaeology of the Human Sciences.*

35. Chandra Talpade Mohanty, "Feminist Encounters: Locating the Politics of Experience," 31.

36. Allen, "Building a Movement," 97–98. Further quotations from this article in this section are cited parenthetically in the text.

37. For a discussion of this egalitarian ethic and its problematic implications, see Kaplan, *The Erotics of Talk.*

38. See Virginia Woolf, *A Room of One's Own.*

39. Redstockings, "Redstockings Manifesto," 113.

40. Ibid. For analysis of the consciousness-raising-as-therapy issue, see Carol Hanisch, "The Personal Is Political."

41. Simone de Beauvoir, *The Second Sex,* especially 63.

42. Kathie Sarachild, "A Program for Feminist 'Consciousness Raising,'" 78.

43. Sarachild, "Consciousness-Raising," 145.

44. See especially Hartsock, "Fundamental Feminism," 77–78.

45. Susi Kaplow, "Getting Angry," 17.

46. Sarachild, "Consciousness-Raising," 147.

47. Ibid., 149.

48. Radical Feminist 28, "The Women's Movement."

49. *Women's Center Newsletter of Nassau County,* 4–5; emphasis in original.

50. Sarachild, "Consciousness-Raising," 145.

51. Carol Hanisch, "A Critique of the Miss America Protest," 88.

52. Robin Morgan, "Three Articles on WITCH," 72; emphasis in original. Further quotations from this source in this section are cited parenthetically in the text.

53. Morgan has a somewhat different take on the relationship between the consciousness-raising movement and the WITCH collective's approach to zap actions. Both WITCH and the Redstockings collective originated in the group New York Radical Women, but whereas WITCH was the group of "self-styled 'politicos,'" the Redstockings were the radical feminists. The two groups, Morgan contends, were very different: "I was a founder of WITCH, of course, and I was proud that we were not man-haters like those dreadful Redstockings women. While they quietly went about doing steady consciousness-raising and writing papers which were destined to become new feminist classics ('The Politics of Housework,' 'Resistance to Consciousness,' 'Techniques of Consciousness Raising,' 'The Personal Is Political,' 'The Redstockings Manifesto,' and 'The Pro-Woman Line,' to name a few), WITCH became an action group" (ibid., 71). Despite Morgan's ambivalence about the Redstockings' project, Redstockings and WITCH shared more than a common origin: both groups were committed to making visible the connections of the personal and the political, and both groups mobilized discourses of the symbolic and of personal emotion in that effort.

54. Karla Jay's account of the bridal-fair demonstration differs from Morgan's in its conclusions. Succeeding in their symbolic critique of the bride as the apex of a feminine ideal, activists were nevertheless, in the end, conscious that their actions pitted them against the women who were shopping at the bridal fair. Jay writes, "I was thrilled by the boldness of the action but felt it, like the Miss America protest, was antiwoman. . . . Marriage might be slavery, but we had to offer a positive alternative before we encouraged women to abandon matrimony" (*Tales of the Lavender Menace,* 38).

55. Sarachild, "Consciousness-Raising," 145.

56. Juliet Mitchell's response to this charge is typically cogent: she wonders why "there is (a) anything wrong with people imitating 'group therapy' and (b) why they

don't know what group therapy is? . . . Of course, the apparent denigration of therapy is really only a concealed put-down of women: oh, they're moaning again, gossiping their complaints, having a nag . . . what they need is a good therapist (twentieth-century parent-surrogate punisher)" (*Woman's Estate*, 61–62).

2. The Activist Unconscious

1. For further analysis of "unreason" as a subversive political tactic, see Frantz Fanon, *Black Skin, White Masks*, 123–24.

2. See especially Diana Fuss, *Essentially Speaking: Feminism, Nature, and Difference*.

3. Sigmund Freud, "Observations on Transference-Love," 163.

4. Linda Nussbaum (Kingsman), "Female Sexuality."

5. Dana Densmore, "Mr. Freud's Castration Fantasy," 114; emphases in original.

6. Ibid., 116; emphasis in original.

7. Germaine Greer, *The Female Eunuch*, 111.

8. Valerie Solanas, *S.C.U.M. Manifesto*, 6.

9. Laurel Limpus, *Liberation of Women: Sexual Repression and the Family*, 61.

10. Vivian Gornick, introduction to Solanas, *S.C.U.M. Manifesto*, xxxiv–xxxv.

11. See, for example, *Notes from the Third Year*, an annual periodical published by the New York Radical Women, in which theories of feminist action are almost exclusively theories of domesticity and domestic reform.

12. Naomi Weisstein, "'Kinde, Küche, Kirche' as Scientific Law: Psychology Constructs the Female," 228.

13. Alice S. Rossi, "Equality between the Sexes: An Immodest Proposal," 612, 613.

14. Greer, *The Female Eunuch*, 4.

15. Weisstein, "'Kinde, Küche, Kirche,'" 231, 232.

16. See especially Kate Millett, *Sexual Politics*, 177–78. Millett's analysis of the "masculine" qualities of scientific objectivity takes place on p. 202. All subsequent quotations from Millett in this section refer to this edition, and page numbers are cited parenthetically in the text.

17. See especially Sigmund Freud, "Female Sexuality." For a comprehensive analysis of the feminist implications of the phallus, see the introductions by Juliet Mitchell and Jacqueline Rose respectively in their edition of *Feminine Sexuality: Jacques Lacan and the École Freudienne*.

18. See Dorothy Dinnerstein, *The Mermaid and the Minotaur: Sexual Arrangements and Human Malaise*, especially 4–5.

19. Simone de Beauvoir, *The Second Sex*, 42.

20. Gayle Rubin, "The Traffic in Women: Notes on the 'Political Economy' of Sex," 185, 200.

21. Ibid., 188.

22. Juliet Mitchell, *Psychoanalysis and Feminism: Freud, Reich, Laing, and Women*, xiii. All subsequent quotations from Mitchell in this section refer to this edition, and

page numbers are cited parenthetically in the text. Mitchell is writing from a British, rather than a North American, feminist intellectual tradition in which both Marxism and psychoanalysis were, from the first, more central.

23. Greer, *The Female Eunuch*, 92.

24. For more on the relationship between psychoanalysis and biology, see Mari Jo Buhle, *Feminism and Its Discontents: A Century of Struggle with Psychoanalysis,* 194–205.

25. On metaphor as symptom, see Jacques Lacan, "The Agency of the Letter in the Unconscious," 166.

26. Jeffrey Moussaieff Masson, *The Assault on Truth: Freud's Suppression of the Seduction Theory,* 144.

27. See Susan Brownmiller, *In Our Time: Memoir of a Revolution,* 105, within her chapter on the abortion-rights movement, "Abortion Is a Woman's Right," 102–35.

28. Rubin, "The Traffic in Women," 177. All subsequent quotations from Rubin in this section refer to this edition, and page numbers are cited parenthetically in the text.

29. In the essay "Femininity," Freud writes, "Pathology has always done us the service by making discernable by isolation and exaggeration conditions which would remain concealed in a normal state" (121). For a compelling reading of Freudian psychoanalysis and questions of the normal, see Teresa de Lauretis, *The Practice of Love: Lesbian Sexuality and Perverse Desire,* particularly her introductory chapter, "Freud, Sexuality, and Perversion," 3–28. Especially useful for my purposes is de Lauretis's recuperation of the terminology of "perversion" as constitutive of Freud's theory of sexuality rather than as aberrant from the norm; see especially 23–38. On this topic, also see Jonathan Dollimore, *Sexual Dissidence: Augustine to Wilde, Freud to Foucault.*

30. Rubin, in an interview with Judith Butler published in 1998, describes the process that produced "The Traffic in Women" between 1972 and 1974 in terms of a desire to intervene in Marxist feminism and, as Butler puts it, to "make feminism something other than a kind of subsidiary movement in Marxism" (Rubin, "Sexual Traffic: Gayle Rubin Interviewed by Judith Butler," 39). "The Traffic in Women," written at a time when very little French theory, and especially that of Lacan, was available in English, was an attempt to think through psychic structures in relation to social structures. In the early 1980s, in response to the dramatic ascendancy of the New Right in U.S. politics, Rubin produced the essay "Thinking Sex: Notes for a Radical Theory of the Politics of Sexuality," which, more than "The Traffic in Women," returned to the question of erotic diversity and offered a corrective to feminism, which she contended had "dealt inadequately with sexual practice, particularly diverse sexual conduct" (40). For an account of the complex relationship between lesbian theories and queer theories, see Carolyn Dever, "Either/And: Lesbian Theories, Queer Theories."

31. Dinnerstein, *The Mermaid and the Minotaur,* 4. All subsequent quotations from Dinnerstein in this section refer to this edition, and page numbers are cited parenthetically in the text.

32. For more on Melanie Klein, see Juliet Mitchell's introduction to *The Selected Melanie Klein,* as well as Carolyn Dever, "Psychoanalytic Cannibalism," in *Death and the Mother from Dickens to Freud: Victorian Fiction and the Anxiety of Origins,* 39–77.

33. Dinnerstein engages Beauvoir's theory of the phallus as social prerogative rather than bodily organ (*The Mermaid and the Minotaur,* 52 n).

34. Nancy Chodorow, *The Reproduction of Mothering: Psychoanalysis and the Sociology of Gender,* 3. All subsequent quotations from Chodorow in this section refer to this edition, and page numbers are cited parenthetically in the text.

35. Louis Althusser, "Ideology and Ideological State Apparatuses (Notes towards an Investigation)," 164–65.

36. Sigmund Freud, *The Interpretation of Dreams*; J. Mitchell, *Psychoanalysis and Feminism,* 368.

37. Jane Gallop, *The Daughter's Seduction: Feminism and Psychoanalysis,* xii. All subsequent quotations from Gallop in this section refer to this edition, and page numbers are cited parenthetically in the text.

38. Millett, *Sexual Politics,* 183.

39. *Notes from the Second Year,* 1; emphasis in original.

40. Jacques Lacan, "The Signification of the Phallus," 287; also cited in Gallop, *The Daughter's Seduction,* 19.

3. The Feminist Body Politic

1. Audre Lorde, "The Uses of the Erotic: The Erotic as Power."

2. Diana Fuss has suggested an essentialism informing even antiessentialist feminisms. In a sense, I am reversing her argument here, not to disagree with it but to reflect the terms circulating in this particular feminist discourse; I suggest that this deliberately essentialist discourse is continually frustrated by its encounter with de-essentializing abstractions. See Fuss, *Essentially Speaking: Feminism, Nature, and Difference,* especially chapter 1, "The 'Risk' of Essence," and chapter 2, "Reading like a Feminist." Feminist work on the topic of the body has ranged widely. See especially Ann Fausto Sterling, *Sexing the Body: Gender Politics and the Construction of Sexuality*; Anne Balsamo, *Technologies of the Gendered Body: Reading Cyborg Women*; Elizabeth Grosz, *Volatile Bodies: Toward a Corporeal Feminism*; Susan Bordo, *Unbearable Weight: Feminism, Western Culture, and the Body*; Jana Sawicki, *Disciplining Foucault: Feminism, Power, and the Body*; Jane Gallop, *Thinking through the Body*; Zillah Eisenstein, *The Female Body and the Law*; and Helena Michie, *The Flesh Made Word: Female Figures and Women's Bodies.*

3. Alfred C. Kinsey and the Staff of the Institute for Sex Research, Indiana University, *Sexual Behavior in the Human Female,* 22. This book followed the 1948 publication of *Sexual Behavior in the Human Male.* Further quotations from Kinsey in this section refer to this edition and are cited parenthetically in the text.

4. Ruth Brecher and Edward Brecher, "The Work of Masters and Johnson," 43–44.

5. Kinsey's critique is milder than that of the feminist writers who would later

demonize Freud in this context: "It is difficult, in the light of our present understanding of the anatomy and physiology of sexual response, to understand what can be meant by a 'vaginal orgasm.' . . . Freud recognized that the clitoris is highly sensitive and the vagina insensitive in the younger female, but he contended that psychosexual maturation involved a subordination of clitoral reactions and a development of sensitivity within the vagina itself; but there are no anatomic data to indicate that such a physical transformation has ever been observed or is possible" (582).

6. William H. Masters and Virginia E. Johnson, *Human Sexual Response,* 45.

7. Daniel G. Brown, "Female Orgasm and Sexual Inadequacy," 131.

8. This is not a universal historical assumption; for material about ancient, medieval, and early modern discourses of female orgasm, see Thomas Laqueur, *Making Sex: Body and Gender from the Greeks to Freud.*

9. Masters and Johnson, *Human Sexual Response,* 67.

10. Ibid., 66.

11. Masters and Johnson write, "Homosexual material, although recorded in both behavioral and physiologic context for both sexes, has not been included in this text. The returns from this facet of human sexual response are too inadequate at present to warrant consideration. At the present pace investigative maturity will not be reached in this program for at least another four to five years" (22). It is important to remember that Masters and Johnson were not only scientific researchers but also marriage counselors, and the vast majority of the subjects studied in the central body of *Human Sexual Response* are married couples.

12. For an astute analysis of Masters and Johnson's behaviorist approach to human sexuality, see Lynne Segal, *Straight Sex: The Politics of Pleasure,* especially 95. See also Segal's "Sensual Uncertainty, or Why the Clitoris Is Not Enough." For an analysis of the contrast between psychoanalysis and the behaviorist model of psychology that implicitly underpins liberal feminism, see Elizabeth Wilson, "I'll Climb the Stairway to Heaven: Lesbianism in the Seventies," especially 185–87.

13. Alix Kates Shulman, "Organs and Orgasms," 302.

14. Sigmund Freud, "Female Sexuality," 228. In "The Signification of the Phallus," Lacan argues for a theory of the phallus as a signifier that intervenes in the construction of gender difference. Lacan notoriously refuses to capitulate to the equation of phallus with penis, and indeed suggests explicitly that the clitoris is as "phallic" as the penis is—in other words, the clitoris, like the penis, is in a divorced or secondary relationship of referentiality to phallic signification. The clitoris was unquestionably the "signifier" that early feminists used to attempt to undo the implications of phallic power, yet it is noteworthy to remark that they were relying upon a metaphorical relationship between the clitoral signifier and the clitoral bodily organ. As Fuss suggests in *Essentially Speaking,* the structure of bodily referentiality that Lacan, in theory, refused is the very structure on which feminist theories of power and discourse were founded.

15. Freud, "Female Sexuality," 228.

16. Though her summary of Freud is accurate, if tendentious, Koedt neither quotes from nor cites his argument directly. Rather, she relies on Mary Ellmann's summary

of Freud in *Thinking about Women,* and work by Frank Caprio, *The Sexually Adequate Female,* and Marie Bonaparte, *Female Sexuality,* to draw her conclusions. See Anne Koedt, "The Myth of the Vaginal Orgasm."

17. Koedt, "The Myth of the Vaginal Orgasm," 292. Further quotations from Koedt in this section refer to this essay and are cited parenthetically in the text.

18. G. Lombard Kelly, *Sexual Feelings in Married Men and Women,* 35; quoted in ibid., 39.

19. Shulman, "Organs and Orgasms," 292–93; emphasis in original. Further quotations from Shulman in this section refer to this essay and are cited parenthetically in the text.

20. Shulman returned to the subject of "Organs and Orgasms" in "Sex and Power: Sexual Bases of Radical Feminism," an essay published in 1980: "In ['Organs and Orgasms'] I cited case after case of injustice done to women by bias in the very terminology of sex and suggested that a solution to our sexual problems might be advanced by reexamining our assumptions, definitions, and beliefs about sexuality from a woman's point of view. It was not that I discounted the importance of political struggle, but I believed we would have to change the way we *think* before we could change the way we live. The ideas of the movement were spreading so fast that it seemed to many of us in those days that it would not be difficult to organize women to revolt" (32; emphasis in original).

21. The Boston Women's Health Book Collective, *Our Bodies, Ourselves: A Book by and for Women,* 13. Further quotations from *Our Bodies, Ourselves* in this section refer to this volume and are cited parenthetically in the text.

22. Jane Gallop, *The Daughter's Seduction: Feminism and Psychoanalysis,* 58.

23. Wendy Sandford, with Paula Brown Doress, "Relationships and Sexuality," 122.

24. The Boston Women's Health Book Collective, *The New Our Bodies, Ourselves,* 171.

25. Ibid., 172.

26. Nancy Friday, *My Secret Garden: Women's Sexual Fantasies,* 6. Further quotations from Friday in this section refer to this volume and are cited parenthetically in the text.

27. Kate Millett, *Sexual Politics,* 5.

28. Shere Hite, *The Hite Report: A Nationwide Study of Female Sexuality,* xi. Further quotations from Hite in this section refer to this volume and are cited parenthetically in the text.

29. For her theory of the "apparitional lesbian," see Terry Castle, *The Apparitional Lesbian: Female Homosexuality and Modern Culture.*

30. For a convincing critique of Hite's polemic and an analysis of the imposition of assumptions about sexual and racial normativity in Hite's book, see Segal, *Straight Sex,* especially 106–9.

31. Andrea Dworkin, *Pornography: Men Possessing Women,* 23.

32. In addition to Dworkin, ibid., see Susan Griffin, *Pornography and Silence: Culture's Revenge against Nature*; Kathleen Barry, *Female Sexual Slavery*; Catharine A.

MacKinnon, *Feminism Unmodified: Discourses on Life and Law*; and Catharine A. MacKinnon and Andrea Dworkin, eds., *In Harm's Way: The Pornography Civil Rights Hearings*. On the term "cultural feminism," see Alice Echols, "The Taming of the Id: Feminist Sexual Politics, 1968–83."

33. See especially the anthology *Pleasure and Danger: Exploring Female Sexuality,* ed. Carole S. Vance, especially Vance's "Pleasure and Danger: Toward a Politics of Sexuality," 1–27, and Echols's "The Taming of the Id," 50–72; as well as Lisa Duggan and Nan D. Hunter, *Sex Wars: Sexual Dissent and Political Culture*; and Ann Snitow, Christine Stansell, and Sharon Thompson, eds., *The Powers of Desire: The Politics of Sexuality.*

34. Amber Hollibaugh and Cherríe Moraga, "What We're Rollin around in Bed With: Sexual Silences in Feminism," 401; emphasis in original.

35. Vance, "Pleasure and Danger," 21.

36. Ibid.

37. Hollibaugh and Moraga, "Rollin around in Bed," 404–5.

38. Wilson, "I'll Climb the Stairway to Heaven," 180.

4. The Feminist Abject

1. Lisa Alther, *Kinflicks,* 331. Further quotations from this novel refer to this edition and are cited parenthetically in the text.

2. Though this chapter focuses on the importance of popular realist novels to the consolidation of categories of theory and practice in the women's movement, it builds from a related critical discourse on the importance of science fiction to feminism. See, for example, Marleen S. Barr, *Lost in Space: Feminist Science Fiction and Beyond*; Libby Falk Jones and Sarah Webster Goodwin, eds., *Feminism, Utopia, and Narrative*; Donald Palumbo, ed., *Erotic Universe: Sexuality and Fantastic Literature*; Marleen S. Barr and Nicholas D. Smith, eds., *Women and Utopia: Critical Interpretations*; Marleen S. Barr, *Future Females: A Critical Anthology,* which includes Joanna Russ's "Recent Feminist Utopias"; and Kathryn Seidel, "Envisioning the Androgynous Future."

3. Scholarship on this influential subgenre includes Elaine Neil Orr, *Subject to Negotiation: Reading Feminist Criticism and American Women's Fictions*; Ellen Peel, "Subject, Object, and the Alternation of First- and Third-Person Narration in Novels by Alther, Atwood, and Drabble: Toward a Theory of Feminist Aesthetics"; Molly Hite, "Writing—and Reading—the Body: Female Sexuality and Recent Feminist Fiction"; James Mandrell, "Questions of Genre and Gender: Contemporary American Versions of the Feminine Picaresque"; Margaret Homans, "'Her Very Own Howl': The Ambiguities of Representation in Recent Women's Fiction"; and Joan Reardon, "Fear of Flying: Developing the Feminist Novel."

4. For an argument concerning *une fiction théoretique,* Nicole Brossard's notion of "fiction/theory" as it occurs in formally experimental feminist and lesbian novels, see Teresa de Lauretis, "Sexual Indifference and Lesbian Representation." See also Dorothy J. Hale, *Social Formalism: The Novel in Theory from Henry James to the Present.*

5. Heilbrun's scholarly work on the genre of detective fiction includes "Nancy Drew: A Moment in Feminist History"; "Gender and Detective Fiction"; "Dorothy L. Sayers: Biography between the Lines"; and "Sayers, Lord Peter, and God." Heilbrun's Amanda Cross series has itself received a great deal of critical attention; see especially Susan Kress, *Carolyn G. Heilbrun: Feminist in a Tenured Position*; Lois A. Marchino, "The Professor Tells a Story: Kate Fansler"; Jeanne Addison Roberts, "Feminist Murder: Amanda Cross Reinvents Womanhood"; Marty S. Knepper, "Who Killed Janet Mandelbaum and India Wonder? A Look at the Suicides of the Token Women in Amanda Cross's *Death in a Tenured Position* and Dorothy Bryant's *Killing Wonder*"; Judith Wilt, "Feminism Meets the Detective Novel"; Helena Michie, "Murder in the Canon: The Dual Personality of Carolyn Heilbrun"; Frances K. Barasch, "Faculty Images in Recent American Fiction"; and J. M. Purcell, "The 'Amanda Cross' Case: Socializing the U.S. Academic Mystery."

6. Amanda Cross, *Death in a Tenured Position*, 10. Further quotations from this novel refer to this edition and are cited parenthetically in the text.

7. See the articles "Who's Come a Long Way, Baby?" and "Women's Lib: A Second Look."

8. Jacques Lacan, "The Agency of the Letter in the Unconscious," 151.

9. Marilyn French, *The Women's Room*, 1. Further quotations from this novel refer to this edition and are cited parenthetically in the text.

10. Emily Martin, *The Woman in the Body: A Cultural Analysis of Reproduction*, 97.

11. Julia Kristeva, *The Powers of Horror: An Essay on Abjection*, 71.

12. Ibid., 3; emphasis in original. See E. Martin, *The Woman in the Body*, 45–50, for an analysis of the cultural and economic construction of menstrual blood as a form of waste.

13. Kristeva, *The Powers of Horror*, 13; emphasis in original. Kristeva argues later that women's use of the abject involves not mastery but the reiteration of an external patriarchal authority: "When a woman ventures out in those regions it is usually to gratify, in very maternal fashion, the desire for the abject that insures the life (that is, the sexual life) of the man whose symbolic authority she accepts" (54).

14. On the constitutive function of the scapegoat, see René Girard, *Violence and the Sacred*. On the gendered politics of abjection, see Judith Butler, *Bodies That Matter: On the Discursive Limits of "Sex."*

15. Kathie Sarachild, "Consciousness-Raising: A Radical Weapon," 145.

16. For a feminist theory of readerly response and identification, see Janice Radway, *Reading the Romance: Women, Patriarchy, and Popular Literature*.

17. On lesbian fictions, see especially Terry Castle, *The Apparitional Lesbian: Female Homosexuality and Modern Culture*; Louise Kawada, "Liberating Laughter: Comedic Form in Some Lesbian Novels"; Jonathan Dollimore, "The Dominant and the Deviant: A Violent Dialectic"; Leslie Fishbein, "Rubyfruit Jungle: Lesbianism, Feminism, and Narcissism"; and Sonya Andemahr, "The Politics of Separatism and Lesbian Utopian Fiction."

18. Of the many critiques of Friedan's class- and race-blind theory of gender, bell

hooks's is perhaps the most influential. In *Feminist Theory from Margin to Center,* she writes, "[Friedan] did not discuss who would be called in to take care of the children and maintain the home if more women like herself were freed from their house labor and given equal access with white men to the professions. She did not speak of the needs of women without men, without children, without homes. She ignored the existence of all non-white women and poor white women. She did not tell readers whether it was more fulfilling to be a maid, a babysitter, a factory worker, a clerk, or a prostitute, than to be a leisure class housewife. . . . She made her plight and the plight of white women like herself synonymous with a condition affecting all American women. In so doing, she deflected attention away from her classism, her racism, her sexist attitudes towards the masses of American women" (1–2).

19. Joan W. Scott, "The Evidence of Experience."

20. For an analysis of critical responses to the question of men in *The Women's Room,* see Lisa Marie Hogeland, *Feminism and Its Fictions: The Consciousness-Raising Novel and the Women's Liberation Movement,* 90–93.

21. On the cost of Val's "failed activism," and on the surprising infrequency of feminist fictional representations of activism, see ibid., 107.

22. There is a critical discourse, however, that situates Jong as a Jewish novelist. See Charlotte Templin, "Erica Jong: Becoming a Jewish Writer"; and Evelyn Gross Avery, "Tradition and Independence in Jewish Feminist Novels." Critical interest also extends to Lisa Alther and Rita Mae Brown as Southern writers; see E. M. Broner, "The Dirty Ladies: Earthy Writings of Contemporary American Women—Paley, Jong, Schor, and Lerman"; Mary Anne Ferguson, "Lisa Alther: The Irony of Return"; Frederick G. Waage, "Alther and Dillard: The Appalachian Universe"; Edward E. Irwin, "Freedoms as Value in Three Popular Southern Novels"; and Martha Chew, "Rita Mae Brown: Feminist Theorist and Southern Novelist."

23. Erica Jong, *Fear of Flying,* 288. Further quotations from this novel refer to the 1995 edition and are cited parenthetically in the text. In an introduction to the novel, "*Fear of Flying* Turns Twenty-One," written in 1994, Jong underscores the novel's useful consciousness of travel: "Every writer has a myth buried in the unconscious—accessible only through the telling of a tale. My myth is picaresque. A woman in trouble takes a journey which unlocks the rest of her life and confirms her as a heroine. The voyage taken is both inner and outer; it changes forever what she thinks of herself and of her life" (xiii). The central oppositional structure at the heart of *Fear of Flying,* Jong argues, "brings us to the prickly question of sex and feminism and whether the two are ever compatible. The novel does not presume to take a position on that. It is descriptive, not prescriptive; a work of imagination, not of polemic. What it strives to do is *show* the many contradictions between passion and freedom in a woman's life and leave the reader to make up her own mind about what to do" (xiv; emphasis in original). See also Robert J. Butler, "The Woman Writer as American Picaro: Open Journeying in Erica Jong's *Fear of Flying.*"

24. On Colette's mixed-race heritage, see Judith Thurman, *Secrets of the Flesh: A Life of Colette.*

25. J. Butler, *Bodies That Matter,* 224.

5. Obstructive Behavior

The italicized epigraphs throughout this chapter are excerpted from definitions of *dyke* in the *Oxford English Dictionary*, 2d ed. (1989).

1. For a discussion of theoretical appropriations of such disparaging terms as "queer," see Judith Butler, "Critically Queer," in *Bodies That Matter: On the Discursive Limits of "Sex,"* especially 226–30.

2. Katie King, "Lesbianism as Feminism's Magical Sign," in *Theory in Its Feminist Travels: Conversations in U.S. Women's Movements,* 135.

3. Radicalesbians, "The Woman-Identified Woman," 166. Authorship of this essay has also been attributed to Rita Mae Brown.

4. Catharine A. MacKinnon, "Feminism, Marxism, Method, and the State: An Agenda for Theory," 247 n. 46.

5. Ti-Grace Atkinson, "Lesbianism and Feminism: Justice for Women as 'Unnatural,'" 132, 134.

6. Ti-Grace Atkinson, "Strategy and Tactics: A Presentation of Political Lesbianism," 138.

7. Ibid., 136–37.

8. Ibid., 135–36.

9. Atkinson, "Lesbianism and Feminism," 131.

10. Miriam Schnier, ed., *Feminism in Our Time: The Essential Writings, World War II to the Present,* 161.

11. Adrienne Rich, "Compulsory Heterosexuality and Lesbian Existence," 244; emphasis in original. Further quotations from this essay in this section refer to this printing and are cited parenthetically in the text.

12. Rich refers to Mary Daly, *Gyn/Ecology: The Metaethics of Radical Feminism,* 15.

13. Jane Gallop, *Around 1981: Academic Feminist Literary Theory,* 10.

14. bell hooks, *Feminist Theory from Margin to Center,* 111. Further quotations from this volume in this section refer to this edition and are cited parenthetically in the text.

15. Cheryl Clarke, "The Failure to Transform: Homophobia in the Black Community," quoted in ibid., 153. Hooks responds again to the emotional, if not the intellectual, implications of this issue in the essay "Censorship from Left and Right," in *Outlaw Culture: Resisting Representations,* 71.

16. Interestingly, hooks herself later criticizes Madonna's book *Sex* for *its* conflation of the heterosexual and the heterosexist: "Even in the realm of male homoeroticism/homosexuality, Madonna's image usurps, takes over, subordinates. Coded always in *Sex* as heterosexual, her image is the dominant expression of heterosexism. . . . In the context of *Sex,* gay culture remains irrevocably linked to a system of patriarchal control framed by a heterosexist pornographic gaze" ("Power to the Pussy," in *Outlaw Culture,* 16–17).

17. Barbara Smith, "Toward a Black Feminist Criticism," 168.

18. See Gallop, *Around 1981,* especially chapter 2, "The Problem of Definition."

19. Judith Roof, *A Lure of Knowledge: Lesbian Sexuality and Theory*, 217. For another reading of the "black and lesbian" analogy, see my analysis of Toril Moi's *Sexual/Textual Politics: Feminist Literary Theory* in the introduction to this book; Roof addresses Moi's use of the term on pp. 226–27 of *A Lure of Knowledge*.

20. Roof, *A Lure of Knowledge*, 216.

21. Elaine Showalter, "The Rise of Gender," 2–3.

22. Ibid., 10.

23. Eve Kosofsky Sedgwick, *Between Men: English Literature and Male Homosocial Desire*, 18.

24. Gayle Rubin, "The Traffic in Women: Notes on the 'Political Economy' of Sex."

25. Sedgwick, *Between Men*, 2.

26. Rich, "Compulsory Heterosexuality and Lesbian Existence," 229.

27. Terry Castle, *The Apparitional Lesbian: Female Homosexuality and Modern Culture*, 71. Castle quotes from Sedgwick's *Between Men*, 3; emphasis Castle's. Further quotations from Castle in this section refer to this edition and are cited parenthetically in the text.

28. For a revisionary reading of Sedgwick's paradigm of triangulated desire, see Castle, *The Apparitional Lesbian*, chapter 4, "Sylvia Townsend Warner and the Counterplot of Lesbian Fiction," 66–91.

29. Teresa de Lauretis, "Queer Theory: Lesbian and Gay Sexualities, an Introduction," v–vi.

30. Ibid., iv.

31. Eve Kosofsky Sedgwick, *Epistemology of the Closet*, 39. Further quotations from this volume in this section refer to this edition and are cited parenthetically in the text.

32. Rich, "Compulsory Heterosexuality and Lesbian Existence," 239.

Conclusion

1. Carol Gilligan, *In a Different Voice: Psychological Theory and Women's Development*, ix. Further quotations from this volume in this section refer to the 1993 reprint and are cited parenthetically in the text.

2. Martha C. Nussbaum, "The Professor of Parody," 38. Further quotations from this article are cited parenthetically in the text.

3. Nussbaum's major book on this topic, *Sex and Social Justice*, was published in 1999, during the same period in which she published her critique of Butler, "The Professor of Parody."

4. Gilligan, *In a Different Voice*, 70–71.

5. Ibid., 100. Nussbaum briefly addresses implications of Gilligan's book in the introduction to *Sex and Social Justice*; see pp. 13–14.

6. Judith Butler, "A 'Bad Writer' Writes Back."

7. Ibid.

8. Margaret Cruikshank, foreword to *The New Lesbian Studies: Into the Twenty-*

First Century, xi–xii. For a more general discussion of this book in relation to several other volumes concerned with the overlap between lesbian and queer studies, see my "Either/And: Lesbian Theories, Queer Theories."

9. Bonnie Zimmerman, "Placing Lesbians," 274.

10. Ibid.

Bibliography

Ackerly, Brooke A. *Political Theory and Feminist Social Criticism.* Cambridge: Cambridge University Press, 2000.

"Ain't I a Woman?" Collective. "More Thoughts on Structuring a Revolution." *Ain't I a Woman?* 2, no. 8 (1972): 2–4.

Allen, Pamela. "Building a Movement: Free Space." *Notes from the Third Year* (1971): 93–98.

Alther, Lisa. *Kinflicks.* New York: Plume, 1996. First published in 1976.

Althusser, Louis. "Ideology and Ideological State Apparatuses (Notes towards an Investigation)." In *Lenin and Philosophy, and Other Essays,* translated by Ben Brewster, 121–73. London: New Left Books, 1971.

Amatniek, Kathie. "Funeral Oration for the Burial of Traditional Womanhood." *Notes from the First Year* (1968): n.p.

Andemahr, Sonya. "The Politics of Separatism and Lesbian Utopian Fiction." In *New Lesbian Criticism: Literary and Cultural Readings,* edited by Sally Munt, 133–52. New York: Columbia University Press, 1992.

Atkinson, Ti-Grace. "Lesbianism and Feminism: Justice for Women as 'Unnatural.'" In *Amazon Odyssey: The First Collection of Writings by the Political Pioneer of the Women's Movement,* 131–34. New York: Links Books, 1974.

———. "Radical Feminism." *Notes from the Second Year* (1970): 32–36.

———. "Strategy and Tactics: A Presentation of Political Lesbianism." In *Amazon Odyssey: The First Collection of Writings by the Political Pioneer of the Women's Movement,* 135–89. New York: Links Books, 1974.

Austin, J. L. *How to Do Things with Words.* Cambridge: Harvard University Press, 1975.

Avery, Evelyn Gross. "Tradition and Independence in Jewish Feminist Novels." *MELUS* 7, no. 4 (1980): 49–55.

Balsamo, Anne. *Technologies of the Gendered Body: Reading Cyborg Women.* Durham: Duke University Press, 1996.

Barasch, Frances K. "Faculty Images in Recent American Fiction." *College Literature* 10, no. 1 (winter 1983): 28–37.

Barr, Marleen S. *Future Females: A Critical Anthology.* Bowling Green, Ohio: Bowling Green State University Popular Press, 1981.

———. *Lost in Space: Feminist Science Fiction and Beyond.* Chapel Hill: University of North Carolina Press, 1993.

Barr, Marleen S., and Nicholas D. Smith, eds. *Women and Utopia: Critical Interpretations.* Lanham, Md.: University Press of America, 1983.

Barry, Kathleen. *Female Sexual Slavery.* Englewood Cliffs, N.J.: Prentice-Hall, 1979.

Baumgardner, Jennifer, and Amy Richards. *Manifesta: Young Women, Feminism, and the Future*. New York: Farrar, Straus & Giroux, 2000.

Baxandall, Rosalyn, and Linda Gordon, eds. *Dear Sisters: Dispatches from the Women's Liberation Movement*. New York: Basic Books, 2000.

Baym, Nina. "The Madwoman and Her Languages: Why I Don't Do Feminist Theory" (1984). In *Feminisms: An Anthology of Literary Theory and Criticism*, edited by Robyn R. Warhol and Diane Price Herndl, rev. ed., 278–92. New Brunswick, N.J.: Rutgers University Press, 1997.

Beauvoir, Simone de. *The Second Sex*. Edited and translated by H. M. Parshley. New York: Vintage, 1989. First published in 1952.

Bellafante, Ginia. "Feminism: It's All about Me!" *Time*, June 29, 1998, 54–60.

Benhabib, Seyla. *Democracy and Difference: Contesting the Boundaries of the Political*. Princeton: Princeton University Press, 1996.

Benhabib, Seyla, and Drucilla Cornell, eds. *Feminism as Critique: On the Politics of Gender*. Minneapolis: University of Minnesota Press, 1987.

Bonaparte, Marie. *Female Sexuality*. Translated by John Rodker. New York: International Universities Press, 1953.

Bordo, Susan. *Unbearable Weight: Feminism, Western Culture, and the Body*. Berkeley and Los Angeles: University of California Press, 1993.

Boston Women's Health Book Collective. *The New Our Bodies, Ourselves: A Book by and for Women*. New York: Simon & Schuster, 1984.

———. *Our Bodies, Ourselves: A Book by and for Women*, 2d ed. New York: Simon & Schuster, 1976.

Brecher, Ruth, and Edward Brecher. "The Work of Masters and Johnson." In *An Analysis of "Human Sexual Response,"* edited by Ruth Brecher and Edward Brecher, 17–107. London: Andre Deutsch, 1966.

Broner, E. M. "The Dirty Ladies: Earthy Writings of Contemporary American Women—Paley, Jong, Schor, and Lerman." *Regionalism and the Female Imagination* 4, no. 3 (1979): 34–43.

Brown, Daniel G. "Female Orgasm and Sexual Inadequacy." In *An Analysis of "Human Sexual Response,"* edited by Ruth Brecher and Edward Brecher, 125–74. London: Andre Deutsch, 1966.

Brown, Rita Mae. *Rita Will: Memoir of a Literary Rabble-Rouser*. New York: Bantam, 1997.

———. *Rubyfruit Jungle*. Plainfield, Vt.: Daughters, 1973.

Brownmiller, Susan. *Against Our Will: Men, Women, and Rape*. New York: Simon & Schuster, 1975.

———. *In Our Time: Memoir of a Revolution*. New York: Dial, 1999.

Buhle, Mari Jo. *Feminism and Its Discontents: A Century of Struggle with Psychoanalysis*. Cambridge: Harvard University Press, 1998.

Butler, Judith. "A 'Bad Writer' Writes Back." *New York Times*, March 20, 1999, A-15.

———. *Bodies That Matter: On the Discursive Limits of "Sex."* New York: Routledge, 1993.

———. *Excitable Speech: The Politics of the Performative*. New York: Routledge, 1997.

———. *Gender Trouble: Feminism and the Subversion of Identity*. New York: Routledge, 1990.

———. "Imitation and Gender Insubordination" (1991). In *The Lesbian and Gay Studies Reader*, edited by Henry Abelove, Michèle Aina Barale, and David M. Halperin, 307–20. New York: Routledge, 1993.

Butler, Robert J. "The Woman Writer as American Picaro: Open Journeying in Erica Jong's *Fear of Flying*." *Centennial Review* 31, no. 3 (1987): 308–29.

Caprio, Frank. *The Sexually Adequate Female*. New York: Citadel, 1953.

Castle, Terry. *The Apparitional Lesbian: Female Homosexuality and Modern Culture*. New York: Columbia University Press, 1993.

Chew, Martha. "Rita Mae Brown: Feminist Theorist and Southern Novelist." *Southern Quarterly: A Journal of the Arts in the South* 22, no. 1 (fall 1983): 61–80.

Chodorow, Nancy. *The Reproduction of Mothering: Psychoanalysis and the Sociology of Gender: With a New Preface*. Berkeley and Los Angeles: University of California Press, 1999. First published in 1978.

Christian, Barbara. "The Race for Theory." *Feminist Studies* 14, no. 1 (spring 1988): 67–79.

Cornell, Drucilla. *At the Heart of Freedom: Feminism, Sex, and Equality*. Princeton: Princeton University Press, 1998.

———. *Beyond Accommodation: Ethical Feminism, Deconstruction, and the Law*. New York: Routledge, 1991.

Cross, Amanda [Carolyn Heilbrun]. *Death in a Tenured Position*. New York: Ballantine, 1981.

Cruikshank, Margaret. Foreword to *The New Lesbian Studies: Into the Twenty-First Century*, edited by Bonnie Zimmerman and Toni A. H. McNaron, xi–xii. New York: Feminist Press at the City University of New York, 1996.

———, ed. *Lesbian Studies: Present and Future*. Old Westbury, N.Y.: Feminist Press, 1982.

Daly, Mary. *Gyn/Ecology: The Metaethics of Radical Feminism*. Boston: Beacon, 1978.

———. *Outercourse: The Be-dazzling Voyage: Containing Recollections from My Logbook of a Radical Feminist Philosopher (Be-ing an Account of My Time/ Space Travels and Ideas—Then, Again, Now, and How)*. San Francisco: Harper San Francisco, 1992.

———. "The Spiritual Dimension of Women's Liberation." *Notes from the Third Year* (1971): 75–79.

———. *Webster's First New Intergalactic Wickedary of the English Language*. Boston: Beacon, 1987.

Davis, Flora. *Moving the Mountain: The Women's Movement in America since 1960*. Urbana: University of Illinois Press, 1999. First published in 1991.

de Lauretis, Teresa. *The Practice of Love: Lesbian Sexuality and Perverse Desire*. Bloomington: Indiana University Press, 1994.

———. "Queer Theory: Lesbian and Gay Sexualities, an Introduction." *differences* 3, no. 2 (1991): iv–xviii.

———. "Sexual Indifference and Lesbian Representation" (1988). In *The Lesbian and Gay Studies Reader,* edited by Henry Abelove, Michèle Aina Barale, and David M. Halperin, 141–58. New York: Routledge, 1993.

de Man, Paul. *The Resistance to Theory.* With a foreword by Wlad Godzich. Minneapolis: University of Minnesota Press, 1986.

Densmore, Dana. "Mr. Freud's Castration Fantasy." *No More Fun and Games* 6 (May 1973): 114–16.

———. *Sex Roles and Female Oppression: A Collection of Articles.* Boston: Movement for a New Society, n.d.

Dever, Carolyn. *Death and the Mother from Dickens to Freud: Victorian Fiction and the Anxiety of Origins.* Cambridge: Cambridge University Press, 1998.

———. "Either/And: Lesbian Theories, Queer Theories." *GLQ: A Journal of Lesbian and Gay Studies* 5, no. 3 (1999): 413–24.

Dinnerstein, Dorothy. *The Mermaid and the Minotaur: Sexual Arrangements and Human Malaise.* New York: Other Press, 1999. First published in 1976.

Dollimore, Jonathan. "The Dominant and the Deviant: A Violent Dialectic." In *Homosexual Themes in Literary Studies,* edited by Wayne R. Dynes and Stephen Donaldson, 87–100. New York: Garland, 1992.

———. *Sexual Dissidence: Augustine to Wilde, Freud to Foucault.* Oxford: Clarendon, 1991.

Donovan, Josephine. *Feminist Theory: The Intellectual Traditions of American Feminism.* New York: Continuum, 1986.

Duggan, Lisa. "Scholars and Sense" (1992). In *Sex Wars: Sexual Dissent and Political Culture,* by Lisa Duggan and Nan D. Hunter, 173–78. New York: Routledge, 1995.

Duggan, Lisa, and Nan D. Hunter. *Sex Wars: Sexual Dissent and Political Culture.* New York: Routledge, 1995.

DuPlessis, Rachel Blau, and Ann Snitow, eds. *The Feminist Memoir Project: Voices from Women's Liberation.* New York: Three Rivers, 1998.

Dworkin, Andrea. *Pornography: Men Possessing Women.* New York: G. P. Putnam's Sons, 1979.

Eagleton, Terry. *Literary Theory: An Introduction.* Minneapolis: University of Minnesota Press, 1983.

Echols, Alice. *Daring to Be Bad: Radical Feminism in America, 1967–1975.* Minneapolis: University of Minnesota Press, 1989.

———. "The Taming of the Id: Feminist Sexual Politics, 1968–83." In *Pleasure and Danger: Exploring Female Sexuality,* edited by Carole S. Vance, 50–72. Boston: Routledge & Kegan Paul, 1984.

Editorial Collective. "Variations on Common Themes." Translated by Yvonne Rochette-Ozzello. In *New French Feminisms: An Anthology,* edited by Elaine Marks and Isabelle de Courtivron, 212–30. Amherst: University of Massachusetts Press, 1980. First published in *Questions féministes* 1 (November 1, 1977).

Eisenstein, Zillah. *The Female Body and the Law*. Berkeley and Los Angeles: University of California Press, 1988.

Ellmann, Mary. *Thinking about Women*. New York: Harcourt, Brace & World, 1968.

Fanon, Frantz. *Black Skin, White Masks*. Translated by Charles Lam Markmann. New York: Grove, 1967.

Ferguson, Mary Anne. "Lisa Alther: The Irony of Return." *Southern Quarterly: A Journal of the Arts in the South* 21, no. 4 (summer 1983): 103–15.

Feyerabend, Paul. *Against Method*. New York: Verso, 1993.

Fishbein, Leslie. "Rubyfruit Jungle: Lesbianism, Feminism, and Narcissism." *International Journal of Women's Studies* 7, no. 2 (1984): 155–59.

Foucault, Michel. *The Archaeology of Knowledge*. Translated by A. M. Sheridan Smith. New York: Harper & Row, 1972.

———. *The Order of Things: An Archaeology of the Human Sciences*. New York: Vintage, 1973. First published in 1970.

Fraser, Nancy. *Unruly Practices: Power, Discourse, and Gender in Contemporary Social Theory*. Minneapolis: University of Minnesota Press, 1989.

Freeman, Jo. "The Building of the Gilded Cage." *Notes from the Third Year* (1971): 44–55.

French, Marilyn. *The Women's Room*. New York: Ballantine, 1988. First published in 1977.

Freud, Sigmund. "Female Sexuality." In *The Standard Edition of the Complete Psychological Works of Sigmund Freud*. Edited and translated by James Strachey. Vol. 21, 223–43. London: Hogarth, 1971. First published in 1931.

———. "Femininity." In *The Standard Edition of the Complete Psychological Works of Sigmund Freud*. Edited and translated by James Strachey. Vol. 22, 112–35. London: Hogarth, 1971. First published in 1933.

———. *The Interpretation of Dreams*. In *The Standard Edition of the Complete Psychological Works of Sigmund Freud*. Edited and translated by James Strachey. Vol. 4, 1–338; vol. 5, 339–627. London: Hogarth, 1953. First published in 1900.

———. "Observations on Transference-Love." In *The Standard Edition of the Complete Psychological Works of Sigmund Freud*. Edited and translated by James Strachey. Vol. 12, 159–71. London: Hogarth, 1968. First published in 1915.

Friday, Nancy. *My Secret Garden: Women's Sexual Fantasies*. New York: Pocket, 1973.

Friedan, Betty. *The Feminine Mystique*. With a new introduction. New York: Norton, 1997. First published in 1963.

Fuss, Diana. *Essentially Speaking: Feminism, Nature, and Difference*. New York: Routledge, 1989.

Gallop, Jane. *Around 1981: Academic Feminist Literary Theory*. New York: Routledge, 1992.

———. *The Daughter's Seduction: Feminism and Psychoanalysis*. Ithaca: Cornell University Press, 1982.

————. *Reading Lacan*. Ithaca: Cornell University Press, 1987.

————. *Thinking through the Body*. New York: Columbia University Press, 1988.

Gilligan, Carol. *In a Different Voice: Psychological Theory and Women's Development*. With a new preface. Cambridge: Harvard University Press, 1993. First published in 1982.

Girard, René. *Violence and the Sacred*. Translated by Patrick Gregory. Baltimore: The Johns Hopkins University Press, 1977.

Godzich, Wlad. "The Tiger on the Paper Mat." Foreword to *The Resistance to Theory*, by Paul de Man, ix–xviii. Minneapolis: University of Minnesota Press, 1997.

Gornick, Vivian. Introduction to *S.C.U.M. Manifesto,* by Valerie Solanas. London: Olympia, 1971.

Gramsci, Antonio. *Selections from the Prison Notebooks*. Translated by Quinton Hoare and Geoffrey Nowell Smith. New York: International, 1971.

Greer, Germaine. *The Female Eunuch*. New York: Bantam, 1972. First published in 1970.

Griffin, Susan. *Pornography and Silence: Culture's Revenge against Nature*. New York: Harper & Row, 1981.

Grosz, Elizabeth. *Volatile Bodies: Toward a Corporeal Feminism*. Bloomington: Indiana University Press, 1994.

Gubar, Susan. "What Ails Feminist Criticism?" *Critical Inquiry* 24, no. 2 (summer 1998): 878–902.

Guillory, John. "Literature after Theory: The Lesson of Paul de Man." In *Cultural Capital: The Problem of Literary Canon Formation*, 176–265. Chicago: University of Chicago Press, 1993.

Habermas, Jürgen. *Between Facts and Norms: Contributions to a Discourse Theory of Law and Democracy*. Translated by William Rehg. Cambridge: MIT Press, 1998.

Hale, Dorothy J. *Social Formalism: The Novel in Theory from Henry James to the Present*. Stanford: Stanford University Press, 1998.

Hanisch, Carol. "A Critique of the Miss America Protest." *Notes from the Second Year* (1970): 86–88.

————. "The Personal Is Political." *Notes from the Second Year* (1970): 76–78.

Haraway, Donna. "A Cyborg Manifesto." In *Simians, Cyborgs, and Women: The Reinvention of Nature*, 149–81. New York: Routledge, 1991.

Hartman, Joan E., and Ellen Messer-Davidow, eds. *(En)Gendering Knowledge: Feminists in Academe*. Knoxville: University of Tennessee Press, 1991.

Hartsock, Nancy. "Fundamental Feminism: Process and Perspective." *Quest* 2, no. 2 (fall 1975): 67–80.

Heilbrun, Carolyn. "Dorothy L. Sayers: Biography between the Lines." *American Scholar* 51, no. 4 (autumn 1982): 552–61.

————. "Gender and Detective Fiction." In *The Sleuth and the Scholar: Origins, Evolution, and Current Trends in Detective Fiction*, edited by Barbara A. Rader and Howard G. Zettler, 1–8. Westport, Conn.: Greenwood, 1988.

————. "Nancy Drew: A Moment in Feminist History." *Armchair Detective* 29, no. 1 (winter 1996): 62–67.

———. "Sayers, Lord Peter, and God." *American Scholar* 37 (1968): 324–34.

Hirsch, Marianne, and Evelyn Fox Keller, eds. *Conflicts in Feminism*. New York: Routledge, 1990.

Hite, Molly. "Writing—and Reading—the Body: Female Sexuality and Recent Feminist Fiction." *Feminist Studies* 14, no. 1 (spring 1988): 121–42.

Hite, Shere. *The Hite Report: A Nationwide Study of Female Sexuality*. New York: Macmillan, 1976.

Hogeland, Lisa Marie. *Feminism and Its Fictions: The Consciousness-Raising Novel and the Women's Liberation Movement*. Philadelphia: University of Pennsylvania Press, 1998.

Hollibaugh, Amber, and Cherríe Moraga. "What We're Rollin around in Bed With: Sexual Silences in Feminism." In *Powers of Desire: The Politics of Sexuality*, edited by Ann Snitow, Christine Stansell, and Sharon Thompson, 394–405. New York: Monthly Review Press, 1983.

Homans, Margaret. "'Her Very Own Howl': The Ambiguities of Representation in Recent Women's Fiction." *Signs* 9, no. 2 (1983): 186–205.

hooks, bell. *Ain't I a Woman: Black Women and Feminism*. Boston: Beacon, 1981.

———. *Feminist Theory from Margin to Center*. Boston: South End, 1984.

———. *Outlaw Culture: Resisting Representations*. New York: Routledge, 1994.

Hunt, Lynn. *The Family Romance of the French Revolution*. Berkeley and Los Angeles: University of California Press, 1992.

Irwin, Edward E. "Freedoms as Value in Three Popular Southern Novels." *Proteus: A Journal of Ideas* 6, no. 1 (spring 1989): 37–41.

Jaggar, Alison, and Paula R. Struhl, eds. *Feminist Frameworks: Alternative Accounts of the Relations between Men and Women*. New York: McGraw-Hill, 1978.

Jameson, Fredric. *The Political Unconscious: Narrative as a Socially Symbolic Act*. Ithaca: Cornell University Press, 1981.

Jardine, Alice. *Gynesis: Configurations of Women and Modernity*. Ithaca: Cornell University Press, 1985.

Jay, Karla. *Tales of the Lavender Menace: A Memoir of Liberation*. New York: Basic Books, 1999.

Johnson, Barbara. *The Feminist Difference: Literature, Psychoanalysis, Race, and Gender*. Cambridge: Harvard University Press, 1998.

———. *A World of Difference*. Baltimore: The Johns Hopkins University Press, 1987.

Jones, Ann Rosalind. "Writing the Body: Toward an Understanding of *L'Écriture féminine*." In *The New Feminist Criticism: Essays on Women, Literature, and Theory*, edited by Elaine Showalter, 361–77. New York: Pantheon, 1985.

Jones, Libby Falk, and Sarah Webster Goodwin, eds. *Feminism, Utopia, and Narrative*. Knoxville: University of Tennessee Press, 1990.

Jong, Erica. *Fear of Flying*. With an introduction. New York: Signet, 1995. First published in 1973.

Kaplan, Carla. *The Erotics of Talk: Women's Writing and Feminist Paradigms*. New York: Oxford University Press, 1996.

Kaplow, Susi. "Getting Angry." *Notes from the Third Year* (1971): 15–17.

Kawada, Louise. "Liberating Laughter: Comedic Form in Some Lesbian Novels." In *Sexual Practice, Textual Theory: Lesbian Cultural Criticism*, edited by Susan J. Wolfe and Julia Penelope, 251–62. Cambridge: Blackwell, 1993.

Kelly, G. Lombard. *Sexual Feelings in Married Men and Women*. New York: Pocket Books, n.d.

King, Katie. *Theory in Its Feminist Travels: Conversations in U.S. Women's Movements*. Bloomington: Indiana University Press, 1994.

Kinsey, Alfred C., and the Staff of the Institute for Sex Research, Indiana University. *Sexual Behavior in the Human Female*. Philadelphia: Saunders, 1953.

Knepper, Marty S. "Who Killed Janet Mandelbaum and India Wonder? A Look at the Suicides of the Token Women in Amanda Cross's *Death in a Tenured Position* and Dorothy Bryant's *Killing Wonder*." *Clues: A Journal of Detection* 13, no. 1 (spring–summer 1992): 45–58.

Koedt, Anne. "The Myth of the Vaginal Orgasm." *Notes from the Second Year* (1970): 37–42.

Kress, Susan. *Carolyn G. Heilbrun: Feminist in a Tenured Position*. Charlottesville: University Press of Virginia, 1997.

Kristeva, Julia. *The Powers of Horror: An Essay on Abjection*. Translated by Leon S. Roudiez. New York: Columbia University Press, 1982. First published in 1980.

Lacan, Jacques. "The Agency of the Letter in the Unconscious." In *Écrits: A Selection*, translated by Alan Sheridan, 146–78. New York: Norton, 1977.

———. "The Mirror-Stage." In *Écrits: A Selection*, translated by Alan Sheridan, 1–7. New York: Norton, 1977.

———. "The Signification of the Phallus." In *Écrits: A Selection*, translated by Alan Sheridan, 281–91. New York: Norton, 1977.

Laqueur, Thomas. *Making Sex: Body and Gender from the Greeks to Freud*. Cambridge: Harvard University Press, 1990.

Lerner, Gerda. *The Creation of Feminist Consciousness: From the Middle Ages to Eighteen-Seventy*. New York: Oxford University Press, 1993.

Lévi-Strauss, Claude. *The Elementary Structures of Kinship*. Edited by Rodney Needham. Translated by James Harle Bell, John Richard von Sturmer, and Rodney Needham. Rev. ed. Boston: Beacon, 1969.

"Liberate Women to Liberate Society." *Lesbians Fight Back* 1, no. 1 (1972): 1.

Limpus, Laurel. *Liberation of Women: Sexual Repression and the Family*. Boston: New England Free Press, n.d.

Lorde, Audre. "The Uses of the Erotic: The Erotic as Power" (1978). In *The Lesbian and Gay Studies Reader*, edited by Henry Abelove, Michèle Aina Barale, and David M. Halperin, 339–43. New York: Routledge, 1993.

MacCannell, Juliet Flower. *Figuring Lacan: Criticism and the Cultural Unconscious*. Lincoln: University of Nebraska Press, 1986.

MacKinnon, Catharine A. "Feminism, Marxism, Method, and the State: An Agenda for Theory" (1973). In *The Signs Reader: Women, Gender, and Scholarship*, edited by Elizabeth Abel and Emily K. Abel, 227–56. Chicago: University of Chicago Press, 1983.

———. *Feminism Unmodified: Discourses on Life and Law*. Cambridge: Harvard University Press, 1988.

MacKinnon, Catharine A., and Andrea Dworkin, eds. *In Harm's Way: The Pornography Civil Rights Hearings*. Cambridge: Harvard University Press, 1998.

Madonna. *Sex*. Photographed by Steven Meisel. Art directed by Fabien Baron. Edited by Glenn O'Brien. Produced by Callaway. New York: Warner, 1992.

Mandrell, James. "Questions of Genre and Gender: Contemporary American Versions of the Feminine Picaresque." *Novel: A Forum on Fiction* 20, no. 2 (1987): 149–70.

Marchino, Lois A. "The Professor Tells a Story: Kate Fansler." In *In the Beginning: First Novels in Mystery Series,* edited by Mary Jean DeMarr, 155–70. Bowling Green, Ohio: Bowling Green State University Popular Press, 1995.

Marcus, Sharon. "The Profession of the Author: Abstraction, Advertising, and *Jane Eyre*." *PMLA* 110, no. 2 (March 1995): 206–19.

Marks, Elaine, and Isabelle de Courtivron, eds. *New French Feminisms: An Anthology*. Amherst: University of Massachusetts Press, 1980.

Martin, Biddy. *Femininity Played Straight: The Significance of Being Lesbian*. New York: Routledge, 1996.

Martin, Emily. *The Woman in the Body: A Cultural Analysis of Reproduction*. Boston: Beacon, 1987.

Marx, Karl. *Capital*. Edited by Frederick Engels. Translated from the third German edition by Samuel Moore and Edward Aveling. Vol. 1. New York: International, 1967.

Masson, Jeffrey Moussaieff. *The Assault on Truth: Freud's Suppression of the Seduction Theory*. New York: Pocket, 1998. First published in 1984.

Masters, William H., and Virginia E. Johnson. *Human Sexual Response*. Boston: Little, Brown, 1966.

McCarthy, Mary. *The Group*. New York: Harcourt, Brace & World, 1963.

McDowell, Deborah. "Transferences; Black Feminist Discourse: The 'Practice' of Theory." In *Feminism beside Itself,* edited by Diane Elam and Robyn Wiegman, 93–118. New York: Routledge, 1995.

Messer-Davidow, Ellen. *Disciplining Feminism: From Social Activism to Academic Discourse*. Durham: Duke University Press, 2002.

Meyers, Diana Tietjens, ed. *Feminist Social Thought: A Reader*. New York: Routledge, 1997.

Michie, Helena. *The Flesh Made Word: Female Figures and Women's Bodies*. New York: Oxford University Press, 1987.

———. "Murder in the Canon: The Dual Personality of Carolyn Heilbrun." *Massachusetts Studies in English* 9, no. 3 (1984): 1–12.

———. *Sororophobia: Differences among Women in Literature and Culture*. New York: Oxford University Press, 1992.

Miller, Nancy. *Getting Personal: Feminist Occasions and Other Autobiographical Acts*. New York: Routledge, 1991.

Millett, Kate. *Flying*. New York: Simon & Schuster, 1990. First published in 1974.

————. *Sexual Politics.* New York: Simon & Schuster, 1969.

Mitchell, Juliet. Introduction to *Feminine Sexuality: Jacques Lacan and the École Freudienne,* by Jacques Lacan. Edited by Juliet Mitchell and Jacqueline Rose. Translated by Jacqueline Rose, 1–26. New York: Norton, 1985.

————. Introduction to *The Selected Melanie Klein,* edited by Juliet Mitchell, 9–32. New York: Free Press, 1986.

————. *Psychoanalysis and Feminism: Freud, Reich, Laing, and Women.* New York: Vintage, 1974.

————. *Woman's Estate.* New York: Vintage, 1973. First published in 1971.

Mitchell, W. J. T., ed. *Against Theory: Literary Studies and the New Pragmatism.* Chicago: University of Chicago Press, 1985.

Mohanty, Chandra Talpade. "Feminist Encounters: Locating the Politics of Experience." *Copyright* 1 (1987): 30–44.

Moi, Toril. *Sexual/Textual Politics: Feminist Literary Theory.* New York: Routledge, 1985.

Morgan, Robin. "Three Articles on WITCH" (1968, 1969, 1969). In *Going Too Far: The Personal Chronicle of a Feminist,* 71–81. New York: Random House, 1977.

————, ed. *Sisterhood Is Powerful: An Anthology of Writings from the Women's Liberation Movement.* New York: Vintage, 1970.

Mouffe, Chantal. *The Return of the Political.* London: Verso, 1993.

Moyer, Marie. "The Female Studies as Joke Syndrome." *Spare Rib* 15 (1973): 33–36.

Muñoz, José Esteban. *Disidentifications: Queers of Color and the Performance of Politics.* Minneapolis: University of Minnesota Press, 1999.

Newton, Esther, and Shirley Walton. "The Personal Is Political: Consciousness-Raising and Personal Change in the Women's Liberation Movement" (1971). In *Margaret Mead Made Me Gay: Personal Essays, Public Ideas,* by Esther Newton, 113–41. Durham: Duke University Press, 2000.

Newton, Judith. "History as Usual? Feminism and the 'New Historicism.'" *Cultural Critique* (spring 1988): 87–121.

Nicholson, Linda J. *The Play of Reason: From the Modern to the Postmodern.* Ithaca: Cornell University Press, 1999.

Notes from the Second Year (1970).

Notes from the Third Year (1971).

Nussbaum [Kingsman], Linda. "Female Sexuality." *Echo of Sappho* 1, no. 3 (1972): 13.

Nussbaum, Martha C. "The Professor of Parody." *New Republic,* February 22, 1999, 37–45.

————. *Sex and Social Justice.* New York: Oxford University Press, 1999.

Orr, Elaine Neil. *Subject to Negotiation: Reading Feminist Criticism and American Women's Fictions.* Charlottesville: University Press of Virginia, 1997.

Paglia, Camille. *Sexual Personae: Art and Decadence from Nefertiti to Emily Dickinson.* New Haven: Yale University Press, 1990.

Palumbo, Donald, ed. *Erotic Universe: Sexuality and Fantastic Literature*. Westport, Conn.: Greenwood, 1986.

Peel, Ellen. "Subject, Object, and the Alternation of First- and Third-Person Narration in Novels by Alther, Atwood, and Drabble: Toward a Theory of Feminist Aesthetics." *Critique: Studies in Contemporary Fiction* 30, no. 2 (1989): 107–22.

Pellegrini, Ann. *Performance Anxieties: Staging Psychoanalysis, Staging Race*. New York: Routledge, 1997.

Piercy, Marge. *Small Changes*. Garden City, N.Y.: Doubleday, 1973.

Poovey, Mary. *Making a Social Body: British Cultural Formation, 1830–1864*. Chicago: University of Chicago Press, 1995.

Purcell, J. M. "The 'Amanda Cross' Case: Socializing the U.S. Academic Mystery." *Armchair Detective* 13 (1980): 36–40.

Radicalesbians. "The Woman-Identified Woman." In *Feminism in Our Time: The Essential Writings, World War II to the Present*, edited by Miriam Schnier, 160–67. New York: Vintage, 1994.

Radical Feminist 28. "The Women's Movement." *Ain't I a Woman?* 2, no. 7 (1972): 9.

Radway, Janice. *Reading the Romance: Women, Patriarchy, and Popular Literature*. Chapel Hill: University of North Carolina Press, 1984.

Reardon, Joan. "Fear of Flying: Developing the Feminist Novel." *International Journal of Women's Studies* 1 (1978): 306–20.

Redstockings. "Redstockings Manifesto." *Notes from the Second Year* (1970): 112–13.

Rich, Adrienne. "Compulsory Heterosexuality and Lesbian Existence" (1980). In *The Lesbian and Gay Studies Reader*, edited by Henry Abelove, Michèle Aina Barale, and David M. Halperin, 227–54. New York: Routledge, 1993.

Robbins, Bruce. "The Politics of Theory." *Social Text* 18 (1987–1988): 3–18.

Roberts, Jeanne Addison. "Feminist Murder: Amanda Cross Reinvents Womanhood." In *Feminism in Women's Detective Fiction*, edited by Glenwood Irons, 94–111. Toronto: University of Toronto Press, 1995.

Roof, Judith. *A Lure of Knowledge: Lesbian Sexuality and Theory*. New York: Columbia University Press, 1991.

Rose, Jacqueline. Introduction to *Feminine Sexuality: Jacques Lacan and the École Freudienne*, by Jacques Lacan. Edited by Juliet Mitchell and Jacqueline Rose. Translated by Jacqueline Rose, 27–57. New York: Norton, 1985.

Rosen, Ruth. *The World Split Open: How the Modern Women's Movement Changed America*. New York: Viking, 2000.

Rossi, Alice S. "Equality between the Sexes: An Immodest Proposal." *Daedalus* 93, no. 2 (spring 1964): 607–52.

Rubin, Gayle. "Sexual Traffic: Gayle Rubin Interviewed by Judith Butler." In *Coming Out of Feminism?* edited by Mandy Merck, Naomi Segal, and Elizabeth Wright, 36–73. New York: Blackwell, 1998.

———. "Thinking Sex: Notes for a Radical Theory of the Politics of Sexuality." In *Pleasure and Danger: Exploring Female Sexuality*, edited by Carole S. Vance, 267–319. Boston: Routledge & Kegan Paul, 1984.

———. "The Traffic in Women: Notes on the 'Political Economy' of Sex." In *Toward an Anthropology of Women,* edited by Rayna R. Reiter, 157–210. New York: Monthly Review Press, 1975.

Russ, Joanna. "Recent Feminist Utopias." In *Future Females: A Critical Anthology,* edited by Marleen S. Barr, 71–75. Bowling Green, Ohio: Bowling Green State University Popular Press, 1981.

Sandford, Wendy, with Paula Brown Doress. "Relationships and Sexuality." Introduction to *The New Our Bodies, Ourselves: A Book by and for Women,* by the Boston Women's Health Book Collective. New York: Simon & Schuster, 1984.

Sarachild, Kathie. "Consciousness-Raising: A Radical Weapon." In *Feminist Revolution,* by the Redstockings of the Women's Liberation Movement, abr. ed., edited by Kathie Sarachild, 144–50. New York: Random House, 1978.

———. "The Power of History." Preface to *Feminist Revolution,* by the Redstockings of the Women's Liberation Movement, abr. ed., edited by Kathie Sarachild, 12–43. New York: Random House, 1978.

———. "A Program for Feminist 'Consciousness Raising.'" *Notes from the Second Year* (1970): 78–80.

Sawicki, Jana. *Disciplining Foucault: Feminism, Power, and the Body.* New York: Routledge, 1991.

Schnier, Miriam, ed. *Feminism in Our Time: The Essential Writings, World War II to the Present.* New York: Vintage, 1994.

Scott, Joan W. "The Evidence of Experience" (1991). In *The Lesbian and Gay Studies Reader,* edited by Henry Abelove, Michèle Aina Barale, and David M. Halperin, 397–415. New York: Routledge, 1993.

Sedgwick, Eve Kosofsky. *Between Men: English Literature and Male Homosocial Desire.* New York: Columbia University Press, 1985.

———. *Epistemology of the Closet.* Berkeley and Los Angeles: University of California Press, 1990.

Segal, Lynne. "Sensual Uncertainty, or Why the Clitoris Is Not Enough." In *Sex and Love,* edited by Sue Cartledge and Joanna Ryan, 30–47. London: Women's Press, 1983.

———. *Straight Sex: The Politics of Pleasure.* London: Virago, 1994.

Seidel, Kathryn. "Envisioning the Androgynous Future." *Sun and Moon: A Quarterly of Literature and Art* 3 (1976): 98–101.

Showalter, Elaine. "The Rise of Gender." Introduction to *Speaking of Gender,* edited by Elaine Showalter, 1–13. New York: Routledge, 1989.

———, ed. *The New Feminist Criticism: Essays on Women, Literature, and Theory.* New York: Pantheon, 1985.

Shulman, Alix Kates. "Organs and Orgasms." In *Woman in Sexist Society: Studies in Power and Powerlessness,* edited by Vivian Gornick and Barbara K. Moran, 292–303. New York: Basic Books, 1971.

———. "Sex and Power: Sexual Bases of Radical Feminism." In *Women: Sex and Sexuality,* edited by Catharine R. Stimpson and Ethel Spector Person, 21–35. Chicago: University of Chicago Press, 1980.

Simpson, David. *Romanticism, Nationalism, and the Revolt against Theory*. Chicago: University of Chicago Press, 1993.

Smith, Barbara. "Toward a Black Feminist Criticism" (1977). In *The New Feminist Criticism: Essays on Women, Literature, and Theory*, edited by Elaine Showalter, 168–85. New York: Pantheon, 1985.

Snitow, Ann, Christine Stansell, and Sharon Thompson, eds. *The Powers of Desire: The Politics of Sexuality*. New York: Monthly Review Press, 1983.

Solanas, Valerie. *S.C.U.M. Manifesto*. London: Olympia, 1971.

Spivak, Gayatri Chakravorty. *In Other Worlds: Essays in Cultural Politics*. New York: Methuen, 1987.

Sterling, Ann Fausto. *Sexing the Body: Gender Politics and the Construction of Sexuality*. New York: Basic Books, 2000.

Templin, Charlotte. "Erica Jong: Becoming a Jewish Writer." In *Daughters of Valor: Contemporary Jewish American Women Writers*, edited by Jay L. Halio and Ben Siegel, 126–40. Newark: University of Delaware Press, 1997.

Thurman, Judith. *Secrets of the Flesh: A Life of Colette*. New York: Knopf, 1999.

Vance, Carole S. "Pleasure and Danger: Toward a Politics of Sexuality." In *Pleasure and Danger: Exploring Female Sexuality*, edited by Carole S. Vance, 1–27. Boston: Routledge & Kegan Paul, 1984.

———, ed. *Pleasure and Danger: Exploring Female Sexuality*. Boston: Routledge & Kegan Paul, 1984.

Waage, Frederick G. "Alther and Dillard: The Appalachian Universe." In *Appalachia/America: Proceedings of the 1980 Appalachian Studies Conference*, edited by Wilson Somerville, 200–208. Johnson City, Tenn.: Appalachian Consortium, 1981.

Walker, Alice. *In Search of Our Mothers' Gardens: Womanist Prose*. San Diego: Harcourt Brace Jovanovich, 1983.

———. *Meridian*. New York: Harcourt Brace Jovanovich, 1976.

Weisstein, Naomi. "'Kinde, Küche, Kirche' as Scientific Law: Psychology Constructs the Female." In *Sisterhood Is Powerful: An Anthology of Writings from the Women's Liberation Movement*, edited by Robin Morgan, 228–45. New York: Vintage, 1970.

"Who's Come a Long Way, Baby?" *Time*, August 31, 1970, 16–25.

Wiegman, Robyn. "What Ails Feminist Criticism? A Second Opinion." *Critical Inquiry* 25, no. 2 (1999): 362–79.

Wilson, Elizabeth. "I'll Climb the Stairway to Heaven: Lesbianism in the Seventies." In *Sex and Love: New Thoughts on Old Contradictions*, edited by Sue Cartledge and Joanna Ryan, 180–95. London: Women's Press, 1983.

Wilt, Judith. "Feminism Meets the Detective Novel." *Clues: A Journal of Detection* 3, no. 2 (fall–winter 1982): 47–51.

Women's Center Newsletter of Nassau County 1 (1972).

"Women's Lib: A Second Look." *Time*, December 14, 1970, 50.

Woolf, Virginia. *A Room of One's Own*. New York: Harcourt Brace Jovanovich, 1989. First published in 1929.

Young, Iris Marion. *Justice and the Politics of Difference*. Princeton: Princeton University Press, 1990.

Zimmerman, Bonnie. "Placing Lesbians." In *The New Lesbian Studies: Into the Twenty-First Century*, edited by Bonnie Zimmerman and Toni A. H. McNaron, 269–75. New York: Feminist Press at the City University of New York, 1996.

Index

abject, feminist, 118–40; constitutive function of degradations of, 125–26, 127, 128; modeled by fictional deaths, 119, 128–29, 130, 136–37, 139. *See also* novels, feminist popular
abortion-rights activists, 68
abstraction: bodily, xiii, 65–69, 112; feminist collective identity as, 107; feminist critique of, xi; intuition vs., 35; logic of, 5; Marx on, 5–6; as masculine mode, 35, 162; material function within feminist theoretical context, 7; materiality and, xii–xiii, xv, 6; moral imperative of men as, 165, 166; moralized, as betrayal of feminine principles, 167–68; psychological distance achieved in, 41, 42; resistance to, 6–7
academic canonization of theory, 4
academic feminism, xv, 149–50; educational vacuum created by, 22–23, 25; exclusionary language of, 8–9, 149–50, 169; as problem for feminist novelists, 120. *See also* novels, feminist popular
achievement: pleasure located in, 104–5
activism: consciousness-raising as mode of, 28–29, 32–33, 37–38, 46–51; literary criticism as locus of, 149; in mid-1980s, 153; "mindless," 48; as political theater, 49–50; theory building as crucial component of, 46–47
activist unconscious, 54, 85, 90. *See also* psychoanalytic feminism
aesthesis and *theoria*: distinction between, 16–18, 21
African American feminists, 24; "black

and lesbian" analogy, 152–53; black feminist criticism, 14–15; devaluing of works of, 4; race and feminism, 149–53; "womanist" movement proposed by, 20
Against Our Will (Brownmiller), 23
AIDS epidemic, 153; lesbian activists' work in, 159–60
Ain't I a Woman? (journal), 38
"Ain't I a Woman" Collective of Iowa, 46
alienation, 6, 112; from "ownership" of one's body, 132–33
Allen, Pamela, 33, 35, 40–41, 42
Alther, Lisa, 118–19, 122, 137
Althusser, Louis, 81
Amatniek, Kathie. *See* Sarachild, Kathie
Amazon Odyssey (Atkinson), 145–46
Amazons, 145
ambivalence toward theory, 3–4, 16, 20
"American Dream," 133
anger: consciousness-raising actions out of, 48–50
Anglo-American feminist "criticism": French feminist in contrast to, 12–15
Anglo-Saxon psychoanalysis: anatomical-biological bias of, 65. *See also* psychoanalytic feminism
Anthony, Susan B., 22
anthropology: kinship systems described in, 69–70
antiauthoritarian authority: contradictory challenges of feminist, 3
antiessentialism, feminist, 55
antiporn feminism, 113–14, 116
Anzaldúa, Gloria, 169
apparitional lesbian, 112

Paglia, Camille, 23
passivity: dismantling equation of female genitalia with, 100–101; Freudian opposition of masculine activity with feminine, 99–100, 101
patriarchy: abstraction as constitutive trope of, 6–7; abstract vs. intuitive thought in, 35; categories of knowledge in, 50; clitoral sexuality as signifier of women's political agency within erotic economy of, 104; consciousness-raising movement and challenge to, 33–34; distance implied by abstraction as vestige of, 42; family system and, 69–73; literature as direct entrance into structuring principle of culture of, 15–17; as male homosocial construct, 155; marriage and, 32–33; origins within psychodynamics of infancy, 82; power possessed by women within, 77; private home as patriarchy's origin in individual lives, 54; psychic structures of femininity and oppression in, 59; resistance to, 13–14, 53; sacred maternity as part of, 73; separatism as logical extreme of feminist critiques of, 145; unconscious complicity with, 53, 54, 57; vagina demonized as vessel of, 99–100
Pellegrini, Ann, 10
penis, 94. See also phallus
penis envy, 64; Freud's theory of, 56, 59–60, 86; as metaphorical, 63
personal and the political: fusion of the, 38–39, 57; invasive aspects of slogan, 115–16; repoliticization of the personal, 71–72; risk in, 39–46
phallic substitutes in Freudian psychoanalysis, 60
phallogocentrism, 8
phallus: feminist, 69–72, 98–105; feminist discourses of clitoris in terms of, 93; as ideology (patriar-

chy) organized around symbol, 64; in Lacanian psychoanalysis, 88–89, 182n.14; as symbol of cultural power, 60, 61, 62
Philosophy and Literature (journal), 168
Piercy, Marge, 120, 122, 130
pleasure: clitoral orgasm and ideology of, 98; knowledge and, 139; located in achievement, 104–5; power and, 105–12, 115–16. See also sexual pleasure
pluralism, feminist, 153
political change in feminist theory-practice continuum, 38–39
political empowerment: grounded in bodily pleasure of clitoral orgasm, 92–93
political lesbianism, 148, 157
political upward mobility, 41–42
political voice, feminist, xv–xvi
politics: fusion of the personal and the political, 38–46, 57, 71–72, 115–16; of promiscuity, 89; racialized identity, 24; textual, 11–15; of theory, 1–11; of theory production, xiii, xvi
pop-cultural feminism, 23
pornography: cultural feminism's discourses against, 113–14, 116
portability: value of theory in its, 7, 45–46
postcolonial feminists, 24
power: with bodily knowledge, 105–8; of consciousness-raising, 30; male mothering and restructuring of power arrangements, 74–77; in marriage relationships, 132–34; phallus as symbol of cultural, 60, 61, 62; pleasure and, 105–12, 115–16; possessed by women within patriarchy, 77
practice: theory and. See theory-practice relationship
primal ambivalence toward women, 75

Solanas, Valerie, 36, 56–57, 87–88
solidarity: ideal of, 24; "sisterhood" as metaphor for women's, 31–32
Speaking of Gender (anthology), 154
Spivak, Gayatri Chakravorty, 8
status symbol: theory as, 11–15
Steinem, Gloria, 22
strategic transgression: tradition of, 88
structuralism: shaping influence of, 70
subjectivity: desire as founding condition of, 88; male and female, 81–82
subjugation: homogenization as mechanism of, 10
Supreme Court: *Roe v. Wade* decision of, 68

textual politics, 11–15
theoria and *aesthesis*: distinction between, 16–18, 21
theory: ambivalence toward, 3–4, 16, 20; consciousness-raising movement as new way of doing, 27–28, 33–39; explanatory and planning functions of, 5, 37; as metalanguage of feminism, 9–10; politics of, 1–11; portability of, 7, 45–46; as practice of language, 15–22; resistance to, 162; as status symbol, 11–15; theorizing as material feminist intervention, 5, 35–36
Theory in Its Feminist Travels: Conversations in U.S. Women's Movements (King), 171n.11
theory-practice relationship, xii, 7, 27, 36–37; clitoris as symbol of theory put into practice, 98; discourses attempting to breach, xiii; feminism-lesbianism distinction and, 145; in feminist novels, 120–21; feminist theory as feminist practice, 44–46; progression of feminist theory-practice continuum, 38–39
theory production: formative dialectic of feminist, 5; politics of, xiii, xvi; as

resistance to patriarchal devaluations of femininity, 35–36
"Thinking Sex: Notes for a Radical Theory of the Politics of Sexuality" (Rubin), 180n.30
Thinking through the Body (Gallop), 90
Time magazine: August 1970 cover story canonizing Millett, xiii, 1–3, 20–21, 171n.1; death of feminism story (1998), 22–23, 24, 25; December 1970 rescinding of Millett's icon status, 2
"Toward a Black Feminist Criticism" (Smith), 152
traffic in women, 155; in kinship system, 69–70
"Traffic in Women, The" (Rubin), 81, 180n.30
transgression, strategic, 88
Trojan-horse strategy, 89

unconscious: activist, 54, 85, 90; Freud's discovery of, 66, 67–68; making conscious the dynamics of, 85; patriarchal system wired into infant's, 73; as political force, feminist appropriation of, 84; shift to emphasis on, 53–55, 63–69. *See also* psychoanalytic feminism
uncontainability of female body, 123–25
universality of female oppression, 133–34
upward mobility, political, 41–42. *See also* consciousness-raising movement

vagina: functions of, 102; in Kinsey's sex studies, 95; as locus of "mature" sexual response (Freud), 99; as vessel of patriarchy and emblem of enthralled femininity, 99–100
vaginal orgasm, 56, 97, 182n.5; myth of natural, mature, 99–103, 105
vaginal victimization, 113–14
Vance, Carole, 115–16

Carolyn Dever is associate professor of English and acting director of women's studies at Vanderbilt University. She is the author of *Death and the Mother from Dickens to Freud: Victorian Fiction and the Anxiety of Origins* and the coeditor (with Margaret Cohen) of *The Literary Channel: The Inter-national Invention of the Novel.*